Working Without a Net

Working Without a Net

A Study of
Egocentric Epistemology

RICHARD FOLEY

New York   Oxford
OXFORD UNIVERSITY PRESS
1993

Oxford University Press

Oxford   New York   Toronto
Delhi   Bombay   Calcutta   Madras   Karachi
Kuala Lumpur   Singapore   Hong Kong   Tokyo
Nairobi   Dar es Salaam   Cape Town

Melbourne   Auckland   Madrid

and associated companies in
Berlin   Ibadan

Published by Oxford University Press, Inc.
200 Madison Avenue, New York, NY 10016

Oxford is a registered trademark of Oxford University Press

Library of Congress Cataloging-in-Publication Data
Foley, Richard
Working without a net : a study of egocentric epistemology /
Richard Foley.
p.   cm.   Includes bibliographical references and index.
ISBN 0-19-507699-0
1. Knowledge, Theory of.   2. Descartes, René, 1596–1650.
I. Title.
BD161.F58   1992   121—dc20   91-48108

2 4 6 8 9 7 5 3 1

Printed in the United States of America
on acid-free paper

Preface

Part of the fascination of philosophy is the way topics blend into one another. You are writing on what you take to be a well-defined topic, but to your surprise you soon find yourself writing about something that antecedently would have seemed to have been a quite different topic. This is the experience I had with this book. As a result, I often found it difficult to say in a simple, unequivocal way what the book was about. I even heard myself giving quite different descriptions of it, sometimes in the course of a single day. Eventually, I came to realize that these various descriptions were equally accurate and that it might be useful to set out at least a few of them in a preface.

I do so with some reluctance. A well enough written book would not need a preface to tell the reader what it is about. Besides, authors who use a preface to explain themselves tend to look either presumptuous or diffident—presumptuous if their explanations are motivated by the assumption that only they are in a position to understand the significance of their views, and diffident if their explanations are motivated by too great a fear of being misunderstood.

So, in providing a list of some of the ways that I have found myself describing my project, I'm going against my better instincts. To make myself feel at least a little better about this, I make the list brief:

1. The project shows how the theory of rational belief can be regarded as a part of a perfectly general theory of rationality. Thus, the first few sections of the book deal with questions of rationality wherever they arise, and then in the later sections questions of rational belief are regarded as instances of these general questions. The search is for a theoretically unified way to think about rationality, so that the rationality of belief does not turn out to be a fundamentally different kind of phenomenon from, say, the rationality of decision or the rationality of action. This also suggests a working procedure, one that stresses parallels between questions, problems, and puzzles that arise for theories of rational decision, rational action, rational strategy, and the like on the one hand and the theory of rational belief on the other. The presupposition is that if a puzzle arises for one, it is likely to have an analogue for the other. Emphasizing these analogies is often a useful first step in finding a way through the puzzles.

2. The project is one of meta-epistemology. I present a way of thinking about the subject matter of an epistemological theory, and this in turn provides us with

some guidance as to what we can expect such a theory to do and what we cannot expect it to do. These might seem to be relatively straightforward matters, but it is one of my themes that a variety of projects are done under the name of epistemology. Although these projects report their conclusions using the same cluster of epistemic terms—terms such as "rationality," "justification," "warrant," and "evidence,"—in fact they have different aims and different contents. As a way of making sense of this variety, I propose a way to think about judgments of rationality wherever they arise and a corresponding way to think about philosophical accounts of these judgments. The result is a taxonomy for epistemology. And the taxonomy itself is suggestive; it suggests promising ways of thinking about a range of epistemological issues, such as the distinction between epistemic and nonepistemic reasons for belief, the epistemic significance of simplicity and other theoretical virtues, the relevance of radical skeptical hypotheses, the difference between a theory of rational belief and a theory of knowledge, the difference between a theory of rational belief and a theory of rational degrees of belief, and the limits of idealization in epistemology.

3. The book is an extended essay on Cartesian epistemology. "Cartesianism" has become something of a dirty word in philosophy. To convict someone of Cartesian views, whether it be in epistemology or philosophy of language or some other area, is thought to be equivalent to a *reductio*. It is to implicate the person in a way of thinking about philosophical issues that the history of philosophy shows to be dead-ended.

My view is that the history of philosophy has no such simpleminded lessons for us, but it does have its share of ironies. One of its ironies is that despite the fact that Descartes is the most influential of all modern epistemologists, there are no Cartesian epistemologists. Perhaps there never were. In the entire history of philosophy, perhaps Descartes was the only Cartesian. Indeed, there are those who doubt whether even Descartes was a Cartesian in the usual sense of the term. Be this as it may, the Cartesian project does have its appeal, in part because of its dramatic quality but also for philosophically more respectable reasons. My task is to inquire into these reasons. It is to ask what if anything is worth doing of the Cartesian project. No one thinks that it can be done in its entirety, and this has provoked some into proclaiming the death of epistemology, as if epistemology just were Cartesian epistemology. But of course, even if not everything in the Cartesian project can be done simultaneously, there may be aspects of the project that can be done individually and that are worth doing. This is what I will be arguing. In particular, I will be defending an egocentric approach to epistemology. However, I will insist, contrary to Descartes, that egocentric epistemology be done in a nondefensive manner—one that resists the temptation to search for guarantees of truth or even likely truth.

Acknowledgments

There are many people whose help I want to acknowledge: Robert Audi, Kent Bach, Marian David, Michael DePaul, Richard Fumerton, Gary Gutting, Mark

Kaplan, Richard Kirkham, Peter Klein, Jonathan Kvanvig, Ernest LePore, Alasadair MacIntyre, Eileen O'Neill, Alvin Plantinga, Phillip Quinn, William Ramsey, John Robinson, Stephen Ruth, David Solomon, Ernest Sosa, Bas van Fraassen, and Nicholas Wolterstorff.

In preparing this book, I have made use of some previously published material. Section 1.4 is based on "Rationality, Belief and Commitment," *Synthese 89* (December 1991), 365–392; section 1.5 on "Evidence and Reasons for Belief," *Analysis* 51 (1991), 98–102; sections 2.1 and 2.2 on "Skepticism and Rationality," in G. Ross and M. Roth (eds.), *Doubting: Contemporary Perspectives on Skepticism* (Dordrecht: Kluwer, 1990), 69–82; section 3.3 on "What Am I to Believe?" in S. Wagner and R. Warner (eds), *Beyond Physicalism and Naturalism* (Notre Dame: University of Notre Dame Press, 1992); section 4.3 on "Probabilism," *Midwest Studies in Philosophy* 15 (1990), 114–129; sections 4.2 and 4.5 on "The Epistemology of Belief and the Epistemology of Degrees of Belief," *American Philosophical Quarterly* 29 (1992), 111–124; and section 4.6 on "Being Knowingly Incoherent," *Nous* 26 (1992), 81–203.

New Brunswick, N.J.   R. F.
January 1992

Contents

Working Without a Net

1

Rational Belief

1. Rationality as a Goal-oriented Notion

Rationality is a goal-oriented notion. At least as a starter, we can say that questions concerning your rationality are questions concerning how effectively you are pursuing your goals. More exactly, this is a starter insofar as the questions are ones concerning a full-blooded notion of rationality. In a weak sense, you are rational simply because you are capable of being rational or irrational in the full-blooded sense. Being rational in the weak sense contrasts with being arational; stones, buildings, and artichokes are arational, whereas you are not. Being rational in the full-blooded sense contrasts with being irrational, and it is this notion of rationality that is goal-oriented.

Any such view invites the question of what makes something a goal. One answer is that your goals are those things that you intrinsically value. This answer manages to be at once too strong and too weak. It is too weak because it implies that anything you intrinsically value is a goal, however feebly you might value it and however trivial it may be. It makes your every passing whim into a goal—a whim for pistachio ice cream, for instance. The answer is too strong because it implies that something might not be a goal even if it is one of the dominating concerns of your life. If you do not intrinsically value the acquisition of wealth, it cannot be one of your goals, no matter how much time and effort you devote to its pursuit.

Suppose we say instead that your goals are those things that you significantly value, or perhaps better, those things that you would significantly value were you to be acquainted with all the relevant facts and were you to deliberate carefully about these facts. This avoids the above difficulties, but it does so at the cost of being vague. Still, a vague but otherwise adequate notion is better than none.

But is it otherwise adequate? An alternative approach is to think of goals not in terms of what is valued but rather in terms of what is valuable, where what is valuable need not be something that you either value or are disposed to value. Some will find this suggestion obvious, noting that it is common for people not to value their true ends, but others will find it unsettling. They will prefer to say of those things that are valuable without being valued by you not that they are among your goals but rather that they should be; valuing such things is part of a good life. Or they will deny altogether that something can be valuable for you if it is not valued by you.

I will glide over these issues. In what follows, one can pretty much presuppose one's favorite account of goals. I am primarily concerned here not with the theory of goals but rather with the theory of rationality, and my proposal is that it is best to think about judgments of rationality as judgments concerning how effectively individuals or groups are pursuing their goals. This is so regardless of what it is that we are rationally evaluating. Questions of rationality arise about many things—people, groups, beliefs, actions, decisions, strategies, methods, plans, and so on. A desideratum of a theory of rationality is that it provide a uniform way of thinking about all such questions. Rational belief, for example, should not turn out to be a fundamentally different phenomenon from rational action, as if the two shared only a common name. A goal-based approach to rationality , as I will try to show, can satisfy this desideratum. So, there is at least this much to recommend it.

But of course, it has its share of difficulties as well. An especially pressing one is that if questions about your rationality are essentially questions about how effectively you are pursuing your goals, it would seem that we cannot sensibly ask whether your goals are the sorts of things that it is rational for you to pursue. This alone might seem to warrant a fundamentally different approach. Perhaps it would be preferable to take a rules approach, one that makes rationality a matter of following a certain set of rules, rules that are constitutive of the notion of rationality.[1] Or perhaps we could take a virtue-based approach, one that understands rational actions, rational beliefs, rational plans, and so on as being the products of such intellectual virtues as thoroughness, impartiality, judiciousness, and the like.[2]

Both a rules approach and a virtue-based approach can and should leave room for means–end reasoning, just as a goal-based approach can and should leave room for rule-following and virtues. It's a question of what is taken to be fundamental.[3] But by taking rules or virtues as basic, the former two approaches provide us with a way of understanding how it might be irrational for you to pursue your goals. It is irrational if doing so would violate the rules constitutive of rationality or if doing so would be intellectually unvirtuous.

Even so, it is hard to escape the feeling that these approaches will strike us as plausible just to the extent that we are convinced that the proposed rules or the proposed virtues standardly promote our goals. Imagine a case in which this isn't so. Suppose you realize that you almost always are unlikely to achieve your goals if your actions, plans, and beliefs conform with the proposed rules—the rules that are supposed to be constitutive of rationality. Or suppose you realize that you almost always are unlikely to achieve your goals if your actions, plans, and beliefs are products of the proposed virtues. Would such actions, plans, and beliefs nonetheless be rational for you?

Quick remarks such as these are not enough to refute rule-based and virtue-based accounts of rationality, but they are enough to indicate that these accounts have problems of their own and that their superiority cannot be established by equally quick remarks to the effect that goal-based accounts make it impossible to question whether it is rational for you to pursue your goals. The depth of understanding an approach provides is more important than any quick counterargument against other approaches, and in the final analysis it is this that most recommends a goal-based approach over other approaches. It sheds more light on questions of rationality than they do.

Even so, something must be said about the charge that on a goal-based approach, no sense can be made of the idea that you might have goals that are irrational for you to pursue. The first thing to say is that the charge is untrue. There is, for one, the pedestrian point that it can be irrational for you to pursue one or more of your goals if doing so would worsen your chances of satisfying your other goals. Circumstances are typically such that you cannot simultaneously satisfy all of your goals. For lack of time and resources if nothing else, the pursuit of any given goal is likely to preclude the active pursuit of at least some others. Choices have to be made, and if you make these choices badly, you will be pursuing goals that are irrational for you to pursue.

The most obvious cases of this sort occur when your first-level goals come into conflict, but there are also cases in which the potential for irrationality is deeper because the conflict is deeper. Conflicts can arise across levels, for example. You might have meta-goals, goals about what kind of goals it is best for you to have, and these meta-goals might make it irrational for you to pursue some of your first-level goals. They might even make it rational for you to purge yourself of one or more of these goals, assuming that this is possible. For instance, you might have a preference for goals that if followed would generate a balanced, well-rounded life, but some of your first-level goals might encourage just the opposite kind of life. They might even encourage behavior that borders on being obsessive. If so, it may be rational for you to purge yourself of these goals or at least to diminish their importance. Your other goals and your meta-goals may give you a reason to do so.

Moreover, it is not just systemic conflicts among your goals that can make it irrational for you to pursue one or more of them. Some goals may be intrinsically irrational, in the sense that it is irrational for you to pursue them regardless of what your other goals are. This will be the case, for example, if the goal is a recognizably contradictory one, such as being present at your own funeral or belonging to clubs that will not have you as a member. Not every theory of goals will allow these to be among your goals, but if a theory does, it cannot be rational for you to pursue them, since you yourself realize that nothing can possibly satisfy them.

So, a goal-based approach to rationality does leave room for the irrational pursuit of goals. Indeed, there is even room for such irrationality to be pervasive. It would be pervasive if, as Sartre claims, our most fundamental projects typically involve self-contradictory goals, such as that of simultaneously being both wholly an object and wholly a subject.

Nevertheless, there may be an uneasy feeling that any goal-based view of rationality limits too severely our ability to criticize one another's goals. But insofar as there is this kind of uneasiness, it may arise not so much from a goal-based theory of rationality as from the theory of goals that is being presupposed. Suppose the theory is one that understands your goals in terms of what you value rather than in terms of what is objectively valuable. Such a theory allows you to have goals that seem weird or even perverted to the rest of us; but then, a goal-oriented way of thinking about rationality will imply that it is rational, all else being equal, for you to pursue these weird or perverted goals. If this is thought to be an unacceptable result, it can be avoided by rejecting a theory of goals that allows what is weird or perverted to be among your goals. For a variety of motivations, however, ranging from a healthy respect for diversity in the eyes of some to an unhealthy relativism in the eyes of others, many of us are uncomfortable with placing substantive restrictions upon what can count as a genuine goal. Nevertheless, what we give with one hand we may try to take away with the other. We are tempted instead to quibble with a theory of rationality that allows the pursuit of these goals to be rational.

This temptation arises from a misplaced impulse, but it is an impulse that is common in much of philosophy, to be found in traditions as otherwise dissimilar as the Aristotelean and Kantian ones. It is the impulse to turn every human shortcoming into a failure of rationality. The way to thwart this impulse is to remind ourselves that the charge of irrationality is not the worst, much less the only, criticism we can hurl at one another. We can criticize others as being unimaginative or hypocritical or self-pitying or cowardly or even unintelligent without implying that they are thereby irrational.

This observation may sound trivial when stated in isolation, but an assumption to the contrary does have a hold on many of us. If we cannot say of those who are pursuing weird, perverted, or otherwise unacceptable goals that they are irrational, we have a tendency, especially when doing philosophy, to be puzzled as to what we can say of them by way of criticism. Witness the tradition in ethics that is concerned with proving that egoists must be irrational. The hunt for such a proof is motivated in part by a desire to have a tool for changing the behavior of egoists, as if argument were the best way to alter behavior. This would be merely quixotic were it not for the fact that in the midst of such a hunt, it is easy enough to slide into the idea that the charge of irrationality is the only criticism of egoists worth anything. But insofar as the problem is having something to say by way of criticism of egoists, there is an easy solution. We can say of them that they are pursuing unacceptable goals. Their failures are failures of character or of outlook, failures that result in their caring for the wrong things. They are not necessarily failures of rationality.

Does this demean the role of reason in our lives? Suppose we think of our reason as something like the collection of all those cognitive abilities whose products are subject to rational assessment—the ability to deliberate, evaluate, plan, calculate, form beliefs, and so on. The worry, then, is that goal-based views of rationality tend to eviscerate reason by limiting its scope. Since our goals are subject only to weak kinds of rational assessments—concerning their contradictory nature or their mutual satisfiability, for example—the most fundamental questions of our existence are not the concern of reason. Reason's role in determining how we are to live our lives is thus a puny one. Its function is simply to find effective means to goals that are given to us independently of reason. As a result, the most fundamental questions of human existence become immune to rational investigation: they are located outside the realm of reason.

There is nothing in a goal-based approach, however, that makes this kind of evisceration of reason inevitable. On the contrary, such an approach leaves plenty of room for rational investigation of the most fundamental questions of our existence, if for no other reason than that questions always arise as to whether something really is a goal or merely appears so.[4] The only way to avoid such questions is to assume that our goals are always utterly transparent to us, but any such view of goals is implausible. Consider, for example, a view that makes our goals simply a function of what we want for its own sake, where it is further assumed that we can unproblematically discover what we want by introspection. Or consider a view that makes our goals a function of our fundamental choices, which are not made with the idea of securing something else that we want but rather are wholly unconstrained; choices made without reason and with complete freedom, and moreover completely transparent to us. On either of these views, reason's role is severely limited and essentially passive. It does not even play an active role in discovering what our goals are. It simply waits for goals to be given to it from some other source, whether it be human nature or human freedom. Then and only then does reason have a role to play, a role of finding effective means to these goals.

But once these kinds of views are rejected as implausible, nothing prevents the most basic issues of our lives from being the objects of rational inquiry. This is so whether our goals are in some manner given to us or whether we somehow create them in our free choices or whether a combination of the two. If our goals are not simply a matter of our surface wants or choices, if they are instead a matter of, say, our deepest wants and needs (ones that may be a function of the kind of creatures we are or the kind of society in which we live) or our deepest choices (ones that we may have made long ago in a not fully conscious way), and if in addition these needs or choices can change over time (as we mature or as the community in which we find ourselves is altered), then it is no trivial matter to determine what our goals are. We cannot do so simply by looking inward. Nor can we read them off in any easy way from our behavior or our preferences. Rather, discovering our goals is one of our intellectual projects, arguably our most important one, and it is a project that makes use of the entire range of our intellectual faculties.

Moreover, the way we conduct this project is itself open to rational assessment. The goal of the project is to determine what our most fundamental goals are, and questions concerning whether we are conducting the project in a rational way are questions concerning how effectively we are pursuing this goal. So, given a goal-based view of rationality, this project, like others, is one that can be conducted more or less reasonably.

On the other hand, any goal-based view of rationality does rule out attempts to define goals in terms of what it is rational for us to do or believe. There is an analogy here with realistic views of truth. The realist with respect to truth insists that although reason can help us discover the truth, it cannot be used to define it. Truth is one thing; what it is rational for creatures such as us to believe is another. A goal-oriented approach to rationality requires a similar distinction. Reason can help us discover our goals, and moreover being rational may even be one of our goals, but what makes something a goal cannot itself be defined in terms of rationality.

2. Reasons and Perspectives

A different kind of problem for goal-based approaches concerns the bearing that a decision, action, belief, plan, or whatever must have on your goals if it is to be rational. Consider decisions, for example. It is too stringent to insist that a decision of yours is rational only if it in fact will satisfy your goals. We want to allow the possibility of rational decisions turning out badly. It even seems too stringent to say that the decision is rational only if it is likely to satisfy your goals. After all, it might be that neither you nor anyone else in your position could have been reasonably expected to see that your decision was likely to have unwelcome consequences. Suppose we say, at least as a way of beginning, that your decision is rational provided that it will apparently satisfy your goals. We will then want to know straight off to whom this is supposed to be apparent. To you? To the members of your community? To a reasonably knowledgeable observer? The question is what the appropriate perspective is for making judgments of rationality.

This is not the only question that will arise. We will also want to know the extent to which something must apparently satisfy your goals if it is to be rational. Shall we say that your decision is rational only if it seems from the appropriate perspective to satisfy your goals better than any of the alternatives, or might something less than the very best do? Let me make some stipulations. As I use the terms, *reasonability* admits of degrees whereas *rationality* does not. Reasonability is a matter of the relative strength of your reasons. The rational consists of that which is sufficiently reasonable. This leaves open the possibility of a number of decisions being rational for you, even though some are more reasonable than others. A decision is rational as long as it apparently does an acceptably good job of satisfying your goals.

What is an acceptably good job? There are many complications here, the most pressing of which is that you have many goals, not all of which are equally important. This makes it natural to treat the rationality of a decision in terms of its estimated desirability, where this is a function of both the apparent effectiveness of the decision in promoting your goals and the relative value of these goals.⁵ We are thus driven to the issue of how, if at all, these values are to be measured. For the most part I will take the coward's path and ignore this issue, since it has received a good deal of attention from others. For the discussion at hand, it will do simply to say that a decision of yours is rational if its estimated desirability is acceptably high given the context, where the context is defined by the relative desirability of your alternatives and their relative accessibility. The fewer alternatives there are with greater estimated desirabilities, the more likely that your decision is rational. Moreover, if these alternatives are only marginally superior or if they are not readily accessible, then it will be all the more likely that your decision is rational. It will be rational because it is good enough, given the context.

Of course, this characterization of rationality is vague, but for purposes here it can be left vague. Indeed, it is probably best left vague for any purpose. In any event, the vagueness need not hinder the discussion of the points in which I am primarily interested, one of the most important of which has to do with the previously posed question of what the appropriate perspective is for making judgments of rationality.

There is no simple answer to this question. Judgments of rationality are judgments about how things look from some perspective, but in making these judgments, we can try to project ourselves into any one of a number of perspectives. Moreover, the same is true of the corresponding judgments that we make about what reasons there are to decide, to do, or to believe something. They too can presuppose various perspectives.

A perspective is essentially a set of beliefs, but it is convenient to identify these beliefs by identifying the individual, real or imaginary, whose beliefs they are. Thus, your perspective is constituted by your beliefs, your reflective perspective is constituted by the beliefs that you would have on reflection, the perspective of a knowledgeable observer is constituted by the beliefs that such a observer would have, and so on. What perspective we adopt in making a judgment of rationality depends upon our interests and the context.

We are sometimes interested in evaluating your decisions from your own egocentric perspective. Our aim is to assess whether or not you have lived up to your own standards. We try to project ourselves into your perspective, or perhaps the perspective you would have had were you to have been carefully reflective, and we evaluate your decision from it. We then give expression to our evaluations using the term 'rational' or one of its cognates. We are especially prone to project ourselves into your perspective when reconstructing a past decision of yours that from our more informed position we know has turned out badly. It may even be obvious in retrospect why the decision was likely to have turned out as it did. Accordingly, we are perplexed by it. It bewilders us. Dismissing it as irrational does not remove the bewilderment; it merely puts a name on it. Besides, we are inclined to be charitable, assuming that there probably was something in your situation, not immediately apparent to us, that resulted in your missing what now seems so obvious. We try to enter into your situation and see the decision from your perspective. We bracket to the extent possible any information that is now available to us but that was not then available to you. In addition, we try to identify the method that you thought was appropriate to use in interpreting the available information, a method that we perhaps regard as unreliable but one we nonetheless might grant was natural for you to employ, given your situation. If we discover such a method and if it identifies the decision you made as a satisfactory one, relative to the information available to you, we are likely to think we have shown why this decision was a rational albeit mistaken one for you to make. It was rational by your lights.

Similarly, when we are evaluating the decision of someone from a different culture, perhaps far removed from us in both time and place, it will often seem appropriate to adopt the decision-maker's egocentric perspective. Or short of this, it may seem appropriate to adopt a sociocentric perspective, whereby we evaluate the decision with respect to some standard that is relative to the community of the decision-maker. This perspective can be particularly attractive when the decision-maker belongs to a culture that we judge to be less advanced than our own. The method generally used in the decision-maker's culture may not be the method that we now think is best. Indeed, it might even be that his or her method encountered difficulties that led to the development of ours. Even so, we may think that it is unfair to evaluate the decision in terms of our more sophisticated standards.[6] After all, our method had not yet been developed. However, it is not unfair, we may think, to judge the that person's decision in terms of the ancestor of our method, the one that was standard in his or her community.[7]

In adopting a sociocentric perspective, we are concerned to see the decision not so much through the eyes of the individual as from the point of view of the individual's community. The main question is whether the decision is consistent not so much with the personal standards of the decision-maker but rather with the standards that were "in the air". Once again, we may very well give expression to the results of such an inquiry by using the language of rationality. We may say that decisions that were not in accord with these standards were irrational, even if they were in accord with the decision-maker's personal standards. They were irrational because they failed to meet the standards of excellence embraced by the community.[8]

The simplest versions of such a stance are ones in which we make a generalization about the egocentric perspectives of the individuals who make up the relevant community. We first identify the community, and we then identify what most members of the community would regard as an effective strategy for the decision-maker to use in trying to secure the goal in question. This result then becomes the standard by which we evaluate the decision. In negligence cases, for example, judges instruct juries to decide the issue by employing the standard of what a reasonably prudent individual would have done in the defendant's circumstances. The reasonably prudent person is an abstraction. It is an imaginary individual who embodies the community's standards of behavior and belief, but these standards are not just a matter of statistically normal behavior. They reflect what the community "feels ought ordinarily to be done, and not necessarily what is ordinarily done, although in practice the two would very often come to the same thing."[9] The aim is not for juries to evaluate the defendant's behavior in terms of the defendant's own egocentric standards but to use the views of ordinary members of the community to generate a standard that "eliminates the personal equation and is independent of the idiosyncrasies of the particular person whose conduct is in question".[10]

Evaluations of this sort place great emphasis on the standards of ordinary individuals. For some of our purposes, this emphasis may be too great, especially if there is an institutionalized division of intellectual labor, with it being the responsibility of one group to think carefully about issues of a certain sort and the responsibility of another group to think carefully about other sorts of issues. This division of labor can encourage us to evaluate certain kinds of decisions and beliefs, as well the methods that produced them not from the perspective of ordinary individuals but from the perspective of those who are experts.[11] We take their views, rather than those of ordinary individuals, as providing the best expression of the community's standards of excellence about these matters. The standards of ordinary people may enter into such evaluations but do so only indirectly, by helping determine who the experts are. They then drop out as irrelevant.

Even for such evaluations, however, the issue is one of apparent effectiveness. The concern is with what the experts would regard as the appropriate decision, strategy, or whatever, but of course even the experts can make mistakes. Indeed, like all individuals and groups of individuals, they can make even drastic mistakes. Effectiveness is no more a strict prerequisite of rationality in this sense than it is of rationality in an egocentric sense.

By contrast, effectiveness is a prerequisite of rationality in an objective sense. Nevertheless, even this sense of rationality can be given a perspectival reading. The relevant perspective is that of a knowledgeable observer. A decision of yours is rational in an objective sense only if a knowledgeable observer would take it to be an effective means to your goals. The observer need not be thought of as omniscient. We need not imagine that the observer knows with certainty the consequences of each of the options that are available to you. Rather, we need to imagine "only" that the observer has access to the objective probabilities of the various options yielding various outcomes. Thus, an option is rational for you, at least in the simplest of cases—for example, in which only one of your goals is involved—if the probability that this kind of observer would assign to its bringing about the goal is high enough to make it a satisfactory option.

Our evaluations of decisions that have not yet been made or whose consequences are not yet clear to us are ordinarily best understood in an objective manner. Suppose, for example, that in an upcoming race all the horses are running at the same odds, and we are discussing with our friends the question of which horse they have the best reason to bet on. If we know that all but one of the horses is less than healthy and that therefore the healthy horse is more likely to win than any of the others, then regardless of what our friends may believe, we will be inclined to think that we have what we need to answer the question: our friends have reason to bet on the healthy horse, since this is most likely to get them what they want—a winning bet.

Had we been considering one of their past losing bets, we might have been inclined to proceed differently. There might have been greater pressure to try to see the betting decision through their eyes, or perhaps through the eyes of the experts—say, those who are skilled at reading racing forms. But in discussing a decision that is still up for grabs, this is unlikely to be our tendency. We are unlikely to be interested in bracketing the information we have or the standards we think best for interpreting this information. Rather, we try to exploit fully whatever resources we have in an attempt to assess the objective probabilities of various options yielding various outcomes. We then give expression to these assessments using the notion of rationality or one of its cognates. We talk of what it is rational for our friends to do or what they have reasons to do or what they ought to do.[12]

We also make judgments with an objective content when we are evaluating our own current decisions. When I say that it is rational for me to do X, I am ordinarily not saying something about how things look from my own egocentric perspective. I cannot plausibly be understood to be asserting that from my perspective, doing X would seem to be an effective way to satisfy my goals. Nor can I plausibly be understood to be asserting something about how things look from an sociocentric perspective. I am not asserting, for example, that from the perspective of an average person in my community, X would seem to be an effective means to my goals. Rather, I am asserting something concerning the objective chances of X's actually satisfying these goals. Of course, whenever I sincerely assert something, you will be able to make inferences about how things look from my perspective, but that is irrelevant to the point here, which is about the content of my assertions.

What is true of my assertions is true *a fortiori* of my deliberations. When I am deliberating about what it is rational for me to do or believe, I am not deliberating about my standards or my community's standards. I am instead deliberating—to be sure, from my perspective—about the objectively correct standards. I am deliberating about what is objectively likely to accomplish my ends or what is objectively likely to be true. Analogous points hold for first-person plural deliberations. When we as a group are deliberating about what it is rational for us to do, we are deliberating about the objective chances of various options' bringing about our goals.

First-person but past-tense ascriptions of reasons are a different matter, however. When discussing our past decisions and beliefs, we often try to project ourselves into our past egocentric perspective. We try to remember how things looked to us then. We are especially inclined to do this if the decision or belief has turned out to be a mistake, since doing so may enable us to present ourselves in a favorable light. But when it comes to present-tense ascriptions of reasons, the pressure is reversed.

Initially it might seem odd to regard present-tense, first-person ascriptions of reasons as objective since it is natural to think of first-person, present-tense concerns as egocentric. However, the oddity disappears when issues of endorsement are clearly separated from those of content. It is easy to imagine contexts in which I project myself into your egocentric perspective and agree that from your perspective you have adequate reasons for X even though I myself do not endorse these reasons, since I do not think that they are objectively adequate. But this distinction between reporting reasons and endorsing them tends to collapse in the first-person. If I judge myself to have reasons for X, I ordinarily cannot withhold my endorsement. I cannot add the qualification that these reasons are not objectively adequate, that they merely appear so from my perspective. I cannot sensibly do this precisely because the contents of my self-assessments are typically objective.[13]

This conclusion points to a limitation of any egocentric or sociocentric account of rationality. Such accounts are inescapably incomplete. Indeed, their proponents cannot plausibly understand their current self-ascriptions of reasons in the way that their own accounts suggest. Ordinarily, only third-person or past-tense evaluations can be interpreted egocentrically or sociocentrically.

To be sure, there are some exceptions, the most notable ones occurring during philosophical moments. One way to conceive of epistemology, for example, is as an inquiry into our methods of inquiry. We make ourselves and our methods into an object of study. Within the context of such a study, it can be natural to make self-ascriptions of reasons that have an egocentric content, or at least this is what I will argue.[14] But for my immediate purposes, I want only to point out that this is so, granting that it is, because the epistemological inquiry has led us to look at ourselves from the outside. We are taking the anthropologist's stance with respect to ourselves, examining our intellectual projects to the extent possible as if they were someone else's. However, this stance cannot be maintained in nonphilosophical moments. It is not a stance, for example, that sane people take when they are deliberating whether they have good reasons to believe that their doctor is competent or their automobile safe. Nor is it the kind of stance that sane people take when they are constructing a list of reasons for, say, staying in a marriage or changing jobs. These judgments must be read as having an objective content.

Nevertheless, this is only to say that egocentric and sociocentric accounts are inevitably incomplete, not that they are to be dismissed as altogether implausible. In particular, it is only to say that the most charitable interpretation of some of our judgments of rationality is not the one that these accounts recommend. However, the same can be said of objective accounts

As I have already suggested, many of our judgments about the rationality of our own past decisions and beliefs cannot be given a charitable objective interpretation, nor can all the judgments of rationality that we want to make when doing epistemology. Moreover, the same is true of the judgments we make about the rationality of individuals far removed from us who are using methods that we consider to be inferior to our own. Indeed, if we weren't prepared to evaluate these individuals in terms of their own standards and if we weren't prepared to give expression to our evaluations using the language of rationality, we would be forced into a dilemma. Either we would have to find some way of insisting that their methods really are our methods after all, the ones that we take to be reliable, or we would be forced to say that there is no interesting sense in which they are rational. In effect, we would be forced either to make them into us or to dismiss them as irrational.

There is no single perspective that is adequate for understanding the entire range of our judgments of rationality. We make such judgments for a variety of purposes and in a variety of contexts, and the kind of judgment we are inclined to make varies with these purposes and contexts.

All of these judgments involve limitations. When we make egocentric and sociocentric evaluations of you, for example, there are limits as to how far we can enter into your perspective or the perspective characteristic of individuals in your culture. These limits are especially obvious when your culture is far removed from ours, but they are present in some form whenever we attempt to take the viewpoint of another. Moreover, all of our judgments are fallible. Egocentric and sociocentric evaluations are at bottom evaluations of you in terms of what we from our perspective take to be your situation and what we from our perspective take to be your standards or the standards of your culture. There can be no guarantee that our judgments about these matters are accurate. And of course, the same is true of the objective evaluations that we make. At bottom these are evaluations of you and your decision in terms of what we from our fallible perspective take to be the objective situation—in terms, for example, of what we take to be the objective probabilities.

None of these limitations, however, affect the recommendation I am making concerning the content of our judgments of rationality and irrationality. It is a truism that we cannot entirely escape our perspective. We make judgments in our perspective-drenched and fallible way concerning how things appear from perspectives other than our own current one.[15] My recommendation is that judgments of rationality or irrationality are best thought of as judgments about whether from some perspective a decision, strategy, belief, or whatever appears to be an effective means for achieving a certain set of ends. Any one of a number of perspectives might enter into these judgments, including, for example, the egocentric perspective of those being evaluated, the perspective of a typical member of their community, the perspective of an expert in the community, or the perspective of a knowledgeable observer.

Our everyday claims of rationality and irrationality do not make explicit the perspective that they are concerned with. They are commonly elliptical. Accordingly, if we are to understand these claims properly, we must take care to identify the perspective. Otherwise, we may find ourselves talking past one another.

Often enough, the context will make it obvious what the relevant perspective is. If, for example, someone says, "I don't care what you or anyone else might think, the rational thing for you to do is _____," then we can be pretty well assured that the perspective being adopted is an objective one. Sometimes the perspective will not be at all obvious, however, but if it is not, we can ask for it. We are always entitled to ask of someone making a claim of rationality or a corresponding claim about reasons, "From what perspective, from what viewpoint, is this supposed to be a rational (or irrational) thing to do?"

3. Reasons, Beliefs, and Goals

For convenience, I will restrict my attention, at least for the moment, to claims of rationality that purport to be objective. We need not worry about identifying the relevant perspective. Nevertheless, there is a second way in which claims about what it is rational for you to do or believe can be elliptical. Depending upon the context and our purposes, we can take into consideration all or only some of your goals.

Often enough, we do the former. We make claims about what is rational for you, all things considered. But for certain purposes and in certain situations, we make claims about a specific kind of rationality. For example, we might be interested in evaluating your decisions with respect to goals that concern your material well-being. If we judge that a decision to do X would be an effective means to these goals, we can say that in a prudential sense this is the rational decision for you to make. We can say this even if, with respect to all of your goals, both prudential and nonprudential, it is not rational for you to decide in favor of X.

Hence, to prevent misunderstandings, we need to be clear about what goals are at issue. Just as we are always entitled to ask of someone making a claim of rationality from what perspective this is supposed to be a rational (or irrational) thing to do, so too we are always entitled to ask, "With respect to what goals, what ends, is this supposed to be a rational (or irrational) thing to do?"

This point is especially important when the rationality of your beliefs is in question, since here as a rule we seem not to be interested in your total constellation of goals. Our interest is only in those goals that are distinctly intellectual. Thus, we typically regard as irrelevant the fact (if it is one) that were you to believe the workmanship on Japanese cars is shoddy, you would be more likely to buy a European or American model and accordingly more likely to promote in your own small way the prospering of Western economies, which, let us suppose, is one of your goals. We may grant that this goal gives you at least a weak reason not to buy a Japanese car, but we would not be inclined to say that it gives you even a weak reason to believe that Japanese automobiles really are shoddily made. More notoriously, in assessing whether it might be rational for you to believe in God, we are unlikely to join Pascal in regarding as relevant the fact (again, if it is one) that you increase your chances of salvation by being a theist.

Nevertheless, despite the claims of so-called evidentialists who insist that there cannot be good nonevidential reasons for belief,[16] there is nothing in principle wrong with evaluating the rationality of your beliefs in terms of how well they promote your nonintellectual goals. Indeed, if anything is mysterious, it is why we do not do so more frequently. After all, your beliefs affect you in a variety of ways and not just intellectually. They have a bearing on your actions as well as your emotions, and they thus have far-reaching implications for the quality of your life as well as for the quality of the lives of those who surround you. Why is it, then, that in our evaluations of beliefs, we are generally not interested in these kinds of considerations?

There are at least two explanations. First, many of our discussions concerning what it is rational for you to believe take place in a context of trying to persuade you to believe some proposition. We point out the reasons that you have to believe it. But for the purpose of getting you to believe something that you do not now believe, the citing of practical reasons is ordinarily ineffective. Even if we convince you that you have good practical reasons to believe a proposition, this usually isn't enough to generate belief. Offering you a million dollars to believe that the earth is flat may convince you that you have a good economic reason to believe the proposition, but in itself it won't be enough to persuade you that the earth really is flat.

By contrast, becoming convinced that you have good intellectual reasons to believe something—in particular, good evidential reasons[17]—ordinarily is enough to generate belief.[18] A belief is a psychological state that by its very nature, in Bernard Williams's phrase,[19] "aims at truth." John Searle expresses essentially the same point in terms of direction of fit. Beliefs, he says, by their very nature have a mind-to-world direction of fit: "It is the responsibility of the belief, so to speak, to match the world . . . "[20] When we propose nonevidential reasons for belief, we are not even trying to meet this responsibility. Our reasons do not aim at truth. As a result, they normally don't prompt belief. At best they prompt you to get yourself into an evidential situation in which belief will be possible. Think again of Pascalians who resolve to attend church regularly, surround themselves with believers, and read religious tracts in an effort to alter their outlook in such a way that belief in God will become possible for them.

Thus, insofar as our concern is to persuade you to believe some proposition, there is a straightforward explanation as to why we are normally not interested in the practical reasons you have to believe it; namely, it is usually pointless to cite them, since they are not the kind of reasons that normally generate belief. Similarly, in your own deliberations about what to believe, you ordinarily don't consider what practical reasons you might have for believing something, and part of the explanation is similar to the third-person case. Deliberations concerning your practical reasons are customarily inefficacious and hence pointless.[21]

There is another kind of explanation as well. Such deliberations tend to be redundant. Although you do have practical reasons as well as evidential reasons for believing, your overriding practical reason with respect to your beliefs is commonly to have and maintain a comprehensive stock of beliefs that contains few false beliefs.

You need such a stock of beliefs because you are continually faced with a huge variety of decisions, but you don't know in advance in any detailed way what kinds of decisions these will be. Consequently, you don't know the kind of information you will require in order to make these decisions well. This lack of advance knowledge might not be terribly important, were it not for the fact that you will need to make a number of decisions relatively quickly, without the luxury of time either to engage in lengthy research or to seek out expert opinion. You will be forced to draw upon your existing resources, and in particular upon your existing stock of beliefs. And if that stock is either small or inaccurate, you risk increasing the likelihood that your decisions will not be good ones.

So ordinarily, the system of beliefs that is likely to do the best overall job of promoting your practical goals is both comprehensive and accurate. Only by having such beliefs are you likely to be in a position to choose effective strategies for achieving your various goals. But then, since your evidential reasons indicate, or at least purport to indicate, what beliefs are likely to be true, you ordinarily have good practical reasons to have beliefs for which you have adequate evidence. Thus, for all practical purposes, taking this phrase literally, you can usually ignore practical reasons in your deliberations about what to believe. You can do so because usually these practical reasons will simply instruct you to acquire beliefs for which you have good evidence.

There are exceptions, to be sure. It is easy enough to imagine cases in which your evidential reasons and your practical reasons for belief are pulled apart. Consider some extreme cases. Suppose that a madman will kill your children unless you come to believe—and not merely act as if you believed—some proposition P for which you now lack good evidence. Then it will be rational for you to find some way of getting yourself to believe P. Similarly, if you are offered a million dollars to believe that the earth is flat, then it may be rational for you to try to acquire this belief.

Finding a way to believe these propositions may not be easy, however. You know that believing them would have beneficial consequences, but this is not the sort of consideration that ordinarily leads to belief. If you are to believe these propositions, you may need to plot against yourself in Pascalian fashion. In particular, you may need to manipulate yourself and your situation so that you come to have what you take to be genuinely good evidence for these propositions, even if doing so involves maneuvering yourself into what you would now regard as a worse evidential situation, that is, a situation in which you have misleading but nonetheless persuasive data about these propositions.

Such plots are unlikely to be narrowly contained. Beliefs ordinarily cannot be altered in a piecemeal fashion. Rather, significant clumps of belief have to be altered in order for any one to be affected. Hence, a project of deliberately worsening your epistemic situation in hopes of getting yourself to believe a proposition for which you now lack good evidence is likely to involve changing your attitudes toward an enormous number of other propositions as well. Furthermore, for such a project to be successful, it must hide its own tracks. A measure of self-deception will be necessary, whereby you somehow get yourself to forget that you have deliberately manipulated your situation in order to garner data favoring the proposition. Otherwise, at the end of your manipulations you won't be convinced by the evidence. You will be aware that it is biased in favor of the proposition.

It will be rational for you to engage in these kinds of desperate manipulations if your children's lives depend on your coming to believe the proposition. But in less extreme cases, the costs of such manipulations are likely to be unacceptably high relative to the benefits of the resulting belief. After all, Pascalian plots require considerable effort, and they are likely to affect adversely the overall accuracy of your beliefs and thus the overall effectiveness of your decision making. So, except in those rare cases in which huge benefits are in the offing, it will be irrational, all things considered, to engage in this kind of plotting against your epistemic self.[22]

Drastic plots against yourself may not always be necessary, however. Suppose that you have reasons to believe that your lover has been faithful despite credible testimony to the contrary, since believing this is the only way, given your attitude toward infidelity, of saving the relationship. Or suppose you have reasons to believe that you will recover from your illness despite clear indications to the contrary, since only this belief will generate the resolve needed to follow a regimen that increases your slim chances for recovery. These kinds of practical reasons for belief are no more capable of directly persuading you to believe the propositions in question than the threat of the madman or the offer of a million dollars. It is not enough for you to be convinced that believing these propositions will be good for you. On the other hand, for you to believe these propositions, it may be not necessary for you to engage in full-fledged self-deception either. More modest deceits may do. You may be able to find ways to take your mind off the evidence of your lover's infidelity or the symptoms of your illness. Simultaneously, you can fasten onto any sign of fidelity and health. You might even unconsciously adjust your standards of evidence. In the case of your lover, you may find yourself insisting upon higher standards of evidence than usual, and as a result it may take more to convince you of the infidelity. In the case of your illness, just the opposite might occur. You might adjust your standards downward, thus making it easier for you to believe in your recovery.

But even these cases confirm the general rule, since it is precisely in these cases, where an important goal pries apart practical and evidential reasons, that we are most prone to take practical reasons for belief seriously. Most of us will admit, for example, that it is not unreasonable for you to believe in your lover's innocence until you have something close to irrefutable evidence to the contrary. If this stance involves closing your ears to the sort of testimony that in other matters you would find credible, then so be it. The not-so-hidden presumption is that in this situation, where the practical consequences of belief are so significant, it is not irrational, all things considered, for you to resist your evidence. In effect, we are saying that although it would be rational for you to believe that your lover has been unfaithful were you exclusively an epistemic being—that is, were you exclusively concerned with the goal of having an accurate and comprehensive system of beliefs—it is important for you in this matter not to view yourself in this way. There are other important goals at stake.[23]

There are still other ways in which evidential and nonevidential reasons for belief might seem to come apart, and some of these ways seem to suggest that the two kinds of reasons might come apart with some frequency. It's not the exception that they are at odds with one another; it's closer to the rule. This suggestion is an especially troublesome one for epistemology, and I will try to argue against it in the next section. But in preparation I need first to take a step backward.

I have been presupposing a rough, intuitive distinction between evidential and nonevidential reasons for belief, but for what follows this distinction needs to be made with more care. No doubt it is hopeless to make it in a way that will satisfy everyone, but a good way to begin is to say that A provides you with an evidential reason to believe B only if you stand in an appropriate relation to A, and only if, in addition, from some presupposed perspective A seems to be a mark of B's truth. The appropriate relation that you must bear to A can be left open for purposes here; perhaps you must know A, or perhaps you must rationally believe it, or perhaps it is enough for you to have some sort of access to its truth. Similarly, the notion of a mark can be left somewhat vague. My purpose here is not to defend a particular account of evidence but rather only to sketch a general approach. Let me simply say, without any illusion that this statement is deeply illuminating, that A's truth is a mark of B's truth just in case A's truth makes B's truth objectively probable, where objective probability is given an empirical reading. It is a frequency or propensity of some sort.

One noteworthy feature of this approach is that it allows a factoring of evidence analogous to the one that I have already proposed for rationality. In an objective sense, A provides you with evidence for B only if, from the perspective of an observer who knows the objective probabilities, A's truth seems to be a mark of B's truth. Alternatively, A provides you with egocentric evidence for B only if, from your own perspective (perhaps on reflection), A's truth seems to be a mark of B's truth; similarly for a sociocentric conception of evidence.

Each of these notions ties evidence to what might be called "a purely epistemic goal." Purely epistemic goals are concerned solely with the accuracy and comprehensiveness of our current belief systems. Thus, the goal of now believing those propositions that are true and now not believing those propositions that are false is a purely epistemic goal. There can be other purely epistemic goals as well, but they all can be regarded as variations on this one.[24] For the time being I will restrict my attention to it.

But first, a terminological remark: when I speak of the goal of now having an accurate and comprehensive belief system and speak also of what might be a means to this goal, I am using "means" in a broad sense. In particular, there are constitutive means as well as causally effective means. A constitutive means to a goal is itself a part of the goal. For example, if we think of good health not just as a state in which you currently lack disease but also one in which you are not disposed to disease, then not having high blood pressure is not so much a causal means to the goal of good health as part of what it means to be in good health. Similarly, getting an A in your philosophy class is not a causal means to getting A's in all your courses but rather part of what is involved in getting all A's. It is a constitutive means to this goal. And so it is with believing a proposition for which you have good evidence. Even if the means cannot be causally effective to the goal of now having an accurate and comprehensive belief system, since the goal is a present-tense one, it can be constitutive to it. Believing the proposition appears, from the presupposed perspective, to be a part of what is involved in now having an accurate and comprehensive belief system.[25]

The important point, however, is that no other goal is tied to your evidence in the way that a purely epistemic goal is. No other goal is such that your evidence invariably purports to indicate what beliefs are likely to satisfy it. This is so even if the goal is an intellectual one, for example, that of believing over the long run those propositions that are true and not believing over the long run those propositions that are false. Although this may be one of your goals, it is not tied to your evidence in the way that a purely epistemic goal is. Your evidence need not even purport to indicate what beliefs are likely to satisfy it. There can be situations in which your long-term prospects for acquiring truths and avoiding falsehoods are apparently diminished by believing those propositions for which you now have evidence. This might be the case, for example, if among these propositions are ones about the intellectual shortcomings of humans. Believing these propositions might discourage you intellectually, thus worsening your long-term intellectual projects. Correspondingly, there can be situations in which your long-term prospects for acquiring truths and avoiding falsehoods are enhanced by believing propositions for which you now lack evidence. For example, let p be the proposition that you alone are a reliable inquirer and hence the future intellectual development of humans depends on you alone. Believing p is likely to increase your intellectual dedication. It's likely to make you a more serious inquirer. As a result, it's also likely to promote your goal of having accurate and comprehensive beliefs in the future. But presumably it is not a proposition for which you now have good evidence. It is the same with other goals. Your evidence indicates, or at least purports to indicate, what beliefs are likely to satisfy your purely epistemic goals, but it need not even purport to indicate what beliefs are likely to satisfy your other goals.

The tie between evidence and purely epistemic goals imposes a restriction upon accounts of evidence, and this is so whether the account is concerned with an objective, egocentric, or sociocentric conception of evidence. Whatever one's criteria of evidence, they must make sense, from the presupposed perspective, of this tie. The criteria must "aim" at identifying beliefs that are likely to satisfy a purely epistemic goal.

This restriction has more bite to it than might appear at first glance. Suppose that an account of rational belief recommends inferences of kind k, and suppose in addition that making such inferences will increase over the long run your chances for true beliefs. Even so, it may be that the account is not best interpreted as trying to describe when you have good objective evidence for believing something. To be so construed, it must be the case that the recommended inferences are likely not just to get you at the truth eventually but also to do so now.

For example, consider an account that recommends the following as an objectively desirable rule of inference: All else being equal, believe the simplest hypothesis that explains all the data in the domain at issue. There are various ways in which simplicity can be understood, some of which might make the above rule border on the trivial. If by definition an explanation is simple to the degree that its elements are not improbable relative to one another, then the above rule is relatively uncontroversial but also relatively uninteresting. In effect, it merely tells us to believe the most probable explanation, when all else is equal.[26] Let us instead say that the simplicity of a hypothesis is a function of such considerations as the number of the entities it postulates, the number of different kinds of entities it postulates, the number of laws it postulates, and the number of variables that are related in these laws.[27]

Since these various facets might be emphasized in varying degrees, this notion of simplicity is somewhat indeterminate, but it at least has the advantage of being nontrivial, which is what is needed for purposes here. The point at issue is that if an account emphasizing nontrivial considerations of simplicity is to be regarded as an account of objective evidence, it is not enough that it provide a rationale for thinking that a policy of believing simple hypotheses is likely to help us get at the truth eventually. There must be a rationale for thinking that the simpler of two hypotheses, all else being equal, is more likely to be true.

For the moment, assume there is no such rationale, or at least no non–question-begging one.[28] Does this assumption then mean accounts of rational belief that emphasize considerations of simplicity are inadequate? Not necessarily. It means only that it is best not to interpret them as evidential accounts, as ones concerned with evaluations of our beliefs in terms of how effectively they satisfy a purely epistemic goal. Rather, it is best to interpret them as being concerned with a wider range of goals, including long-term intellectual goals and perhaps even nonintellectual goals. Considerations of simplicity would seem to find a more natural home in this kind of account. Indeed, it seems easy to provide a plausible rationale for them, namely, simple hypotheses are easier for us to use than complex ones. They are easier to manipulate and easier to test, for example. This in turn suggests that a policy of believing the simplest adequate explanation over the long run will help promote our long-term intellectual goals as well as our nonintellectual goals. But if so, there would seem to be good objective reasons, all else being equal, to believe the simpler of two hypotheses, only these reasons are not evidential reasons. They are reasons based on considerations of theoretical convenience, not on the assumption that truths are apt to be simple.

4. Evidence, Belief, and Commitment

If there are good objective reasons to believe the simpler of two hypotheses but these reasons are not evidential ones, then this is yet another way in which evidential and nonevidential reasons for belief can come apart. All things considered, you might have adequate reasons to believe the simplest hypothesis that is empirically adequate, even though you don't have adequate evidential reasons for thinking that the hypothesis is true. Moreover, cases of this sort may not be particularly unusual. But if they are not unusual, the reassuring idea that your nonevidential reasons for belief ordinarily reinforce your evidential reasons begins to unravel, and it begins to look once again as if your epistemic self might be frequently at odds with your nonepistemic self.

But in fact, we are not forced to this conclusion. We are not forced to it, because we need not grant that when all your goals are taken into account, both intellectual and nonintellectual as well as both short-term and long-term goals, that you really do have adequate reasons to believe the simplest of otherwise equal hypotheses. You need not have adequate reasons, because you need not believe the simplest hypothesis in order to win the benefits of simplicity. Ordinarily, any intellectual or practical benefits of believing simple hypotheses can be won by adopting an attitude that is weaker than belief. They can be won by committing yourself to the truth of the hypothesis. If you are a scientist, for example, you can adopt it as a working hypothesis. You use the hypothesis without actually believing it. You can use it in the design of experiments, the formulation of other hypotheses, and so on.[29]

Admittedly, a policy of commitment may not always be effective. There may be an occasional situation in which the benefits of simple explanations, like the Pascalian benefits of theism, can be won only with genuine belief. Perhaps only belief would generate the perseverance and optimism necessary to win the benefits. But ordinarily, a sufficiently robust attitude of commitment toward the hypothesis will be as effective as genuine belief.

But if so, your evidential reasons for belief (that is, your reasons insofar as your goal is epistemic) and your total reasons for belief (that is, your reasons insofar as all of your goals are taken into account) do not come apart after all. The distinction between commitment and belief keeps them together. Ordinarily it is rational for you, all things considered, to believe only those hypotheses for which you have adequate evidence, even if believing a simple hypothesis for which you lack adequate evidence would produce significant benefits, for ordinarily, committing yourself to the truth of the hypothesis would also generate these benefits, and it would do so without sacrificing the accuracy of your belief system, that is, without sacrificing your epistemic goal.[30]

Problems of this sort arise for simplicity because it isn't a mark of truth, or at least so I have been assuming. Similar problems will arise for any proposed condition of rational belief that purports to be objective but cannot be plausibly construed as an evidential criterion, that is, cannot be plausibly construed as a mark of truth. On the one hand, it won't be possible to provide a plausible rationale for it in terms of a purely epistemic goal, since it is not a mark of truth. On the other hand, with respect to our total constellation of goals, a policy of committing ourselves to the truth of the propositions (hypotheses, theories, and so on) that satisfy the criterion will be preferable to a policy of actually believing these propositions.

For example, consider a criterion that recommends, as objectively desirable, belief in the most fertile of otherwise equal hypotheses; the one that encourages the most research projects of promise. Or consider a criterion that in a more blatant way involves our long-term intellectual interests and pragmatic interests—say, a criterion according to which it is rational for you to believe the hypothesis that most increases your current problem-solving effectiveness.[31] It is at least not obvious that these criteria can be plausibly construed as marks of truth, but if not, they will be subject to the same dilemma to which simplicity is subject. The challenge for the proponents of such criteria is to find some rationale for thinking that the criteria really are marks of truth.

For purposes here the important point is not so much whether this challenge can be met. Maybe it can. The point is rather that accounts emphasizing simplicity, fertility, problem-solving effectiveness, and the like have no chance of fulfilling the aspirations of their proponents unless there is some rationale for regarding these considerations as marks of truth. The proponents of these accounts want such considerations to have a general applicability to questions of rational belief. There is, they think, something that objectively recommends these considerations to us all as reasons for belief. But if so, the considerations must be evidential ones.

This remark isn't merely a terminological one about the term "evidence." It is a point about rational belief. If such considerations are going to make it rational for you to believe something, they must be marks of truth. It must be the case that by believing simple theories or fertile theories or ones that increase your problem-solving capacity, you increase the likelihood of having an accurate and comprehensive belief system. It will not do to argue that by believing such theories, you are likely to win various benefits in the future. The case must be made in terms of your present belief system. Otherwise, the criteria will at best identify hypotheses to whose truth it is rational to commit yourself rather than hypotheses that it is rational for you actually to believe.

The corollary, and this returns us to the thesis with which we began, is that ordinarily you have adequate objective reasons to believe only hypotheses for which you have adequate objective evidence. At first glance, it may seem otherwise. It seems as if considerations of simplicity, fertility, problem-solving capacity, and the like provide you with adequate reasons to believe hypotheses for which you lack adequate evidence. But in fact this isn't so. Either these considerations are marks of truth or they are not. If the former, then they are evidential reasons and there is a no conflict; if the latter, then these considerations are best addressed by a policy of commitment rather than belief, and once again there is no conflict.

The cost to this way of thinking about simplicity is significant, however, and will make many philosophers uncomfortable. The cost is irrationality. For if, as I have been assuming, simplicity is not a mark of truth but we nonetheless have a tendency to believe simple hypotheses, we are to that degree irrational. We have neither adequate evidential reasons nor adequate nonevidential reasons for these beliefs. We are thus less rational than we might have hoped.

In itself this isn't an objection. What we hope for and what is the case are two different things. Still, it is enough to warrant a closer look at the resolution, in hopes of showing that the irrationality here is not as serious as it might initially appear to be. This is precisely what I will be trying to show, but first some preparatory work is needed. A good place to begin is with the notion of commitment.

There are various ways in which you can intellectually commit yourself to the truth of a proposition. You can do so by presupposing it, for example, or by postulating, hypothesizing, or assuming it. Each of these attitudes is distinct from belief, but each is also distinct from merely acting as if the proposition were true. The latter can be entirely a matter of public display. Commitment cannot be: it is a deeper phenomenon, requiring a degree of intellectual engagement that need not be present when you are merely acting as if a claim were true. Commitment requires intellectual resolve, for instance, to think about matters in a certain way.

Nevertheless, committing yourself to the truth of a proposition and merely acting as if it were true have much in common, especially in the ways that they contrast with belief. For example, they are both context-dependent whereas belief is not. When you commit yourself to a proposition, as when you are merely acting as if it were true, you are ordinarily prepared to do so only in a limited range of situations. If you are a scientist, for example, you might commit yourself to the truth of a hypothesis within the confines of your professional life, but if you were asked about the hypothesis in a social setting, you might be reluctant to take its truth for granted. Likewise, in your deliberations about, say, a political problem to which the hypothesis is relevant, you might be reluctant to assume its truth.

Genuine belief is not like this. You don't believe a hypothesis relative to a context. You either believe it or you don't. As a result, belief is neither necessary nor sufficient for commitment. Just as you can commit yourself to a hypothesis that you do not really believe, so too you can refuse to commit yourself to a hypothesis that you do believe, since commitment might have unwelcome consequences. Perhaps it would be politically, even intellectually, unwise. Suppose you believe in the truth of a novel hypothesis but recognize that the case to be made for it, while strong, is not yet overwhelming. Then it might be premature for you to commit yourself to it. It might be premature, for instance, to assume it in the design of experiments and the formulation of other hypotheses. Doing so might impede rather promote its acceptance, and as a result impede rather than promote intellectual progress.

There are other parallels between committing yourself to the truth of a proposition and merely acting as if it were true. Consider situations in which you have objective reasons to act as if some proposition were true. Our daily lives are filled with such situations. You may have reasons to act as if the tie that has just been given to you really is your favorite color, despite the fact that you avoid buying ties of that color for yourself. You may have reasons to act as if the fish that has been especially prepared for you really isn't overcooked, despite its dryness. You may have reasons to act as if your colleague's presentation really wasn't overly repetitive, despite the obvious restlessness of the audience. Fear of giving offense may give you an adequate reason to act as if you believed that these propositions were true, but on the other hand it does not give you an adequate reason to believe that they are true.

Even so, you may have a tendency to believe such propositions and not merely a tendency to feign belief. You are touched by the gift, and perhaps this emotion causes you to disregard, at least momentarily, the fact that you have avoided ties of this color in the past. You get caught up in the good spirits of the table, and only later does it occur to you that contrary to your sincere compliments, the fish really wasn't very good. You want your colleague to do well and this wish prompts you to discount the restlessness of the audience, taking it to be a consequence of the hard, uncomfortable seats rather than an indication of boredom.

In a similar way, considerations of simplicity can play a role in shaping our beliefs, even if they do not provide us with adequate reasons for belief. At the very least, simplicity plays a role in initially filtering hypotheses. Some hypotheses are so complex that we do not take them seriously. We don't even reflect much about their merits, much less go to the trouble of testing them. It would be too time consuming to do so. Thus, these hypotheses are filtered out. The result is that sufficiently simple hypotheses become candidates for belief while sufficiently complex ones do not.

It is sometimes argued that considerations of simplicity also play a more positive and detailed role in our theorizing. They don't just eliminate hypotheses; they also play a role in determining the particular hypothesis that we end up believing. They might seem to play such a role, for example, in some parts of contemporary physics and some parts of mathematics, and perhaps they play such a role in philosophy as well.[32]

Even more strongly, it is sometimes asserted that all of us make use of considerations of simplicity in all of our theorizing and that if we did not, we would believe only a fraction of what we do.[33] We make use of simplicity, it is said, when we postulate atoms, electrons, and quarks, but also when we try to explain our friend's rudeness and when we refuse to take seriously the conspiracy theories of the flat earth society. This is perhaps an exaggeration.[34] No matter. It is clear that considerations of simplicity do play some significant role in shaping our beliefs, even though, we are now assuming, we don't have good objective reasons to believe simple hypotheses. At most we have reasons to commit ourselves to their truth.

Nevertheless, this role may be no more worth worrying about than your belief about the tie. Believing that the tie really is your favorite color encourages you to act in a way that does not give offense, and even though you lack adequate evidence for this proposition, your believing it need not have widespread detrimental effects. Of course, we can imagine situations in which it would have unwelcome effects; it might somehow prompt you to make a bad decision about some other, more important matter. But this need not be the case, and presumably it often is not.

Similarly for your beliefs in simple hypotheses: even if you do not have adequate evidence for these hypotheses and the benefits that accrue to you from these beliefs could have been secured by committing yourself to the hypotheses instead, none of this may matter much. As long as the beliefs do not adversely affect the rest of your life, as they ordinarily do not, there is no need for great concern.

This compromise will not be enough to satisfy those who think that believing the simplest of otherwise equal hypotheses is positively desirable. For them, it is not enough to point out that having such beliefs is not harmful. There must also be a positive rationale, a rationale for thinking that believing simple hypotheses is preferable to committing ourselves to them.

The problem is that there doesn't seem to be any such rationale, at least if we continue to assume that simplicity is not a mark of truth. Given this assumption, there is no way to provide the rationale in terms of a purely epistemic goal, and there seems to be no way of doing so in terms of our practical or long-term intellectual goals either. These goals can be won, and at no epistemic cost, by committing ourselves to the truth of simple hypotheses rather than genuinely believing them.

Even so, the point that needs emphasizing here is that the irrationality involved in believing simple hypotheses, if that be what it is, is of a very weak kind. One way to appreciate this point is to make a distinction between the beliefs it is irrational for you to acquire and those it is irrational for you to retain. Even if you did not have adequate reason to acquire a belief, it need not be rational for you to go to the trouble of ridding yourself of it, given that you do have it. This may be the case for belief in a simple hypothesis. If no significant harm is done by your believing rather than merely committing yourself to the hypothesis, it may not be irrational for you to continue believing it, even though you don't have adequate evidence for it and even though you had no adequate reason to begin believing it either. Going to the trouble of ridding yourself of the belief may not be worth the effort.

Moreover, you may not even have an adequate reason to try to change yourself so that you won't believe simple hypotheses in the future. After all, doing so may not be easy. If you have an inclination to believe simple hypotheses, then given that simplicity isn't a mark of truth, you have a disposition to be irrational, that is, a disposition to believe hypotheses that you don't have adequate reasons to believe. Nevertheless, it might not be rational for you to try to rid yourself of this disposition. Doing so may not be worth the trouble, especially if the disposition is a deep-seated one.

An even stronger and more interesting result may be possible. The set of cognitive dispositions that is best for you, given the kind of creature that you are, may include a disposition to believe rather than merely commit yourself to simple hypotheses. All other sets, or at least all those that are real possibilities for you, might be worse. They might be worse even though this set inclines you to acquire one kind of belief that you lack adequate reasons for acquiring—belief in simple hypotheses. Even so, all the other sets might have more serious drawbacks that would make your overall situation worse. Perhaps they would result in your spending more time deliberating over whether to believe or merely commit yourself to the truth of various hypotheses, thereby decreasing the amount of time you have to devote to other more important matters. If so, it may be rational for you to keep the set of dispositions that you now have, despite the fact that these dispositions tend to produce some irrational beliefs. In other words, it may be rational for you to be irrational in this way.

None of these points, not even the last one, implies that it is rational for you to believe, as opposed to commit yourself to, the simplest of otherwise equal hypotheses. On the contrary, they all acknowledge that it is not rational for you to do so. However, they do take much of the sting out of this kind of irrationality. They suggest that it can be rational for you to put up with this kind of irrationality in yourself. It might even be rational for you to encourage it, since the best overall set of cognitive dispositions for you would include the disposition to believe simple hypotheses.

Points of this sort are enormously important for our everyday assessments of beliefs. For the moment, however, these quick remarks will have to do,[35] since pursuing them would blur the main point at issue, which is that neither a crude evidentialism nor a crude pragmatism with respect to our reasons for belief will do. The evidentialist is right to insist that ordinarily it is deeply irrational to undertake a project of worsening our epistemic situation in hopes of securing a belief that will generate pragmatic or long-term intellectual benefits. On the other hand, the pragmatist is right in refusing to dismiss such benefits as altogether irrelevant to questions of rational belief. The correct position is one between evidentialism and pragmatism: pragmatic and long-term intellectual benefits are relevant to questions of rational belief, but in general these benefits are best won by believing that for which we have adequate evidence.

5. *Evidence and Reasons for Belief*

It is natural to think that evidence and epistemic reasons for belief go hand in hand. When you have one, you have the other. Having adequate evidence for the truth of a proposition always gives you an adequate epistemic reason to believe it, insofar as one of your ends is to have accurate and comprehensive beliefs. Correspondingly, if you lack adequate evidence for the truth of a proposition, you do not have an adequate reason to believe it insofar as your ends are epistemic.

This is an attractive idea, but unfortunately it isn't quite right. Belief in accordance with the evidence can itself affect the evidence, and when it does, evidence and epistemic reasons for belief can come apart. This can happen whether evidence is construed objectively, sociocentrically, or egocentrically. For convenience, I will ignore the sociocentric case and discuss the other two together.

Suppose you know that you will get your degree if you pass the final exam. You currently neither believe nor disbelieve that you will get the degree, but you do nonetheless have adequate evidence that you will pass the exam. You know that you have studied hard and that there is relatively little that you do not understand, and moreover you would concede, at least if you took the time to think about it, that this makes it likely that you will pass and thus get your degree.

So far there is nothing particularly unusual about the case. It's just another case in which you fail to believe a proposition for which you have good evidence. But now, add this wrinkle. In an attempt to teach you humility, your examiners will alter the exam, making it much more difficult, if you come to believe that you will get your degree. Indeed, they will make the exam so difficult that you are unlikely to pass. Moreover, the examiners are able to anticipate your belief, and thus they are able to ensure that if you come to believe that you will get your degree, the onslaught of belief and the alteration of the exam will be simultaneous. Finally, suppose you know all of this. You know that the examiners are prepared to act in this way.[36]

Then you are in a bind. You cannot believe that for which you have good evidence without undermining that evidence and thereby making your belief irrational. But notice, the problem is not with your evidence. By hypothesis, the evidence that you will get your degree is perfectly adequate and you realize this. Nor is the problem like those encountered in the familiar paradoxes of belief. The proposition that you believe P and P is false is a proposition that can be true, but there is a legitimate question as to whether you could genuinely believe it to be true. By contrast, there isn't any question of your being able to believe the proposition that you will get your degree. The problem lies elsewhere. It lies in the fact that belief in accordance with your evidence would destroy that evidence.[37]

Insofar as your goal is epistemic, what attitude is it rational for you to take toward the proposition that you will get your degree? Is it rational for you to believe or disbelieve or withhold judgment on this proposition?

It's hard to say. None of these options is epistemically desirable. If you disbelieve the proposition—that is, if you believe that you won't get the degree—you would then be believing what you realize is unlikely to be true. But you won't do any better by believing that you will get the degree. You realize that if you were to believe this, the exam would be altered, thus making it unlikely that you will get the degree. So once again, you would be believing something that you realize is unlikely to be true. The remaining option is to withhold judgment on the proposition that you will get the degree, but this option too is undesirable, since you would then be withholding judgment on a proposition that you realize is likely to be true.

Thus, insofar as your goal is epistemic, you really are in a bind. There isn't much to choose among the three options. Appealing to other goals may help some. In particular, you have pragmatic reasons not to believe that you will get the degree, since this belief is likely to have undesirable consequences. It is likely to result in your not getting the degree. So, this would seem to favor not believing over believing.

Still, the main point here has nothing to do with nonepistemic reasons for belief. The point is that believing you will get the degree would be epistemically undesirable, despite the fact that you have adequate evidence for the truth of this proposition. It would be a belief that is unlikely to be true, given what your evidence would be.[38]

This is an important point for epistemology. It illustrates that evidence for the truth of a proposition, whether it be objective or egocentric, need not invariably generate a corresponding reason to believe the proposition, because belief in accordance with the evidence might itself eliminate the evidence.[39]

The reverse is also possible. Belief against the evidence can itself create evidence, as is the case with self-fulfilling prophecies. Consider another exam case. Suppose you don't have strong evidence for thinking that you will pass the exam. The evidence indicates that your current chances of passing are about the same as your chances of failing. However, you know if you were to believe that you will pass, this would increase your confidence, and you also know that if you were confident, you would do much better on the exam. Indeed, you would do well enough to pass.

Here again, evidence and reasons for belief come apart, only from the other direction. You currently lack adequate evidence for the proposition that you will pass but you nonetheless have a reason to believe it, and not just a pragmatic reason. Believing this proposition is defensible insofar as your goal is to have accurate and comprehensive beliefs. You yourself realize that in believing that you will pass, you would be believing a proposition that is likely to be true.

On the other hand, it is also epistemically desirable to withhold judgment on the proposition that you will pass the exam. After all, you realize that your current chances of passing are only about 50–50, and you realize also that if you withhold judgment on whether you will pass, these chances won't be altered.

So, with respect to the epistemic goal alone, there is nothing to choose between withholding belief and believing. If you were to believe, then believing would be the best option. But equally, if you were to withhold belief, this also would be the best option.

Is there something to choose between these two options if we take into consideration other kinds of goals? Perhaps, but even here there are considerations on both sides. Since passing the exam is important to you and since believing that you will pass will help you pass, you have practical reasons to acquire this belief, all else being equal. But all else need not be equal. By hypothesis, you realize that you are likely to pass the exam if you come to believe that you will, but this realization need not be enough in itself to prompt belief, especially since you are convinced that your current chances of passing are only 50–50. Thus, if you are to acquire the belief, you may have to plot against yourself in a Pascalian manner so as to get yourself into a position where you can believe. This maneuver may have significant costs, and if the costs are great enough, they will outweigh the benefits of belief, making it irrational, all things considered, to engage in such plottings.

In any event, this discussion is a side issue. The most important point for epistemology is that this and the previous case illustrate that evidence and epistemic reasons for belief do not invariably go hand in hand. They can come apart. Since belief itself can create evidence, you can have an adequate epistemic reason to believe a proposition for which you lack sufficient evidence, and since belief itself can destroy evidence, you can lack an adequate epistemic reason to believe a proposition for which you do have sufficient evidence.

There is nonetheless a general, albeit more complicated, way in which evidence and epistemic reasons for belief are linked. They are subjunctively linked. Having sufficient evidence for a proposition gives you an adequate epistemic reason to believe it, unless believing the proposition would itself undermine the evidence. Correspondingly, if you don't have sufficient evidence for a proposition, then you don't have an adequate epistemic reason to believe it, unless believing it would itself create adequate evidence for the proposition.[40]

6. An Evaluation Procedure for Epistemology

The procedure I used to discuss evidential and nonevidential reasons for belief contains the beginnings of an evaluation procedure for epistemology. It is a procedure that can be used whenever we wish to assess an account of rational belief. It tells us, first, how to identify the subject matter of the proposed account and, second, how to assess the account given its subject matter. Moreover, the procedure flows naturally out of what I have urged is the best way to think about claims of rationality.

Claims of rationality, I have said, are to be understood in terms of a goal (or a set of goals) and a perspective. Every claim makes a proposal concerning how effectively an individual's or group's actions, beliefs, strategies, or whatever seem from the presupposed perspective to satisfy the presupposed goal. However, the perspective and goal can vary with the context and our purposes.

It is not surprising that this same variety is to be found in philosophical accounts that propose criteria for rational belief, rational action, or whatever. They too typically do not wear their subject matter on their sleeves. The way to make their contents explicit is analogous to the way in which the contents of particular claims of rationality are made explicit. It is done by identifying the perspectives and goals that they implicitly adopt. For example, if it is an account of rational belief that is in question, the way to make its subject matter transparent is to identify an important goal and important perspective such that beliefs fulfilling the criteria of rational belief laid down by the account seem from that perspective to be an effective way of satisfying that goal. If we find such a perspective and goal, we have a charitable interpretation of the proposed account.

This procedure also makes it easy to see how we can ridicule an account. We can do so by uncharitably interpreting its subject matter. Suppose an account implies that a belief is rational if it has characteristic X. If we so wish, we can display the account in an unflattering light by evaluating it in terms of a perspective P and goal G, such that from P having beliefs with X does not seem to be a particularly effective way of satisfying G.

Ridicule of this sort is a thriving industry in epistemology. Consider, for example, the debate between externalists and internalists. The former propose conditions of rational belief that need not be introspectively accessible to individual believers (for example, reliability conditions), and the latter tend to favor conditions that are easily accessible. Correspondingly, internalists adopt subjective-leaning perspectives in order to criticize the criteria of their externalist rivals; externalists return the favor by adopting objective-leaning perspectives in order to criticize the criteria proposed by internalists. In short, each side adopts a perspective that is guaranteed to make the least sense of the criteria of rational belief proposed by the other side and then triumphantly concludes that the criteria look implausible from its adopted perspective.[41]

Of course, none of this is made explicit. It is done under the guise of intuitions. Each side describes a number of cases and then bases its criticisms of the other side upon intuitions about what it is rational for someone to believe in these cases. Appeals to intuitions do have a place in epistemology, but the intuitions that are appealed to in these controversies are unhelpful, since epistemologists can, and do, tailor their cases to generate the intuitions they want.

Internalists can generate intuitions that make it seem as if what it is rational for us to believe is a matter of how things look from our own perspective. One way of doing so is to describe situations that we would not be able to distinguish from our current situation but in which, it is stipulated, the procedures that we now take to be reliable are unreliable, and vice versa. For example, the situation might be one in which ordinary perception is not reliable and the reading of tea leaves is, but where we have no indication of this whatsoever. Internalists can further encourage the intuitions they want by dropping clues as to what kind of perspective they want us to adopt in thinking about this situation. For instance, they might ask whether in such a situation we wouldn't be *entitled* to rely upon our senses in just the way that we ordinarily do. Wouldn't this still be a *responsible* way for us to proceed? And wouldn't it be *irresponsible* for us to resort to reading tea leaves, even if, unbeknownst to us, this procedure turns out to be reliable?

Externalists can play the same game. They can encourage intuitions that make it seem as if what it is rational for us to believe is a matter of the objectively correct standards. One way of doing so, for example, is to focus upon situations where the issue is which of two methods it is rational for a contemporary of ours to use, where we know full well that one of these methods is reliable and the other is not. And externalists, like their internalist opponents, can further encourage the intuitions they want by providing us with clues about the perspective they want us to adopt. They will avoid asking, "Which method would it be responsible for this person to use?" and will instead ask a question such as "Which method would put the person in a position to have knowledge?" A question of the latter sort has the effect of shaping our intuitions about what is rational for the person to believe, especially if it is assumed, as it commonly is in the literature, that knowledge is something close to rational true belief.

The intuitions that are elicited by such means cannot be of much value in settling the dispute between internalists and externalists. They cannot help because the intuitions themselves are shaped by the perspective that we implicitly adopt and because, depending upon the context and the clues we are given, it is sometimes natural for us to adopt one perspective, sometimes another. To have a convincing argument that externalism is the right approach and internalism the wrong one, or vice versa, we would need independent considerations—that is, considerations independent of our intuitions about concrete cases—to defend some perspective as the privileged one for making claims of rationality. But there are no such considerations, and no privileged perspective for making claims of rationality.[42]

In assessing a proposed account of rational belief, the only alternative is to be charitable. The search should be for the perspective that makes the most sense of the account's recommendations. There are limits, of course. The interpretation of an account should be in terms of an important perspective and, moreover, an important goal as well. This restriction is needed because for any proposed criteria of rational belief, it will be possible to find some bizarre perspective and some bizarre goal such that beliefs that satisfy the criteria will seem from that perspective to be an effective means to that goal. For example, if the criteria imply that beliefs with characteristics C are rational, the goal might be that of having beliefs that would have pleased de Gaulle and the perspective that of an individual, say, Smith, who thinks that beliefs with C would have pleased de Gaulle. If the only interpretation of an account is one that adopts a perspective and goal that are this peculiar, the account can be dismissed, but not so much because it is straightforwardly false. There is, after all, an interpretation of the account, one that makes sense of the recommended criteria. Rather, it can be dismissed because it will be what in philosophy is worse than false: it will be uninteresting—both because the goal is one that few if any of us have, de Gaulle himself perhaps having been the exception, and because the perspective is one that we don't think is an enlightening one from which to make evaluations of an individual's beliefs, Smith himself perhaps being the exception.

What we want is an interpretation in terms of goals and a perspective that can be interestingly generalized. The goals must be important for us all, or at least almost all of us. Moreover, they must not be gerrymandered. By this I mean that we cannot arbitrarily ignore certain kinds of goals in order to get the results we want. It is easy enough to see why we might be interested in evaluating an individual's beliefs with respect to a purely epistemic goal, and it is also easy to see why we might be interested in evaluations with respect to the total constellation of the individual's goals. But if something more than an epistemic goal and something less than the total set of goals are taken into account, there must be a point to this restriction, namely, something that we find particularly useful or interesting about evaluating the individual's beliefs with respect to how effectively they seem to satisfy this restricted set of goals.

Similarly, the perspective must be the kind from which it is interesting to make evaluations. Two dangers are especially to be avoided. One is that of adopting a perspective that is so powerful as to be irrelevant to questions of human rationality. This is the danger of overidealization, and I will discuss it in some detail later.[43]

The other principal danger is that of adopting a perspective that is so specific that we would not be interested in using it to evaluate the beliefs of very many people. This is the danger of idiosyncrasy, and it is primarily a danger for egocentric and sociocentric interpretations. For example, suppose an account of rational belief implies that our beliefs are rational just if they satisfy condition C, and suppose some random individual Smith, but almost no one else, thinks that beliefs with C are likely to be true. Then we can give an interpretation of the account in terms of an epistemic goal and the perspective of Smith. But unless there is reason to think that Smith is in a privileged position to determine what is likely to satisfy the epistemic goal, this interpretation won't be interesting. We are not apt to be interested in using the perspective of Smith to evaluate the beliefs of anyone other than Smith himself. What would be the point?

So, if an egocentric or sociocentric account is to be interesting, it must somehow ensure that its proposed criteria have a general applicability. One way in which this can be done is by making the criteria formal rather than substantive. The criteria can leave open the possibility that the substantive standards that our beliefs must meet if they are to be rational vary from person to person or from community to community. However, the criteria will provide instructions for identifying the relevant standards for each person. They can do so, for example, by explicitly making reference to the perspective that is to be adopted in evaluating an individual's beliefs. Consider an account according to which it is rational for individuals to believe propositions that they themselves would think defensible, if they were to be adequately reflective and their only goal was to have comprehensive and accurate beliefs.[44] Or consider an account according to which it is rational for individuals to believe whatever their communities would let them get away with believing.[45] Or an account according to which individuals' beliefs are to be measured against the standards of those who are the experts in their communities.[46] Each of these is an egocentric or sociocentric account, but each is also generalizable in a nonidiosyncratic way, precisely because each proposes formal rather than substantive criteria of rational belief. Each gives us a recipe for identifying the perspective that we are to adopt in assessing the rationality of an individual's beliefs.

By explicitly making reference to the perspective we are to adopt, these accounts go a long way toward providing their own interpretation.[47] But for

other accounts, the interpretations won't be so transparent. We will need to
search for an important perspective and an important goal (or set of goals) that
make sense of the proposed criteria. Actually, the task is a bit more complicated
than this. We also need to identify what the account takes to be the relevant
resources of the individual whose beliefs are being evaluated. A claim about the
rationality of your beliefs, when made fully explicit, has the following form: It is
rational for you to believe _____ because you have resources R and because
from perspective P it seems that, given R, believing _____ is an effective way
to satisfy goal G.

For example, on some reliabilist accounts your resources are perhaps best
understood as the collection of those cognitive processes and methods that are
available to you for use. The proposal, as least roughly, is that it is rational for
you believe _____ if method M would cause you to believe _____ and if a
knowledgeable observer (that is, one who knows the objective probabilities)
would regard M is the best available method for you to use insofar as your goals
are epistemic.[48] On some foundationalist accounts, by contrast, your resources
are perhaps best understood as the collection of your current psychological
states—all your beliefs, experiences, thoughts, memories, and so on. The concern, in other words, is to ask whether from some perspective P it seems that
believing _____ is an effective way for you to satisfy an epistemic goal G,
relative to the information contained in your total psychological state.[49] On still
other accounts, your resources are perhaps best construed as being more limited,
consisting perhaps only of your beliefs or your degrees of belief. So, if it is
possible for you to have experiences that are not represented in any way in your
beliefs, they will not be part of your current resources, even if they could easily
could made so, say, by drawing your attention to them.[50]

Whatever these resources are, they, like the perspective and the goal, must be
important ones, and in particular, we must in fact be apt to have them. Otherwise, the interpretation will be of no help in understanding the evaluations in
which we are most interested, namely, evaluations of our fellow human beings.

There is room for flexibility in providing an interpretation. There are three
elements with which to work: a goal, a perspective, and a set of resources.
Different combinations of these three elements can be said to constitute different
points of view, and more than one point of view may be capable of generating an
interpretation of an account. This presents no difficulty, however. One of these
points of view is likely to seem less strained than the others, and even if this isn't
the case, it will be an interesting property of the account that more than one point
of view can make sense of its recommendations. A problem arises only when
there is not even one plausible interpretation of the account.

There is an additional desideratum. We should try to avoid an interpretation
that itself makes use of the notion of rational belief or any of its cognates.[51]
Suppose an account implies that a belief is rational just in case it has characteristic X. Then it will not do to interpret the account as saying that from the
perspective of someone who is rational it seems that having beliefs with charac-

teristic X is an effective way for individuals with resources R to satisfy some goal G. The problem with such an interpretation is obvious. It leaves us with the task of providing an interpretation for the notion of rational belief that it itself employs. What we want is an interpretation that allows us to escape from the circle of notions having to do with rationality, reasons, and the like.[52]

This evaluation procedure encourages tolerance. It provides a framework within which a variety of epistemic projects can be seen to have their proper places. At the same time, it provides us with a critical tool, since the framework helps display the limits of tolerance. To illustrate how, consider again accounts that recommend inferences to the simplest adequate explanation. The evaluation procedure tells us to search for a perspective, a goal, and a set of resources such that from this perspective, believing the simplest of otherwise equal hypotheses would seem to be an effective means for individuals with these resources to satisfy this goal. For the sake of the illustration, it won't matter much how we construe the believer's resources. Let me simply stipulate that they are roughly a matter of the individual's current psychological states, plus the cognitive processes that are available to the individual for processing these states.

Suppose that simplicity can be plausibly regarded as a mark of truth. Then these accounts can be construed as accounts of objective evidence. They can be interpreted in terms of the purely epistemic goal and an objective perspective. On the other hand, if simplicity is not a mark of truth, we will need to look for some other interpretation. Suppose we try interpreting the account in terms of an objective perspective and the individual's total constellation of goals (or at least a range of goals wider than just the purely epistemic goal). Then we will have to find some way of avoiding the objection that committing oneself to the truth of simple hypotheses would also achieve these goals but would do so without sacrificing the epistemic goal.

Perhaps, then, we should look for a nonobjective interpretation. The major drawback, however, is that no such interpretation will satisfy the proponents of simplicity. They do not want merely to claim that from some egocentric or sociocentric perspective there appears to be something to recommend simple hypotheses. They want to claim that a policy of believing simple hypotheses really is a satisfactory means to some important goal.[53]

Even so, a plausible nonobjective interpretation will be better than none. However, there are problems even in providing this kind of interpretation. For convenience, I will discuss only interpretations that presuppose the perspectives of individual believers, but analogous problems would arise for sociocentric interpretations.

The simplicity of a hypothesis, we are assuming, is a matter of the number of entities it posits, the number of kinds of entities it posits, the number of fundamental laws it requires, the number of variables related in these laws, and other like considerations. But presumably at least some of us do not think, and moreover would not think even if we were deeply reflective, that simplicity in this sense is a mark of truth. Besides, presumably at least of us some of us also would not think that believing the simplest of otherwise equal hypotheses is, all things considered, a satisfactory means to any other important goal. Some of us, for example, may think that committing ourselves to such hypotheses is preferable to believing them, and still others of us may have no opinion on the issue. But if so, there is no interesting, that is, no generalizable, egocentric interpretation of these accounts—in other words, no interpretation that gives us all a reason to believe simple hypotheses. So, if there are no objective reasons to do so either, the most that can be said in favor of believing the simplest adequate explanation is that some misguided individuals have egocentric reasons to have such beliefs. This conclusion is neither very surprising nor very interesting.

Moreover, it does not help to assert that we all make constant use of considerations of simplicity in acquiring beliefs. I have suggested that this assertion is perhaps an exaggeration, but even if it isn't, this won't be enough to show that it is rational in some interesting sense for all of us to make use of simplicity. It doesn't even show that it is rational in an egocentric sense for all of us to do so, for according to the above assumption, at least some of us do not think, and would not think even on deep reflection, that believing the simplest of otherwise equal hypotheses is a satisfactory means to an important goal. Hence, at least some of us don't even have good egocentric reasons to have such beliefs. This puts us into an awkward position, given the assumption that we do make constant use of simplicity. It means that we are with some regularity irrational, and not just objectively irrational but also egocentrically irrational. We do not live up even to our own standards. Sometimes, however, the truth is awkward.

The conclusion, then, is that there is not obviously any promising interpretation of accounts that recommend belief in the simplest of otherwise equal hypotheses. There are three main possibilities, but none seems particularly likely. First, we could try to interpret the accounts in terms of a purely epistemic goal and an objective perspective, in which case we need to find some rationale for regarding simplicity as a mark of truth. Alternatively, we can try to argue that believing simple hypotheses effectively promotes our total constellation of goals (or at least a wide variety of our goals), in which case we need to find some way of dealing with the objection that committing ourselves to the truth of such hypotheses often seems preferable to believing them. Or finally, we could try to provide an interesting nonobjective interpretation, in which case we need to be able to assert that a policy of believing simple hypotheses is universally (or close to universally) regarded as desirable.

Thus, the proponents of simplicity would seem to be in a bind. However, I have already suggested that the bind may be less severe than it initially appears. In particular, there may be a way, albeit indirectly, of capturing the importance of simplicity in our intellectual lives without being forced to defend the idea that simplicity is a mark of truth or that it is universally regarded as desirable. And we need not reject the distinction between commitment and belief.[54]

For the moment, however, my aim is not to take a stand on this bind but merely to display it with the help of the above evaluation procedure. The procedure provides a framework within which a discussion of any proposed account of rational belief can take place. The first step is to look for a perspective, a set of goals, and a set of resources such that from this perspective, having beliefs that meet the criteria recommended by the account seems to be an effective way for individuals with these resources to satisfy these goals.[55] The next step is to compare this interpretation of the account with the aspirations of its proponents, as reported in their remarks about how they themselves want the account to be construed. If the two are at odds, there is an incoherence between the most natural interpretation of the account and the interpretation upon which its proponents insist. The final step is to ask whether the most natural interpretation, albeit perhaps at odds with the purposes of its proponents, is nonetheless an interesting one, where its interest is a function of the importance of the goals, perspective, and resources that provide the interpretation. If they are important, then the proponents of the account will have succeeded in doing something interesting even if they haven't succeeded in doing quite what they thought they were doing. On the other hand, if they are not important, there will be nothing to recommend the account. The most natural interpretation of it is incoherent with the aims of its proponents, and moreover there is nothing in the interpretation that makes the account independently interesting.

Why the talk of incoherence here? It is not unusual for the accomplishments of epistemologists to fall short of their aspirations. When this happens, why not simply say that these epistemologists have made a mistake, that they have taken something to be a condition of rationality that in fact is not?

With questions of rationality, things are rarely this straightforward. If judgments of rationality are essentially judgments concerning how effectively an individual seems from some perspective to be satisfying his or her goals, if there is no privileged perspective for making these judgments, and if, finally, either some or all of an individual's goals can be taken into account in making such judgments, it will be rare for a proposed account of rationality to be mistaken in any simple-minded way. There will be some perspective and some goal that make sense of the account's recommended criteria. But if so, the crucial questions to ask of the proposed account will not concern its truth or falsity; rather, they will concern the importance of the point of view that provides the most plausible interpretation of it, and they will concern whether this interpretation is at odds with the aspirations of the account's proponents. There will be a shift away from talk of the account's truth or falsity and toward talk of its importance and coherence.

7. Further Illustrations of the Procedure

The evaluation procedure tells us how to interpret an account of rational belief charitably. We are to seek the point of view that makes the most sense of the criteria that the account proposes. But frequently this interpretation will be at odds with the one that the proponents of the account endorse.

Consider the view of Descartes. According to him, it is rational for you to believe a proposition only if it is impossible for you to doubt its truth if you think carefully enough about it.[56] Descartes asserted that much of what you believe meets this criterion. For example, it is impossible for you to doubt your own existence and impossible as well for you to doubt the truth of your beliefs about your current, conscious mental states. He went on to state, more notoriously, that if you reflect carefully enough, you will find it impossible to doubt the existence of God and, as a result, the truth of many of your other beliefs as well.

It is now a commonplace that, contrary to what Descartes suggested, relatively few of our beliefs are impossible to doubt, and hence, given his criterion, relatively few are rational. I will return to this problem shortly, but for the moment I want to concentrate instead on a problem of interpretation. The problem arises because the most natural interpretation of Descartes's criterion is at odds with the way that he himself apparently thought of it. He seemed to think that his criterion guarantees the acquisition of only true beliefs.[57] In so doing it also guarantees that fully rational people will not disagree, at least when they have similar evidence. However, the criterion is not most charitably interpreted in this thoroughly objective fashion. After all, we might be psychologically constituted in such a way that we find it impossible to doubt the truth of propositions that are in fact false. But if so, there is no non-question-begging guarantee that what we cannot doubt is true.[58] Likewise, there is no guarantee that you and I cannot be rational and have similar evidence and yet still disagree, since you may be psychologically able to doubt what I cannot doubt, or vice versa.

This suggests that the most charitable interpretation of Descartes's criterion is not the one upon which he seems to insist but, rather, one that is more egocentric. In particular, his criterion is most naturally interpreted as presupposing the point of view of what individual believers on careful reflection, using all their resources of thought, imagination, and the like, would take to be an effective strategy to attain the goal of their now having a belief system that is as comprehensive as it can be without encountering any risk of error. Thus, what it is rational for me to believe is a matter of what I would take to be an effective strategy to reach the goal, what it is rational for you to believe is a matter of what you would take to be an effective strategy, and so on. This is a natural interpretation of Descartes's criterion because from each of our individual perspectives on reflection, the beliefs that we should have insofar as we are interested in having a comprehensive yet risk-free belief system are just those that we cannot imagine being false.

The goal appealed to in this interpretation is extremely demanding. The goal is not to balance the comprehensiveness of a belief system against its riskiness. Rather, the avoidance of risk operates as an absolute constraint. There must be no risk of error whatsoever, regardless of the benefits in increased comprehensiveness that might result from incurring some risks. Indeed, this is such a demanding goal that it would not seem to be of much interest. The problem isn't that we would not value an altogether risk-free belief system. We obviously would. The problem, rather, is that this isn't a realistic goal for us, given the kind of creatures we are. As a result, it is not all that interesting to evaluate our beliefs in terms of how effectively they satisfy this goal.

An analogous suspicion will arise about any account of rationality according to which there is little if anything that we can rationally do or believe. The suspicion will be that the account is presupposing an unrealistic point of view. When we are evaluating one another's actions, beliefs, and strategies, we are ordinarily interested in points of view that provide us with a realistic chance of being able to sort them in terms of their desirabilities. We recognize that people sometimes find themselves in situations in which all of their options are equally ineffective at promoting their goals. On the other hand, we normally won't be interested in a point of view that makes all options equally ineffective as a matter of course.

Yet, this is precisely what some epistemologies do. They adopt points of view that preclude or at least minimize any sorting of beliefs. All of our beliefs, or at least almost all of them, are ones that from the presupposed perspective do not seem to satisfy the presupposed goal. Descartes's epistemology, with its insistence that you believe only what you cannot doubt on reflection, is but one example of this. The most natural interpretation of his criterion is in terms of the goal of having a belief system that is as comprehensive as it can be, subject to the constraint that it be utterly risk-free. But even from your own egocentric perspective, it will seem that insofar as you have such a goal, you ought to have few if any of the beliefs that you in fact have. As a result, all or at least almost all of your beliefs will seem lacking from this point of view. Indeed, we can be pretty well assured in advance that this will be the case for all of your beliefs other than a few trivial ones. Thus, there won't be any significant sorting of your beliefs, and just because of this, the criterion threatens to become uninteresting.

This threat may not arise for every position with skeptical overtones,[59] but it will arise for those that try to achieve their skeptical aims simply by stipulating that your beliefs must meet impossibly demanding standards if they are to be rational. Any such position will face a threat analogous to the one faced by Descartes. The threat is not so much that it can be proven false as that it can be proven boring. Indeed, it is likely to be every bit as boring as an account whose criteria imply that your beliefs, whatever they may be, cannot help but be rational. For either kind of account, there is likely to be some point of view that is capable of making sense of the recommended criterion. So, it is not as if either account is straightforwardly false. The problem, rather, is that the points of view capable of making sense of their recommendations will not be ones that we are interested in using to evaluate one another's beliefs.[60]

Accordingly, the above interpretation of Descartes's criterion, with its emphasis on the egocentric perspectives of individual believers, does not solve the problems for Descartes's account. But unlike his own interpretation, it at least has the virtue of satisfying his proposed criterion of rationality. Hence, charity dictates that it be preferred over the official interpretation, the objective one that Descartes himself usually seems to favor. The cost of this charity, however, is incoherence, an incoherence between Descartes's own interpretation of his project and the most plausible interpretation of it.[61]

It is not hard to explain how this incoherence arises. It is a direct consequence of Descartes's attempt to collapse into one another two perspectives that cannot be collapsed, the reflective egocentric perspectives of individual believers and an objective one. The method of doubt is supposed to allow the two to be collapsed, the idea being that there is introspectively available to every normal adult a method of belief acquisition, namely, the method of believing only that which is impossible to doubt, that is guaranteed to generate only true beliefs. In this method Descartes thinks he has found a method of belief acquisition that is not only subjectively convincing but also guaranteed to be objectively flawless. The failure of his project results from the fact that he cannot have it both ways. There is no such method.

Descartes is not the only epistemologist with a meta-epistemology that is at odds with his epistemology. A number of contemporary epistemologists have also proposed interpretations of their criteria of rational belief that are at odds with most charitable intepretation of those criteria.

Consider, for example, Laurence Bonjour, who says that "the goal of our distinctively cognitive endeavors is *truth*," and who then goes on to add that "being epistemically responsible in one's believings is the core of the notion of epistemic justification."[62] This statement sounds as if Bonjour is interested in a notion of epistemic justification that emphasizes a purely epistemic goal and the perspectives of individual believers, albeit perhaps the perspectives that they would have had were they to have been sufficiently careful, sufficiently thorough, sufficiently unbiased, and so on. Thus, what it is rational for you to believe is a matter of what you would believe were you to be responsible in your efforts to believe truths, and what it is rational for me to believe is a matter of what I would believe were I to be responsible in my efforts to believe truths, and so on for every other individual.

The actual criterion of justified belief that Bonjour defends, however, has little to do with how things would look from the perspective of a responsible believer. According to Bonjour, if your beliefs are to be justified, they must be coherent, and coherence for Bonjour has both negative and positive aspects. For a set of beliefs to be coherent, they must not be inconsistent, and they must have a minimum of what he calls "probabilistic inconsistency." But this feature is not enough. The beliefs must also positively support one another, where this is a matter of there being objectively valid, inferential relations among the beliefs: "The basic requirement for such an inference relation . . . is that it be to some degree truth-preserving; any sort of relation which meets this requirement will serve as an appropriate positive connection between beliefs, and no other connection seems relevant here."[63]

If coherence is understood in this way, however, it often will not be easy for you to tell whether or not your beliefs are coherent. It is not always easy, for example, to discern inconsistency, much less probabilistic inconsistency. It may even be less easy to tell whether there are objectively valid, positive inferential relations among your beliefs. Thus, even if you are careful, thorough, and unbiased—even if, in other words, you are a perfectly responsible believer— you might make mistakes about these matters. You might think your beliefs are coherent when they are not. Bonjour himself admits as much. Indeed, he admits that his recommended criterion is so demanding that perhaps no one has ever satisfied it.[64] But then, we want to know, what has happened to the idea that being epistemically responsible is at the core of the notion of epistemic justification?

Similar tensions can be found in the epistemological system of Roderick Chisholm. At the heart of Chisholm's system is a set of interrelated epistemic principles, and with the help of years of refinement and qualification, the set now has a formidable complexity. This complexity ensures that Chisholm's critics will have ample opportunity to quibble over the implications of his principles, but for purposes here, the most interesting issue is not how such principles might be best formulated but rather how they might be best interpreted.

Chisholm himself provides plenty of hints. He remarks, for example, that one of the fundamental issues that his epistemology is meant to address is how to balance what William James called "our [two] great commandments as would-be knowers": know the truth and avoid error.[65] So, Chisholm's concern, like Bonjour's, is with a purely epistemic goal. In addition, he intends his principles to express necessary truths.[66] As such, they are meant to describe how it is rational for all of us to proceed intellectually, insofar as our aims are epistemic. On the other hand, the principles are also such that there is no guarantee that we won't fall into serious error, even if we proceed in accordance with them. Most roughly expressed, the principles give expression to the idea that in general it is rational for us to trust memory, perception, introspection, and the like. Most of us would be prepared to admit that this intellectual advice is sound, but it is not advice that altogether immunizes us against either error or the likelihood of error.[67]

Once this is noticed, it becomes tempting to think of Chisholm's principles in a more subjective fashion than he himself does. We can admit that in at least one important sense it is rational for us to have beliefs that conform to Chisholm's principles, but the sense would seem to be a subjective one. These principles, or something similar to them, reflect our own deep standards about how best to reach our primary intellectual end, namely, truth.

But of course, this interpretation is at odds with the interpretation that Chisholm himself insists upon, which is to interpret the principles in an objective manner. He regards them as necessary truths. Thus, he would say that they would apply even to people whose reflective, stable views about how to seek truth are quite different from those held by most of us. They too are rationally required to proceed in the way dictated by the principles.

The more subjective and, I am suggesting, more plausible interpretation of his principles suggests otherwise. According to this interpretation, the principles are best regarded as generalities that we from our perspective regard as plausible.

Intellectual procedures that conform to the principles are procedures that most of us on reflection would take to be generally reliable. Ultimately it is this feature that makes it reasonable for us to have the kind of beliefs that the principles recommend. On the other hand, were there to be people whose stable, reflective views about how to seek truth are very different from ours, then the principles would not describe what it is reasonable for them to believe. What it would be reasonable for them to believe would depend upon their deep standards, not ours.

Finally, consider Alvin Goldman. In *Epistemology and Cognition*, he says that he is interested in defending what he calls a "reliable process" account of epistemic justifiedness, where in the most simple case, reliability is "a tendency to produce a high truth ratio of beliefs."[68] He adds that he favors an objective notion of epistemic justifiedness, because it is only such a notion that can make sense of our intellectual practices and methodologies. He observes, for example, that statisticians in thinking about their methods worry about relative rates of errors or the probability of error, and these, says Goldman, are "objective benchmarks, not simply the statistician's personal opinion."[69] This way of thinking about epistemic justifiedness is further reinforced by Goldman's account of knowledge. He says that for a true belief to count as knowledge, it must be the product of a reliable process, but it must also be justified. But this, he reassures us, is not out of spirit with the reliabilist account of knowledge that he favors, since justification, he says, can be understood in terms of elements similar to those that he uses to understand knowledge.[70]

All this would lead one to assume that in thinking about issues of epistemic justification, Goldman is presupposing an objective perspective and a truth-related goal. However, the criteria of epistemic justification that Goldman actually defends makes the justifiedness of our beliefs a matter of whether they are produced by processes that, relative to the other processes at our disposal, have a high propensity to produce true beliefs in worlds that are "normal." A normal world is one that has the general features we take the actual world to have. But of course, if we are mistaken about the general features of the actual world, then these normal worlds, so defined, might be only distantly related to the actual world. As a result, our beliefs might be justified even if they were the products of processes that in fact had a very low propensity to generate true beliefs in the actual world. It is enough that they would be reliable in normal worlds. Similarly, our beliefs might not be justified even if they were products of the processes that in fact had a high propensity to generate true beliefs in the actual world. What matters, once again, is whether these processes would be reliable in normal worlds.[71] But then, an objective perspective and a truth-related goal will not be able to provide a satisfactory interpretation of this criterion. Indeed, the criterion cannot plausibly be regarded as reliabilist anymore.[72]

The most natural interpretations of the criteria that Bonjour, Chisholm, and Goldman propose are at odds, then, with how they themselves want their criteria to be understood. Something has to be revised, either their proposed criteria or their proposed meta-epistemology, or both. There may be relatively painless ways of making these revisions, and the evaluation procedure can be of help in telling us what these ways might be. Indeed, frequently this will be the real value of the procedure. It is obvious enough even without the procedure that the proposals of Chisholm, Bonjour, and Goldman must be altered in some way, but how to do so is likely to stay unclear until we have a plausible interpretation of their proposed criteria. We need some way of understanding the point of Chisholm's principles and the point of Bonjour's and Goldman's recommendations, especially since what they take to be the point of their principles and recommendations is at odds with a sympathetic interpretation of them. In particular, we need to describe a point of view from which their principles and recommendations make sense. If we find such a point of view and it is an important one, we will be able to pinpoint why the interpretation that each of these philosophers places upon his criteria is misguided. We will also be able to see why they have succeeded in doing something important, even if it is not exactly what they thought they were doing.

On the other hand, if we fail to find an important point of view that satisfies the announced criteria, this too will be significant. It will indicate that something has gone wrong with the criteria, and often enough we will have clues as to what this something is. Maybe the only point of view that satisfies the criteria makes use of a strange perspective. Or maybe there is a waffling between two perspectives, the result of which is that no unified point of view can make sense of the entire account. Various aspects of the account are best understood in terms of different goals and perspectives.

So, the procedure has both heuristic and therapeutic value. It provides us with a way of identifying the subject matter of a proposed account of rational belief, and in so doing also provides us with a way of diagnosing and correcting any tensions within the account. Just as our everyday claims of rationality are not readily transparent, so too our philosophical accounts of these claims are not readily transparent. We need some procedure that will help us understand them. The above procedure does this, and it has the additional virtue of tolerance. It allows us to see that questions of rational belief can give rise to a variety of projects.

This variety creates opportunities for confusion, and at no time have the opportunities been greater than at present. Epistemologists, philosophers of the physical sciences, philosophers of the social sciences, decision theorists, and many others are concerned with broadly normative issues about the formation and sustenance of beliefs, and they all give expression to their views on these issues by using the term 'rational' and its cognates. Even so, these accounts are not always rivals of one another. Often their proponents have different aims, despite their shared terminology.

Why there is this variety deserves attention. Part of the answer is simply that there is an enormous diversity in our everyday claims of rationality. We evaluate one another's beliefs in a range of contexts for a range of purposes, and the point of view we think is most appropriate for making these evaluations will depend upon these contexts and purposes. This variety is then reflected in the accounts of these evaluations that philosophers propose.

For a deeper explanation, however, we need to look at the history of the notion of rationality, and there is no better way to do so than to look at the history of philosophy. In large measure, its history is just the history of our notion of rationality.

The history of philosophy is doubly relevant for contemporary epistemologists. First, it has helped shape our current, everyday judgments of rationality, which are the touchstones of philosophical accounts of rationality. In addition, it has given us the discipline of epistemology with its characteristic puzzles. The problems and concerns with which contemporary epistemologists are occupied have in large measure been passed down to them by their philosophical ancestors. Every contemporary project on rational belief is to some extent a descendant of the great epistemological projects of the past, projects of the sort found in the works of Descartes and Locke, for example, just as Descartes's and Locke's projects were the descendants of still earlier ones.

These projects of the past were intricate. They had various aims and background assumptions, some of which we now think do not fit particularly well with one another and others that we find implausible on independent grounds. Contemporary philosophers who are interested in questions of rational belief are inclined to retain some aspects of these older projects while rejecting others. However, what one philosopher retains and rejects is not always the same as what another retains and rejects—hence the differences in their projects.

The Cartesian project, for example, involves a search for a method of belief acquisition that is Janus-faced . The aim is to find a method that is guaranteed to be both subjectively persuasive, thereby making us invulnerable to intellectual self-criticism, and objectively reliable, thereby putting us in a good position to have knowledge. This is a conjunction of aims that must be rejected. Considered individually, each is defensible. We can ask what has to be the case in order for us to have beliefs that are immune to self-criticism. Likewise, we can ask what has to be the case in order for us to have knowledge. The mistake is to think that the answer to the first question provides an answer to the second, or vice versa.[73]

Whereas Descartes saw only one project with two aspects, an egocentric one and an objective one, we must see two projects, and in doing epistemology, we must choose between them. Without always realizing that they are doing so, some epistemologists choose one way, some the other. Some choose to pursue the more subjective aspect of the Cartesian project, the one that sees rationality essentially as a matter of having beliefs that are defensible, given our own individual perspectives. The result is some kind of egocentric-leaning account of rational belief. Others take the opposite tack, embracing the more objective aspect of the Cartesian project, the part that is more closely connected with the search for conditions of knowledge. The result is some kind of externalist account of rational belief, one that deemphasizes the perspective of the individual believer.

An analogous story can be told about the influence of Locke. Again, the tendency is to try to separate various aspects of his project. The problem, however, is that the aspects we are inclined to separate are not so easily separable. Locke placed great emphasis on the idea that we all have an obligation to be rational, as well as on what he took to be the indispensable accompanying ideas that we have access to the conditions of rationality and that we have a good deal of control over what we believe. Many contemporary epistemologists are reluctant to endorse the latter two ideas. They resist voluntaristic conceptions of belief, and they resist as well the idea that the conditions of rational belief are such that we always have access to them. Nevertheless, the Lockean idea that questions of rationality are intimately linked to questions of obligation and responsibility is pervasive, both in our everyday lives and in philosophy. These same epistemologists find it natural to conceive their projects in this way. They assert that their accounts tell us what a *responsible* inquirer would believe or what an inquirer is *obligated* to believe. Often the result is incoherence, an insistence on the part of an account's proponents that the account be understood in terms of such notions as intellectual responsibility, intellectual duty, and the like, even though the actual criteria of rational belief proposed in the account cannot be charitably interpreted in these terms.

In any event, whether or not these quick historical remarks are ultimately defensible, the important point here is that the above evaluation procedure provides a framework within which the otherwise bewildering variety of past and contemporary projects on rational belief can be understood. It is a framework within which their similarities and differences can be precisely but also charitably articulated. It allows us to see how each might have its proper place. In addition, the procedure has therapeutic value. For one, it provides a tool for displaying incoherence. This is especially useful for accounts that are relatively complete, in the sense that their proponents not only put forward specific criteria of rational belief but also describe what they take to be the nature of their projects. The procedure shows us how some such accounts can be deconstructed. Take epistemologists to be narrators and their theories to be stories. The procedure can help us illustrate that the narrator's intended reading of the story is at odds with the story as it is actually told.

The procedure also provides us with a straightforward way to raise questions about the importance of an account of rational belief. There are a variety of such projects that can be done, but not all of them will be of equal importance. For an account to be significant, it is not enough for there to be some plausible interpretation of the criterion it recommends, and it is not even enough for this interpretation of the account to mesh with what its proponents say about it. Internal coherence is only the least we should expect. The account must also be linked in a natural way with our theoretical or practical concerns.

Epistemology is not meant to stand in splendid isolation. It is not simply an interesting intellectual puzzle. There must be some point to the criteria of rational belief that the epistemologist proposes. The evaluation procedure helps us to understand what this point might be. The procedure tells us to interpret the proposed criteria in terms of a point of view—a perspective, a goal, and a set of resources. The account is a significant only if this point of view is significant. The resources must be ones that we in fact are apt to have, and the perspective and goal must be central to our practical or theoretical concerns.

Notes

1. Kant can be interpreted as trying to give expression to some such notion of rationality with his categorical imperative. Among contemporary theorists, see Jürgen Habermas's notion of communicative rationality, Jon Elster's notion of formal rationality, and Herbert Simon's notion of procedural rationality. Habermas, *The Theory of Communicative Action*, trans. T. McCarthy (Boston: Beacon Press, 1981); Elster, "Rationality," in *Contemporary Philosophy: A New Survey*, vol. 2 (The Hague: Martinus Nijhoff, 1982), 111–31; and Simon, "From Substantive to Procedural Rationality," in S. Latsis (ed.), *Method and Appraisal in Economics* (Cambridge: Cambridge University Press, 129–48).

2. For a virtue-based approach to questions of rational belief, see Ernest Sosa, "The Raft and the Pyramid: Coherence vs. Foundations in the Theory of Knowledge," in P. French, T. Uehling, and H. Wettstein (eds.), *Midwest Studies in Philosophy*, vol. 5 (Minneapolis: University of Minnesota Press, 1980), 3–26, especially 23; Sosa, "Knowledge and Intellectual Virtue," *Monist* 68 (1985), 224–45; and Sosa, "The Coherence of Virtue and the Virtue of Coherence," *Synthese* 64 (1985), 3–28. See also Jonathan Kvanvig, *The Intellectual Virtues and the Life of the Mind* (Totowa, N.J.: Rowman and Littlefield, 1991).

3. Thus, just as the field of competitors in moral theory can be divided among consequentialist views, deontological views, and virtue-based views, so too there is a roughly analogous field of competitors in the theory of rationality.

4. Compare with Alasdair MacIntyre, *Whose Justice? Which Rationality?* (Notre Dame: University of Notre Dame Press, 1988).

5. The expression 'estimated desirability' is Richard Jeffrey's; see *The Logic of Decision*, 2d ed. (Chicago: University of Chicago Press, 1983).

6. Much of the work on understanding primitive cultures focuses upon the difficulties of avoiding just this kind of unfairness. For a sampling of these discussions, see Bryan Wilson (ed.), *Rationality* (New York: Harper and Row, 1970).

7. It is generally acknowledged that the chess strategies used by Bobby Fischer in 1972 were superior to those used by Paul Morphy in 1861. Does this then mean that Fischer was the better player? Not necessarily. Chess strategies evolve over time, and Fischer had the advantage of being able to draw upon an additional century of developing strategies and counterstrategies, ones that Morphy's play helped generate. See Simon, "From Substantive to Procedural Rationality," 146, who cites this example to make a different point.

8. Sometimes the key to seeing behavior as rational is to view it as a part of a larger practice or policy in which there are reasons to engage. Suppose you have been married three times previously but that you now promise to love and cherish your new spouse "until death do you part," despite there being every indication that this marriage will also be short-lived. When we hear you utter these words, we need not conclude that you are giving expression to a deeply irrational belief or that you are blatantly lying or even that you are deceiving yourself. Rather, your utterance can be "rationalized" by seeing it as a

part of a larger ritual—the marriage ceremony—in which you have reasons to participate. (I owe this example to Larry Simon.) In debates among philosophers of social science concerning the rationality of practices in primitive societies, it is sometimes suggested that what would seem to be blatantly ineffective practices, e.g., rain dances and the like, should be understood in an analogous way. We should emphasize either the symbolic character of the practice (e.g., the rain dance is an expression of the desire that it rain rather than of the belief that the dance is actually likely to produce rain) or the function of the practice (e.g., the rain dance is an activity whose function is to encourage social cohesiveness through communal action). See, e.g., John Beattie, *Other Cultures* (New York: Macmillan, 1964), especially chapts. 5, 12, and 13; and A. R. Radcliffe-Brown, *Structure and Function in Primitive Society* (New York: Macmillan, 1952), especially chap. 7. One of the limitations of these suggestions is that, unlike the often-divorced individual who is marrying once again, nothing we know about the natives suggests that they view their own behavior as being primarily symbolic or functional. They want rain. If we are to show that their participation in the rain dance is rational in their view, we need to tell a different kind of story.

9. Fowler V. Harper and Fleming James, Jr., *The Law of Torts*, vol. 2 (Boston: Little, Brown, 1956), 903.

10. *Glasgow Corporation v. Muir* (1943) A.C. 448, 457: Lord MacMillan.

11. Compare with Stephen Stich, "Could Man Be an Irrational Animal?" *Synthese* 64 (1985), 115–35.

12. "Behaviour is substantively rational when it is appropriate to the achievement of given goals within the limits imposed by given conditions and constraints. Notice that, by this definition, the rationality of behavior depends upon the actor in only a single respect—his goals. Given these goals, the rational behaviour is determined entirely by the characteristics of the environment in which it takes place." Simon, "From Substantive to Procedural Rationality," 130.

13. Compare with Moore's paradox. You can believe as well as say that I believe P but that P is false, and of course you may be right. On the other hand, it is odd or perhaps even impossible for me to believe or think this of myself.

14. See Chapter 2.

15. Compare with Thomas Nagel, *The View from Nowhere* (New York: Oxford University Press, 1986). One of Nagel's theses is that our ability to make judgments about how things appear from perspectives other than our own makes it possible for us to have an objective conception of reality. This same ability, he argues, gives rise to some of our deepest philosophical problems, e.g., ones having to do with personal identity, the nature of the mental, human freedom, and skepticism. Moreover, the intractability of these problems, Nagel argues, is largely due to tensions between egocentric and objective perspectives. What seems plausible from an egocentric perspective seems implausible from an objective perspective, and vice versa.

16. See W. K. Clifford, "The Ethics of Belief," in *Lectures and Essays* , vol. 2 (London: Macmillan, 1879, 183): "It is wrong, always, everywhere, and for anyone to believe anything upon insufficient evidence." Also see John Locke, "An Essay Concerning Human Understanding," in *The Clarendon Edition of the Works of John Locke*, ed. P. Nidditch (Oxford: Clarendon Press, 1975), Book IV, chap. 17, sec. 24: "For he governs his Assent right, and places as he should, who in any Case or Matter whatsoever, believes or disbelieves, according as Reason directs him. He that does otherwise, transgresses against his own Light, and misuses those Faculties, which were given him to no other end,

but to search and follow the clearer Evidence, and greater Probability." For a contemporary evidentialist, see Alan Gibbard, *Wise Choices, Apt Feelings* (Cambridge: Harvard University Press, 1990), especially 36–7.

17. Below I distinguish evidential reasons from the more general category of intellectual reasons.

18. Compare with Thomas Reid, who says, ". . . nor is it in a man's power to believe anything longer than he thinks he has evidence." *Essays on the Intellectual Powers*, in *The Philosophical Works of Thomas Reid* (London: James Thin, 1895), chap. 10, sec. 1.

19. See Bernard Williams, "Deciding to Believe," in Williams, *Problems of the Self* (New York: Cambridge University Press, 1973).

20. John Searle, *Intentionality* (New York: Cambridge University Press, 1983), 8.

21. Compare this with reasons to intend (or to try, or to choose) something. Just as the reasons we cite for believing P are ordinarily ones that purport to show that P is true, so the reasons we cite for intending to do X are ordinarily ones that purport to show that doing X is worthwhile. Still, there can be reasons for intending to do X that do not even purport to indicate that doing X is worthwhile (just as there can be reasons for believing P that do not even purport to indicate that P is true). Think of cases in which the intention to do X will produce benefits even if we don't do X. Here is an extreme example: someone offers you a million dollars if tomorrow you form an intention to drink a toxin on the day after tomorrow; if you form the intention tomorrow, you will get the money whether or not you actually drink the toxin on the day after tomorrow. (This is Gregory Kavka's example. See Kavka, "The Toxin Puzzle," *Analysis* 43 [1983], 33–36.) Something analogous, albeit less dramatic, may be true of everyday intentions, namely, they too may have consequences that are independent of the intended acts. The puzzle, then, like the puzzle for belief, is why we aren't inclined to take much notice of these consequences in arguing about the rationality of our intentions. Part of the solution is similar to the one above for belief. Becoming convinced that you have these kinds of reasons is ordinarily not enough to generate a genuine intention to do X. So, insofar as someone is trying to persuade you to have this intention, it will normally be pointless to cite such considerations. By contrast, if someone convinces you that doing X is worthwhile, you normally will acquire the intention.

22. Again there is a parallel with reasons for intending, trying, choosing, etc. You can have reasons for intending to do X that are not reasons for regarding X as worthwhile, but ordinarily considerations of this sort won't be enough to generate a genuine intention; you need to be convinced that doing X is worthwhile. Still, considerations of this sort might give you a reason to engage in Pascalian manipulations, in hopes of convincing yourself that X is worthwhile, which in turn would lead to the intention. But such a project is likely to have significant costs. It is likely to require even a measure of self-deception. These costs help ensure that ordinarily you have reasons to intend only that which you also have reasons to do. Compare with Michael Bratman, *Intentions, Plans, and Practical Reasons* (Cambridge: Harvard University Press, 1987), especially sec. 6.6.

23. The goals do have to be important ones, however. If we regard a goal as relatively trivial, e.g., the goal of thinking more highly of yourself than your acquaintances, then we will also regard as trivial whatever reasons for belief it might generate. Indeed, insofar as we are convinced that such reasons have shaped your beliefs, we will to that degree be dismissive of the beliefs as merely self-serving. Contrast this with the above cases, where your beliefs are also self-serving, but the "self-serving" goal is one that we regard as more

substantial, i.e., the saving of the relationship or better prospects for health. For a discussion of some related issues, see sec. 3.2.

24. Verisimilitude, for example, is a purely epistemic goal, the goal of now having beliefs that are approximately true. See Karl Popper, *Objective Knowledge* (New York: Oxford University Press, 1972). Likewise, the goal of now having as comprehensive a belief system as one can without encountering the risk of error is a purely epistemic goal (see the discussion of Descartes in sec. 1.7), as is the goal of now having degrees of belief that are calibrated with the objective probabilities (see the discussion of probabilism in sec. 4.4).

25. Still, it is not worth quibbling over terminological points. Suppose someone insists that only future states of affairs can be goals, since (1) all means are causal means, and (2) something cannot be a goal unless there are means of bringing it about. Then I will introduce new terms to capture what I have in mind. I will say, e.g., that now believing those propositions that are true and not believing those that are false is a value or a desideratum, and I will talk about what appears, from various perspectives, to satisfy this value or desideratum.

26. ". . . a hypothesis is complex rather than simple in this sense to the extent that it contains elements within it, some of which are unlikely to be true relative to others, thus making the hypothesis as a whole unlikely on a purely *a priori* basis to be true; it is simple to the extent that this is not the case." Laurence Bonjour, *The Structure of Empirical Knowledge* (Cambridge: Harvard University Press, 1985), 183. Bonjour is well aware that this is a minimalist conception of simplicity. Indeed, that's what makes it suited for his special purpose. His strategy is to use this seemingly innocent notion of simplicity in an attempt to argue against skeptical hypotheses.

27. I take these from Richard Swinburne, "Simplicity and Choice of Theory," unpublished. Compare with Nelson Goodman, *The Structure of Appearance*, 2d edition (Indianapolis: Bobbs-Merrill, 1966).

28. For example, it will not do to argue that the history of the physical sciences is characterized by progressively greater predictive power and that the simplest explanation of this predictive power, to contradict half of Wilde's aphorism, is that the truth is rarely pure but usually simple. This is a common enough argument. It is sometimes argued that the simplest explanation of the increasing predictive power of the physical sciences is in terms of the increasing verisimilitude (i.e., approximate truth) of physical theory. The simplest explanation of this, it is further argued, is that the criteria of theory choice that scientists actually use, among which (it is asserted) is simplicity, are marks of verisimilitude. The problem with this argument is obvious: the explanations being invoked themselves presuppose that simplicity is a mark of verisimilitude. I will later argue (see sec. 2.5) that this kind of question-begging enterprise is not as trivial as it might appear to be, but on the other hand it is also not particularly helpful if we are casting about for some rationale, even a vague one, for thinking that simplicity really is a mark of truth.

29. Compare with Bas van Fraassen, *The Scientific Image* (Chicago: University of Chicago Press, 1985).

30. Of course, it is easy enough to imagine benefits that could be won by belief but not by commitment. Suppose, e.g., that you derive aesthetic pleasure from believing simple, elegant theories but not from merely committing yourself to them. This then gives you a reason for believing such theories as opposed to committing yourself to them. The hitch is that not very many of us actually have such reasons. Although some of us may

find it aesthetically satisfying to use or even merely to contemplate simple theories, there are not very many of us for whom this aesthetic satisfaction is dependent upon believing that these theories are true.

31. Compare with Larry Laudan, *Progress and Its Problems* (Berkeley: University of California Press, 1977).

32. Just because of this role, many philosophers have antirealist views about physics, mathematics, and philosophy. Sometimes these views are expressed in a semantic thesis, according to which the theories in question, strictly speaking, are neither true nor false, and sometimes they are expressed in an epistemological thesis, according to which we don't have adequate reasons to regard them as true. Whether such antirealist theses are defensible hinges in part on the question of how extensively the data have guided the development of the theory, as opposed to how extensively considerations of convenience and simplicity have done so. It hinges on this question precisely because neither side to the debate generally feels comfortable in regarding the latter kinds of considerations as marks of truth.

33. See Goodman, *The Structure of Appearance*; Swinburne, "Simplicity and Choice of Theory"; William Lycan, *Judgement and Justification* (Cambridge: Cambridge University Press, 1988); and Elliot Sober, *Simplicity* (Oxford: Clarendon Press, 1975).

34. Nelson Goodman has suggested that "it is almost a commonplace that it was considerations of simplicity that led to the rejection of the Ptolemaic system." What is a commonplace is that with enough alteration, the Ptolemaic system could have been made adequate to the observations. It is also true that if the existing background theory and information had been held fixed, these alterations would have required a more complex theory. On the other hand, it is far from obvious that if clever enough changes had been made in the background theory, the resulting overall theory, i.e., the Ptolemaic theory plus the background theory, would have been any less simple in an objective sense. Of course, changes in the background theory would have required complex revisions of existing beliefs. So, in this nonobjective, belief-relative sense, retaining the Ptolemaic system would have been less simple, but on the other hand it also would have been lacking in credibility relative to these beliefs. Contrast with Nelson Goodman, "The Test of Simplicity," in Goodman, *Problems and Projects* (Indianapolis: Bobbs-Merrill, 1972), 279.

35. I return to the issue in sec. 3.2.

36. Earl Conee discusses a similar case in "Evident but Rationally Unacceptable," *Australasian Journal of Philosophy* 65 (1987), 316–26.

37. Once again, analogous problems arise with respect to intentions, plannings, choosings, tryings, etc. Ordinarily, if you now have reasons to do X at some later time, you also now have reasons to form an intention to do X at that time. There are exceptions, however. The intention itself might undercut your reasons for doing X and hence your reasons for intending it. For example, you might have adequate reasons to confront your bosses tomorrow with your suspicions of the firm's illegal dealings even though you know that if you were now to form an intention to do so, this would make you nervous. You might also know that when you are nervous, you have a tendency to be more insulting than you mean to be and that this in turn is likely to make your bosses defiant and hence even less willing than they are now to look into the matter. Contrast with the Kavka case discussed in note 21 above.

38. Ordinarily, becoming convinced that you have good evidence for a proposition is enough to prompt belief in it, but the above situation seems to be one of the exceptions to

this general rule. One way of illustrating this is to suppose that it is not an exception. Then the moment you become convinced that your evidence makes it likely that you will get your degree, you will come to believe that you will get it. But then at the next moment, assuming that you are aware of this belief, you will realize that your evidence now makes it likely that you won't get your degree and hence you will come to believe you won't. Moreover, matters won't stabilize there. You will continue to vacillate between belief and disbelief until either the exam is given or exhaustion sets in. The alternative and more plausible suggestion is that in this kind of situation, where you are fully aware of your predicament, you might not believe that you will get the degree despite being convinced that you have good evidence for this. For a contrasting view, see Richard Swinburne, *Faith and Reason* (Oxford: Clarendon Press, 1981), chap. 1, who argues that believing that P is likely to be true is equivalent to believing P.

39. Assume that you cannot believe a proposition without thinking it (i.e., conceiving it). Let P be the proposition that you have never thought, the proposition that $25^2 = 625$, and suppose that you have adequate evidence for P—perhaps, e.g., you know that you have never tried to square any number greater than 15. Then this is another kind of case in which belief in accordance with the evidence might eliminate that evidence (since believing P itself involves thinking the proposition that $25^2 = 625$).

40. Compare with Richard Jeffrey's view that decisions must be ratifiable; see Jeffrey, *The Logic of Decision*.

41. For a painfully clear instance of this kind of criticism, see sec. 1 of my "What's Wrong with Reliabilism?" *Monist*, 68 (1985), 188–20.

42. See sec. 1.2.

43. See especially sec. 4.4.

44. This is at least roughly the kind of account I will be defending in Chapters 2, 3, and 4.

45. See Richard Rorty, *Philosophy and the Mirror of Nature* (Princeton: Princeton University Press, 1979).

46. See Stich, "Could Man Be an Irrational Animal?"

47. Indeed, the first of the above accounts identifies both the relevant perspective and the relevant goal. It entirely provides its own interpretation.

48. See Alvin Goldman's discussion of resource-relative reliabilism in *Epistemology and Cognition* (Cambridge: Harvard University Press, 1986), especially 104–6.

49. See Roderick Chisholm, "Self-Profile," in R. Bogdan (ed.), *Roderick M. Chisholm* (Dordrecht: Reidel, 1986), 3–77, especially the definition of epistemic preferability on p. 53. See also Chisholm, *The Theory of Knowledge*, 3d ed. (Englewood Cliffs, N.J.: Prentice-Hall, 1989), 60.

50. Some versions of coherentism (for beliefs) and probabilism (for degrees of belief) seem to presuppose resources of this sort.

51. Compare with Goldman, *Epistemology and Cognition*, 23; and Jaegwon Kim, "What Is 'Naturalized Epistemology?'," in J. Tomberlin (ed.), *Philosophical Perspectives*, vol. 2, (Atascadero, Calif.: Ridgeview, 1988), 381–405.

52. Of course, it may be desirable to define some epistemic notions in terms of others, but if so, we will want a neutral interpretation of the defining notion, i.e., an interpretation that does not itself make use of the notion of rationality. This is my strategy in sec. 3.2, where I explicate 'responsible belief' in terms of what it is egocentrically rational for us to believe and where 'egocentrically rational belief' is explicated without recourse to any other notion of rationality.

53. See, for example, Lycan, *Judgement and Justification*; Swinburne, *Faith and Reason*; Bonjour, *The Structure of Empirical Knowledge*, especially 180–88; and William H. Newton-Smith, *The Rationality of Science* (N.Y.: Routledge and Kegan Paul, 1981), especially pp. 226–32. Also see Paul Thagard, "The Best Explanation: Criteria for Theory Choice," *Journal of Philosophy* 75 (1978), 76–92; Gilbert Harman, "The Inference to the Best Explanation," *Philosophical Review* 74 (1965), 88–95, and *Thought* (Princeton: Princeton University Press, 1973); Paul Churchland, "The Ontological Status of Observables: In Praise of the Superempirical Virtues," in P. Churchland and C. Hooker (eds.), *Images of Science* (Chicago: University of Chicago Press, 1985), 35–47, and Churchland, *Scientific Realism and the Plasticity of Mind* (New York: Cambridge University Press, 1979), especially secs. 2, 3, 7, and 10; Wilfrid Sellars, *Science, Perception and Reality* (New York: Humanities Press, 1962); and Ernan McMullin, "The Fertility of Theory and the Unity of Appraisal in Science," in R. S. Cohen, P. K. Feyerabend, and M. W. Wartofsky (eds.), *Boston Studies in the Philosophy of Science*, vol. 39 (Dordrecht: Reidel, 1976), 395–432.

54. See the end of sec. 1.4. Also see sec. 3.2.

55. Or more exactly, this is so for accounts that offer substantive criteria. If the criterion proposed by an account itself makes reference to the relevant perspective and/or goal, then it provides at least part of its own interpretation. The criterion is formal. In effect, it is a criterion for identifying substantive criteria (which might vary from person to person or among cultures).

56. This isn't quite right, since Descartes recommended his method of doubt only for science and not for everyday use. But for the discussion here, this qualification can be ignored.

57. This is the standard view of Descartes's intentions, articulated, e.g., by Bernard Williams in *Descartes: The Project of Pure Enquiry* (London: Penguin Books, 1978), especially chap. 2.

58. Of course, Descartes was not unaware of this problem. The question is whether he appreciated its full force. Many discussions of the so-called Cartesian Circle focus on this question. See, e.g., Alan Gewirth, "The Cartesian Circle," *Philosophical Review* 71 (1962), 504–11; Anthony Kenny, "The Cartesian Circle and the Eternal Truths," *Journal of Philosophy* 67 (1970), 685–700; Fred Feldman, "Epistemic Appraisal and the Cartesian Circle," *Philosophical Studies* 27 (1975), 37–55; James Van Cleve, "Foundationalism, Epistemic Principles, and the Cartesian Circle," *Philosophical Review* 98 (1979), 55–91. I return to this issue in sec. 2.5.

59. See sec. 2.3.

60. Suppose it is asserted that (1) a belief is rational only if criterion X is met, (2) criterion X can rarely if ever be met, and (3) knowledge requires rational belief in this sense. Wouldn't this be a criterion of rational belief with skeptical implications that is nonetheless interesting, precisely because together with assumptions (2) and (3) it implies that we know almost nothing? Not necessarily. The real force of the argument may point in the other direction. It may show that questions of knowledge are uninteresting.

61. Indeed, this may cause us to question the standard view of Descartes's intentions. It may make us wonder whether he was really even a Cartesian, one who regards his criterion as providing a guarantee of truth. There are commentators who argue, against the standard view, that he did not. See, e.g., Nicholas Wolterstorff, "The Emergence of Rationality," manuscript; and Harry Frankfurt, *Demons, Dreamers, and Madmen* (Indianapolis: Bobbs-Merrill, 1970). In support of his interpretation, Wolterstorff cites this

passage from *Second Set of Replies*, trans. Cottingham, Stoothoff, and Murdoch, *The Philosophical Writings of Descartes*, vol. 2 (New York: Cambridge University Press, 1985), 103–4:

> What is it to us that someone may make out that the perception whose truth we are so firmly convinced of may appear false to God or an angel, so that it is, absolutely speaking, false? Why should this alleged 'absolute falsity' bother us, since we neither believe in it nor have even the smallest suspicion of it? . . . It is . . . no objection for someone to make out that such truths might appear false to God or to an angel. For the evident clarity of our perceptions does not allow us to listen to anyone who makes up this kind of story.

62. Bonjour, *The Structure of Empirical Knowledge*, 7–8.

63. Ibid., 96.

64. Ibid., 152.

65. See Chisholm, *Theory of Knowledge*, 13.

66. Ibid., 62–63.

67. See secs. 2.1 and 2.2.

68. Goldman, *Epistemology and Cognition*, 26.

69. Ibid., 72–73.

70. Ibid., 54

71. Ibid., 106–7, 113.

72. In "Strong and Weak Justification," *Philosophical Perspectives* 2(1988), 51–69, Alvin Goldman recognizes this problem. As a result, he abandons the criterion he defended in his book and introduces instead two distinct notions of justified belief, one of which is explicitly egocentric and the other of which is objective.

73. See sec. 2.6.

2

Skepticism

1. Rationality and Skeptical Hypotheses

One way of motivating skeptical doubts is by invoking skeptical hypotheses. By 'skeptical hypothesis' I mean a hypothesis that implies that most of our ordinary beliefs are false. For example, if we are under the control of a deceiving demon or if we are brains in a vat being programmed to have misleading perceptual experiences, then much of what we believe is mistaken, and mistaken not just in detail but overwhelmingly.

Not every philosopher who worries about skepticism is worried about such hypotheses. Hume was not, for instance. His concern was that we don't have good reasons for our ordinary beliefs, and of course this is one kind of skeptical worry. But he preferred to raise this worry without having recourse to specific skeptical hypotheses. Indeed, he thought that "only a fool or a madman" would seriously entertain them.

Be this as it may, skeptical hypotheses have been allowed to set the terms of the epistemological debate. They convince no one, and no one is interested in asserting their truth. Yet they still have an enormous influence. It is often influence by provocation. They provoke epistemologists into endorsing metaphysical and linguistic positions that antecedently would have seemed to have had little appeal. Skeptical hypotheses, it is said, cannot even be meaningfully asserted, or if they can, the nature of God or the nature of truth or the nature of thought makes it altogether impossible for them to be true. There are those who refuse to be provoked, but even their epistemologies tend to be dominated by skeptical hypotheses. The hypotheses push them into an overly defensive posture from which it can seem that the test of an epistemology is how well it would fare in a hostile environment.

I will discuss in some detail both of these reactions to skepticism, but for now it will do merely to note that my working assumption is that there must be a third way. There must be a way of thinking about skeptical hypotheses that is neither dismissive nor submissive. I will try to describe such a way. My ultimate suggestion will be that skeptical hypotheses are meaningful and possibly even true, but that they demonstrate not so much the impossibility of knowledge as its irrelevance. More precisely, they demonstrate its irrelevance for a certain kind of epistemology, what I will call 'egocentric epistemology'.

The kind of skeptical challenge that is most familiar to us is the kind that concerned Descartes. To be sure, the skeptical tradition is an ancient one, but the challenges of the ancient skeptics had a different aim from those discussed by Descartes. The followers of Pyrrho of Elis, for example, saw skepticism as a way of life and a desirable one at that. Suspending judgment about how things really are was thought to be a means to tranquillity. There is no hint of this in Descartes. He did think that skeptical doubt could be put to good use. It could help deliver us from our prejudices and thereby help put our beliefs upon a secure foundation.[1] But even for Descartes, skepticism was first and foremost a threat rather than an opportunity, and it remains so for us.

Descartes thought it was a threat, however, that could be successfully met. He thought that by making rational use of our cognitive resources, we can guarantee the truth. Correspondingly, he thought that error is something for which we are always responsible. We have the tools to avoid it. Knowledge is ours for the taking. We need only to be sufficiently reflective and sufficiently cautious. If we are sufficiently reflective, we will come to perceive clearly and distinctly the truth of various propositions; if we are sufficiently cautious, we will refrain from believing anything else. Skeptical hypotheses were of interest to Descartes precisely because they provided him with a dramatic way to illustrate these assumptions. They helped him dramatize the potential power of reason. One need not rely upon tradition or authority for one's opinions. One can stand alone intellectually, deciding for oneself what to make of the world and what to make of one's tradition.[2] And if in doing so one makes proper use of one's reason, one can be assured of knowledge.

An increasing specialization of intellectual labor has made us sensitive, in a way in which Descartes was not, about the extent to which we rely upon the opinions of others, just as a heightened appreciation of cultural relativity has made us more sensitive about the extent to which we are shaped by our traditions. Even so, we are as reluctant to rely uncritically upon our authorities and traditions as Descartes and his Enlightenment successors were upon theirs. We realize how difficult it is to distance ourselves intellectually from our surroundings, but we realize also that even our best scientists can be mistaken and that even our most venerable traditions can be misguided. Hence, we too feel the need to make up our own minds.

This need creates for us an intellectual predicament that is much like the one Descartes describes at the beginning of the *Meditations*. It is an egocentric predicament, prompted by a simple question: What am I to believe? I cannot simply read off from the world what is true, nor can I unproblematically rely upon the acknowledged experts or the received traditions to guide me toward the truth. I instead must marshal my own resources. I must marshal them to determine by my own lights what is true and who is reliable and what if anything is defensible about the intellectual traditions of my community. In this respect the individualism of Descartes has won the day.

What we find unacceptable in Descartes is his unguarded optimism. We think it naive. We no longer think that by properly marshaling our resources we can be assured of the truth. Being sufficiently reflective and sufficiently cautious is no guarantee that we will avoid error. It is not even a guarantee of reliability. Even so, philosophical problems come down to us through time, and today we remain under the spell of the epistemological aspirations of our philosophical ancestors. The cure is to remind ourselves that their aims need not be ours. What they took to be an intellectual problem in need of a solution we can appreciate as part of the human condition. Given the kind of creatures that we are and the kinds of intellectual methods available to us, we cannot help but lack guarantees of the sort they sought. This is no more a problem for us than is that of finding a way to do without oxygen. We just are creatures who need oxygen. Similarly, the lack of intellectual guarantees just is part of our condition. The problem is how to react to that condition.

The reaction need not be one of abandoning egocentric epistemology. Fully embracing reliabilism, for example, would constitute such an abandonment. The egocentric question is, What am I to believe? To answer this question, I must marshal my resources in an effort to determine what methods of inquiry are reliable. So, from the egocentric perspective, it is altogether unhelpful to be told that I am to have beliefs that are the products of reliable methods. Of course, no sensible reliabilist would claim otherwise. The point, rather, is that at least some reliabilists seem satisfied with an epistemology that does not address the problems of the egocentric predicament, despite the fact that such problems have been at the heart of the great epistemological projects of the past. My point, in turn, is that we need not be satisfied with this. We can do better.

If we are to do better, we must give up an assumption that has had a hold on epistemologists from Descartes through Gettier. According to Descartes, rational belief always results in knowledge. It is rational for you to believe that which is clear and distinct for you, and what is clear and distinct for you is true. By contrast, most contemporary epistemologists construe the link between rational belief and true belief in a looser manner than did Descartes. A rational belief can be false. As a result, a rational true belief need not constitute knowledge. As Gettier pointed out, a true belief can be rationally inferred from a rational but false belief, but this true belief will not be an instance of knowledge. Even so, the difference between Cartesian and contemporary epistemologies is not so great, since within the latter it still is commonly assumed that a rational true belief is at least in the vicinity of knowledge. It is this assumption that must be abandoned. More exactly, it must be abandoned if the answer to the question What is it rational for me to believe? is to be relevant to the egocentric predicament. The assumption must be abandoned because it ties rational belief too closely to knowledge, for if by being rational, one cannot be assured of having mostly true beliefs, then a rational true belief need not be even a remotely plausible candidate for knowledge.

Skeptical hypotheses can help illustrate this. Imagine a world in which a demon alters your environment so that you make egregious perceptual errors, without having any indication of this, but suppose also that the demon allows you to have a few true perceptual beliefs. Suppose, for example, the demon permits the existence of a few red tables, but no nonred ones, and he allows you to perceive the red tables without interference. On the other hand, the demon also arranges things so that you seem to see many more nonred tables than red ones. So, most of your perceptual beliefs are false, and even most of your perceptual beliefs about tables are false. Only on those few occasions when you are in the presence of red tables are your perceptual beliefs true. These isolated true beliefs are not good candidates for knowledge. Why not? If we insist the explanation is that these beliefs are not rational—say, because perception is not reliable here— then the sense of rational belief that we are invoking won't be relevant to the egocentric predicament. On the other hand, if we admit that these beliefs are rational, we are admitting that rational true beliefs are not always good candidates for knowledge.

This is not to say that it is impossible to find a fourth condition that when added to rational true belief is sufficient to yield knowledge. But it is to say that any such condition, if it is to be plausible, must somehow rule out the possibility that the belief in question is an isolated true belief. To put the matter loosely, and it may be that it cannot be put any other way, the condition must rule out your being radically deceived about related matters. But then, it is not the rationality condition that is doing the brunt of the work here. After all, your perceptual beliefs, we are now assuming, can be rational even if a demon arranges things so that they are radically mistaken.

Points of this sort raise the suspicion that if a notion of rational belief is relevant to the egocentric question, it won't even be a necessary condition of knowledge, much less one that when combined with truth is nearly sufficient. There are well-known examples in the literature that seem to support just such a claim. There is the example of the chicken sexer who is somehow able to identify reliably the sex of young chickens, and the example of the boy who when he gets on his rocking horse is somehow able to identify the winners at the local track. The intuition is that in these cases, and in others like them, the individuals have knowledge. They somehow manage to have knowledge, even if we don't understand how it is that they do so. On the other hand, there are no assurances that the beliefs of these individuals are rational, especially if we stipulate that they have had no feedback about the reliability of these beliefs. Indeed, under these conditions, it seems far less reasonable for them to trust their beliefs than it is for you, while under the control of the demon, to trust your perceptual beliefs.

In any event, whatever one thinks of these examples, the main point here is that the more closely rational belief is tied to knowledge, the more difficult it is to resist pressures that push us away from the egocentric question. My proposal is that the prerequisites of rational belief are not so closely tied to the conditions of knowledge. Or at least this is so for the sense of rational belief that adopts the egocentric perspective of individual believers. I do not assert that this is the only sense of rational belief. On the contrary, I have already argued that there are different senses of rational belief, presupposing different perspectives. The more objective the sense is, the more plausible will be the idea that a rational true belief is always a good candidate for knowledge.

On the other hand, skeptical hypotheses illustrate why we cannot be content with having only an objective notion of rational belief. The evil demon or the scientist who envats your brain deprives you of knowledge, but neither need deprive you of the opportunity of being rational in at least one important sense. This is the real lesson of the evil demon and the brain in a vat. By hypothesis these are situations that you could not distinguish from what you take to be your current situation. From your skin in, everything about these situations is as it is now, and yet from your skin out, things are drastically different from what you take them to be in the current situation. Still, you would have egocentric reasons in such situations to believe exactly what you do now. The demon does not deprive you of these reasons. Rather, he alters your environment so that these reasons are no longer reliable indicators of truths. In so doing, he deprives you of knowledge.

In this way, epistemology itself reveals the need for an egocentric sense of rational belief. In doing epistemology, we are consciously self-reflective. We make ourselves and our methods into an object of study. We inquire into ourselves as inquirers. Within such an inquiry, skeptical thoughts can arise. We come to see how we might be systematically deprived of knowledge without there being any internal indication of this. Such a possibility helps illustrate the need for a notion of rational belief that is not tied too closely to knowledge. It illustrates that knowledge involves an element of luck, of good fortune. We cannot altogether eliminate the possibility of radical error by being egocentrically rational. We need the world to cooperate. This is what skeptical hypotheses teach us. If contrary to what we think, the world or something in it conspires against us, then so much the worse for us as knowing creatures. Nothing that we can do with respect to getting our own house in order will succeed in bringing us knowledge.[3]

This is not a comforting thought. We like to think of knowledge as part of our birthright. The thought that it might not be is so disturbing that it makes an appeal to idealism in one of its many garbs attractive to some. This is an appeal to be resisted. It has all the advantages of metaphysics over a straightforward assessment of our situation. The better alternative is to give up success as a condition of egocentric rationality, to admit that this kind of rationality in and of itself is not enough to guarantee either truth or reliability.

Many of us will find it difficult to make this admission, especially when doing philosophy. Among philosophers it is often taken for granted that the consequences of being rational must always be desirable. This attitude finds its way into our ethics as well as our epistemology. We resist the idea that egoists can be as rational as the rest of us. We think we must prove that they are irrational, as if their shortcomings could be the product only of irrationality. But not every failing is a failing of rationality. There can be other explanations of our moral and practical failings. They might be the result of inadequate training, for example, a training that did not sufficiently develop our moral sensitivities. As a result, we might not be able to discriminate finely enough among the relevant features of morally difficult situations.[4] Or more seriously, we may have a fundamentally flawed character, one that has us caring for the wrong things. Or it may simply be that we sometimes find ourselves in situations in which we are systematically deprived of crucial information and in which, as a result, even people of good character will collectively produce disastrous results if each acts rationally.[5]

Analogously, we may be tempted to think that those who have grossly mistaken beliefs must be irrational, as if this were the only possible explanation of their being so thoroughly misguided. But again, we need to remind ourselves that not every failing is a failing of rationality. There are other explanations for intellectual error, even widespread error. Like moral failings, the intellectual failings of some people may be largely a matter of bad training. They may have been brought up in a culture whose intellectual traditions encourage error, a tradition that emphasizes magic, for example. Or more ominously, they may have inappropriate cognitive equipment. They may not be cognitively suited to detect truths in the environment in which they find themselves.

Whatever the explanation, the point is that rationality in the theoretical sphere no more guarantees desirable consequences than does rationality in the practical sphere. Just as someone can be rational and yet lacking in virtue, so too can someone be rational and yet lacking in knowledge. And just as we all can be rational and yet collectively produce disastrous results, so too can we all be rational and yet all be radically mistaken. Appreciating this can help cure the preoccupation with skepticism that has dominated modern epistemology; it can allow egocentric epistemology to be done nondefensively.[6]

But this lack of guarantees will also encourage many to ask a more personal question about egocentric rationality. They will want to know why they should be concerned with making themselves egocentrically rational if this does not ensure that most of their beliefs will be true. I will talk about this issue in some detail later,[7] but for now it will do to note that there appears to be an easy answer to their question. They presumably want or at least need to have accurate and comprehensive beliefs, but insofar as they are egocentrically rational, they are by their own lights effectively satisfying this end. That's what's to be said in favor of their being egocentrically rational.

2. The Lack of Guarantees

A nondefensive epistemology is one that refuses to be embarrassed by a lack of non-question-begging guarantees. There is no guarantee that by being egocentrically rational we will avoid error. There is no guarantee that we will avoid extreme error. It need not even be probable that we will avoid extreme error.

Much of the implausibility of the Cartesian project arises from its failure to recognize that this is part of our intellectual condition. It instead insists that by being rational we can be assured of success. This has disastrous consequences for egocentric epistemology, since there is nothing that we can do with respect to marshaling our cognitive resources that will result in such guarantees. However we marshal them, we will still need the world to cooperate. We are convinced that we are not radically mistaken about the nature of the world. We are convinced that there is much that we know. We may well be right, but we have no non-question-begging guarantees of this. Consider the trust that we place in our perceptual equipment. If unbeknownst to us there is a deceiving demon in this world, then many of our perceptual beliefs are false. Moreover, if most other close worlds are also demon worlds, then trusting our perceptual equipment does not even make it probable that we will avoid radical error.[8]

A nondefensive epistemology refuses to be intimidated by the possibility of widespread error. It refuses to make success or even likely success a prerequisite of rationality. It instead says that it can be rational for us to trust our perceptual equipment even if doing so, unbeknownst to us, is likely to result in radical error. The deepest flaw in the Cartesian approach to epistemology is the assumption to the contrary, the assumption that there is a guaranteed link of some kind between rationality on the one hand and truth or likely-truth on the other. It is not just that Descartes tried to guarantee too much, although this too is so. He unrealistically insisted that by being egocentrically rational we can be altogether assured of avoiding error. He was thus forced to regard any skeptical conjecture, no matter how far-fetched, as a *prima facie* defeater, one that itself had to be conclusively defeated before a proposition could be rationally believed. Of course, if this were so, not much of anything would be rational for us to believe.

Thus, it might seem as if the solution is simply to weaken the guarantee, so that being rational guarantees only that we will avoid widespread error or per-haps, even more weakly, guarantees only that it is likely we will do so. There is, after all, a good rationale for some such weakening. Our principal intellectual goal is not, as Descartes would have it, that of having as comprehensive a belief system as we can without encountering any risk of error. It is the more moderate goal of having an accurate and comprehensive belief system, one in which some risk of error is to be tolerated for greater comprehensiveness. But if so, it can be rational to believe that which is not absolutely certain. Suppose we were to say that a proposition needs only to be sufficiently probable in order to be rational. Then skeptical conjectures that are far-fetched need not be *prima facie* defeaters. Mere logical possibilities will not be enough. Our having the beliefs and experiences we do may be logically compatible with our being under the control of an evil demon or our being a brain in a vat, but in itself this is not enough to show that the existence of tables, stars, people, and trees is not highly probable, given these beliefs and experiences.

All this is correct as far as it goes, but it does not go far enough. It still leaves us with a defensive epistemology, one that insists that rationality must bring with it guarantees, albeit of a weaker sort than those Descartes sought. However, any such insistence will produce exactly the same problem that plagues Cartesian epistemology. The problem arises regardless of the strength of the would-be guarantee, and it arises in the exactly the same form as it did for Descartes. It arises if we say that by being rational we can be assured of avoiding widespread error. It arises if we say more cautiously that by being rational we can be assured of avoiding the likelihood of widespread error. It arises even if we say that by being rational we can be assured only that the likelihood of our avoiding error is at least as great as it would be if we were not rational.[9] Regardless of how we marshal our cognitive sources, there can be no non-question-begging assurances that the way we are marshaling them is suitable for our environment. But then, there can be no non-question-begging assurances that we will achieve any of the above levels of success.

After all, the search for such assurances will itself require us to marshal our cognitive resources. It will itself involve the use of methods about which we can sensibly have doubts, doubts that cannot be addressed without begging the question. Any attempt to address them will employ methods either that are themselves already at issue or that can be made so. There is a close analogy with the practical realm. There too self-directed inquiry can raise doubts that cannot be addressed without begging the question. I commit myself to various projects, ones that initially seem worthwhile, but if I examine my commitments and the values implicit in them, doubts can occur to me. I can ask whether I want to be the kind of person who makes these sorts of commitments. Can I endorse my being that kind of person? And even if I answer yes, this does not definitively settle the doubts. I can go on and ask about the values implicit in this latest endorsement. Either they are values that were implicit in the commitments about which I originally had doubts or they are new values about which I can also raise doubts. It is hopeless to search for a non-question-begging way to endorse all our values, including the ones implicit in the endorsement itself. Any such search would be based on the assumption that there is a neutral position from which these endorsements can be made. There isn't. Nor is there in epistemology. There is no intellectually neutral position from which to defend our most fundamental intellectual positions.[10]

This can make it tempting to shift strategies and defend our intellectual views and procedures on pragmatic grounds. Even if our most fundamental beliefs and most basic intellectual procedures cannot be given a non-question-begging intellectual defense, they have nonetheless proved useful for us in the conduct of our lives. Their usefulness, it might be argued, makes skeptical worries about them pointless.

Suppose we set aside the idea that considerations of usefulness at best give us reasons for commitment rather than reasons for belief.[11] Even so, a pragmatic turn can provide no escape from skeptical worries, since there are no assurances of the usefulness of our beliefs and methods either. The mere fact that we have survived is not enough to establish their usefulness. Life, as Nietzsche remarked, is no argument. Perhaps we have survived despite our beliefs and methods. Others might have served us much better. It is a mistake, albeit a tempting enough one, simply to assume that biological evolution rules this possibility out, since evolution can be relied upon to produce systems that approximate optimally well-designed systems, that is, optimally well designed for survival and reproduction. In fact, evolution cannot be counted on to do this, if for no other reason than that factors other than natural selection (for example, genetic drift) can also affect evolution, and these factors need not select optimally well-designed systems.[12] Besides there aren't even any assurances that our intellectual practices are largely the products of biological processes at all. Social forces may be doing much of the work, and there are no guarantees that these social forces will encourage useful intellectual practices.[13] Indeed, some would declare that there is good evidence that they don't, since social forces have encouraged the development of technologies, and associated intellectual practices, that threaten our planet with pollution and nuclear annihilation.

In any event, whatever one thinks of how our intellectual ways came to be, the relevant point for the discussion here is that we no more have guarantees of their usefulness than we do of their reliability. Thus, as a means to dismiss radical skeptical worries, an appeal to the usefulness of our beliefs and methods will itself be useless.

Any other kind of appeal will be useless as well. Epistemology cannot provide us with a recipe that if followed stringently enough will guarantee that we won't fall into great error. The search for such assurances is doomed from the start. And if there are those who nonetheless demand this kind of assurance in the name of rationality, we can say to them that their demand threatens to become uninteresting precisely because it cannot possibly be satisfied. Capitulating to it would have the effect of ensuring that considerations of rationality and irrationality cannot be used to sort our beliefs. Of necessity our beliefs will be largely irrational. We cannot get out of our intellectual skins to provide guarantees of our own reliability, and a theory that demands in the name of rationality that we be able to do so is as uninteresting as one whose conditions are so trivial as to make it impossible for us to have irrational beliefs.[14]

To bemoan our inability to discharge skeptical hypotheses is to give in to a kind self-pity. It is no use whining about the conditions of our intellectual existence. We have no non-question-begging way to guarantee the reliability of our methods and our rationality does not depend upon our having one.

3. Is Skepticism Self-referentially Incoherent?

One way of dealing with radical skeptical worries is to dismiss them as unnatural or perhaps even senseless. This kind of dismissive attitude can have its unwelcome side effects, since it invites complacency. Whatever else there is to be said about skeptical worries—even if they are unnatural or senseless, as charged—they at least do us the favor of discouraging intellectual smugness.

But in fact, skeptical worries are neither unnatural nor senseless. One of our most important intellectual projects is trying to understand our own position in the world, including our position as inquirers. Epistemology is a part of this inquiry into ourselves as inquirers, and within the context of such an inquiry it is natural to raise general doubts about our beliefs and methods. It is natural to entertain even radical doubts.

In most contexts entertaining radical doubts isn't natural because doing so requires some detachment from ordinary concerns. There is no natural way to raise general skeptical doubts when discussing with your mechanic the problems that you are having with your car.[15] Nor can you raise them when you are doing physics or biology or geometry. But in the context of an inquiry into our place in the world, they arise without being forced. We make ourselves into the objects of our study, and we recognize that the creatures whom we are studying have a rich interaction with their environment. They have various beliefs about it and various desires for it, all of which become intertwined in their projects. The intellectual projects that find expression in their sciences, for example, are intertwined with projects aimed at controlling their environment. The projects, we further recognize, can be conducted more or less successfully. In wondering about the relative success of their intellectual projects, we are raising general questions about their beliefs that make it natural to entertain various skeptical hypotheses. We are wondering whether their cognitive equipment and their ways of employing this equipment are sufficiently well-suited for their environment to be prone to produce true beliefs about it. And even when we wonder about the success of their nonintellectual projects, the same questions arise indirectly, for even if we grant that these creatures are mostly successful in dealing with their environment, we will want some explanation for their success. Is it by having largely accurate beliefs about their environment that they are able to be successful or is there some other explanation? But in wondering whether there might not be another explanation, we are once again taking skeptical possibilities seriously. It is perfectly natural for us to do so in this context.

It is not a mistaken philosophical tradition, then, that lures us into skeptical thoughts.[16] It is our natural curiosity. We are curious about these creatures' place in the world, including their place as inquirers. We know that they take themselves to be accurately representing their environment. This leads us to wonder whether they are right in thinking this or whether their representations might be distorted in some systematic way. The hypothesis of the evil demon and the brain in the vat are merely dramatic devices to express these kinds of thoughts in their most radical form.[17]

Of course, there is something else that is unusual about these thoughts. They are about our beliefs, our presuppositions, our methods of inquiry. If we are to make these things the objects of skeptical concern, we must be able to distance ourselves from them in some way. This might make it seem as if the entertainment of skeptical hypotheses is inevitably an exercise in schizophrenia.

If entertaining skeptical hypotheses is schizophrenic, it is of a common enough sort. Indeed, it can be present even when a proposition is indubitable for you. Such propositions are irresistible once you bring them clearly to mind. Clarity about them is enough to command your assent.[18] So, you cannot directly doubt the truth of such a proposition. I may be able to doubt the truth of a proposition that is indubitable for you, but you cannot. Otherwise, it would not be genuinely indubitable for you.

Even so, you can do the next best thing. You can raise questions about its truth indirectly by considering in a general way whether that which is indubitable for you is true. You can wonder whether you might not be the kind of creature who finds certain falsehoods impossible to doubt. Your wondering this does not prove that nothing is really indubitable for you. It does not prove that you really are capable of doubting, say, that you exist and that $2 + 1 = 3$. These propositions and others may be irresistible for you whenever you directly examine them. However, you can refuse to do this. You can refuse to bring them fully and clearly to mind, and by so refusing, you gain the ability to suspend belief in them hypothetically. You need not actually cease believing them. You merely cease focusing your direct attention upon them. In doing this you can distance yourself even from that which is indubitable for you, and thus you can make even these propositions an object of skeptical concern. There is nothing mysterious about your being able to do so.[19]

Similarly, there is nothing mysterious about your being able to entertain general skeptical worries about the other propositions you believe, the ones that are not altogether indubitable for you.. You can wonder in a general way how much of what you believe is true, and you can do so without actually giving up your beliefs. It is enough for you to suspend them hypothetically.

To claim that there is something inevitably puzzling about your being able to entertain general skeptical doubts about yourself is to make human thought into something far less flexible than it is. Even atheists can debate questions that have theological presuppositions, and they can do so without altering their beliefs. For the duration of the discussion they hypothetically suspend a portion of what they believe. In particular, they suspend their belief that God doesn't exist. Similarly, the morally upright can appreciate, admire, and enjoy the ingenuity and resourcefulness of literary villains even when that ingenuity and resourcefulness are put to repugnant purposes. They can do so by hypothetically suspending their moral scruples.[20]

No doubt there are limits as to how much of our beliefs and values we can put into suspension, but the limits are at best distant ones. They are not so constraining as to prevent discussion between atheists and theists, and they are not such as to preclude appreciation of the great literary villains. Nor are they so stringent as to rule out questions about the general reliability of our beliefs.[21]

Even so, it is one thing to be able to entertain the idea that our beliefs are largely mistaken and our cognitive methods largely unreliable—such thoughts come easily enough. It is another thing to try to mount an argument for this conclusion. It might seem as if skeptical arguments, by their very nature, are self-referentially incoherent.

After all, skeptics are themselves engaged in epistemological inquiry, and all inquiry, regardless of its nature, arises against a backdrop of opinion and makes use of cognitive resources. Epistemology is no exception. Indeed, since epistemology is an inquiry into our role as inquirers, it of necessity comes at a late stage. It is preceded and inspired by an immense range of opinion about ourselves and the world, and it makes use of an immense range of our intellectual resources. If in the course of this inquiry we try to mount a skeptical challenge about this backdrop or these resources, the very backdrop that prompted the inquiry and the very resources that have been used in the inquiry, we would seem to be undermining the force of our own challenge. If our presuppositions and methods really aren't to be trusted, then any argument we might muster on the basis of such presuppositions and methods isn't to be trusted either—hence, the threat of incoherence.[22]

Part of the force of this argument can be deflected by noting that skeptical worries come in varying degrees of generality. They need not be categorical. They can be limited, and in fact most are. Thus, even if sensible inquiry requires that we not challenge the reliability of the presuppositions and resources we have made use of in the inquiry, it will nonetheless be possible to mount strong skeptical challenges without fear of incoherence. We can do so with the aid of presuppositions and resources that we are not currently challenging. There will be disagreements about how much must be left unchallenged, but as a rule, the threat of incoherence diminishes as skeptics narrow the scope of their challenge—narrow it from a challenge of all our methods, resources, and opinions to a challenge of "merely" a sizeable subset of them.

But this kind of response doesn't address the more basic question, namely, Is it always incoherent for would-be skeptics to marshal arguments against the reliability of the very opinions, methods, and resources that they are employing in these arguments? The answer is no, since the aim of skeptical arguments can be purely negative. The aim need not be to provide us with positive reasons for believing some thesis, not even the thesis that our opinions and methods are not to be trusted. Any attempt on the part of the skeptic to find such reasons would undermine itself. Consistent skeptics will realize this. It is not as if they think that the resources they are challenging are such that they but no one else, can use them reliably. On the contrary, they think we are all in the same boat, the only difference being that the rest of us labor under the pretense of reliability. Their strategy is to relieve us of this pretense. They can coherently try to do so by confining themselves to negative argumentative strategies—in effect, by intellectual ju-jitsu. They try to use the presumed strength and weight of our presuppositions and methods against us. They adopt our opinions and methods and then try to use them to find considerations that will undermine the idea that these opinions and methods are to be trusted.

The strategy of these skeptics, in other words, is to convict us of just the sort of incoherency that we so often try to pin on them. They are able to defend themselves against the charge of incoherency by pleading the negative character of their arguments, but this kind of defense will not be open to those of us interested in positive intellectual results. We need to be able to trust our favorite intellectual methods, but according to the skeptic, this is just the problem. If we take these methods seriously and rigorously adhere to them, they will reveal their own inadequacies.

This is a familiar strategy of skeptics, and unlike some other kinds of skeptical strategies, it is an interesting one. The idea is not simply to insist that our beliefs and methods meet some impossibly demanding standard that skeptics themselves have stipulated as appropriate. Skepticism by stipulation always threatens to become boring. That is not the strategy here. The strategy, rather, is to let others say what methods, resources, and presuppositions they regard as reliable and then to try to turn these methods, resources, and presuppositions against them.

For example, after recommending the method of doubt as a way to avoid error, Descartes plays the skeptic's advocate and wonders whether a consistent application of this method might not undermine our trust in it. After all, at least at first glance it seems possible to doubt whether that which we find impossible to doubt is true. Descartes doesn't regard this kind of challenge as incoherent, and he was right not to regard it as such. If the method itself indicates that the method is not to be trusted, then so much the worse for it. Descartes realizes that he cannot dismiss this challenge out of hand. Rather, he must try to meet it. Famously, he tries to do so with his proof of God and his argument that God wouldn't allow us to be deceived about what we cannot doubt. If we keep these arguments in mind, he says, it won't be possible for us to doubt whether that which we find indubitable is true.

Or consider the response of the Academic skeptics to the proposals of Chrysippus. According to Chrysippus, we should assume that the way things perceptually appear to us is the way they are. In response, the skeptics argued that if we take this recommendation seriously, it leads to contradictory judgments. It does so because of perceptual relativity. When viewed from one angle, the coin appears perfectly round. From another angle it appears oval rather than round. But not even Chrysippus thinks that the coin is both round and nonround. Thus, the skeptics concluded, to see the inadequacies of Chrysippus's recommendation, we need only adopt the recommendation and take it seriously. If we do so, we will find that the recommendation undermines itself.

Analogously, it is sometimes argued that if we apply the scientific method to itself, its pretensions of reliability are undermined. After all, the best empirical data we have about the reliability of the method are to be found in the history of science, but this history, it is asserted, is largely a history of error. Hence, the empirical methods recommended by science itself seem to indicate that these methods are not to be trusted.

In each of these cases, a skeptical challenge is mounted by presupposing the reliability of the method under attack. Skeptics do so in hope of undermining the presupposition. Whether they succeed is not the issue at the moment. The issue, rather, is that this is a perfectly respectable strategy, even though the suspicions that skeptics manage to raise in this way may apply to some of their own arguments as well.[23] There is nothing self-defeating about this. Quite the opposite. Insofar as their attack is supposed to be a general one about the method of doubt or the method of perception or the method of science, it would be self-defeating for their arguments not to apply to any use that they themselves make of these methods.

4. Can Metaphysics Solve the Problem of Skepticism?
The kind of errors we can imagine others making we can imagine ourselves making as well. This is one of the ways in which skeptical thoughts arise. After all, we have no trouble imagining situations in which others make modest errors. Indeed, we have no trouble imagining situations in which we manipulate them or their environment so as to induce error in them. Our literature, our movies, and our everyday lives are filled with examples of successful deceits. It is natural to think that if we had the requisite skill and knowledge, we could extend these deceits so as to induce radical error in others. But if this is so, someone with the requisite skill and knowledge might do the same to us. We too might be radically deceived without being aware of it.

I think that this line of reasoning is essentially correct, but there are those who believe that the reasoning should be reversed. Donald Davidson, for example, argues that we could have reasons to think that others are radically deceived if and only if we could have reasons to think that they have beliefs radically different from ours. Moreover, if and only if this were possible could we have reasons to think that the tables might possibly be turned, with others' being largely right and our being largely wrong. But in fact, Davidson asserts, we cannot possibly have reasons for thinking that others have beliefs radically different from ours. Accordingly, it is impossible for us to have reasons for thinking that they are radically deceived. But then, we cannot have reasons to think that we could ever be radically deceived either.[24]

Why is it that we cannot have reasons for thinking that the beliefs of others are radically different from ours and hence radically mistaken? Because, says Davidson, assigning beliefs to others is a theoretical enterprise, and the only way to conduct this enterprise is for us, by our own lights, to look for systematic correlations between their behavior, most important, their verbal behavior, and the features of their environment. Our most plausible theory of what others believe is the one that does the best overall job of revealing and explaining the correlations we find, but this, Davidson insists, is always the theory that makes what we take to be the salient features of their environment both the causes and the contents of their utterances and the beliefs that these utterances express. This means that the interpretation must be one that by our lights makes their beliefs mostly true.

The interpretation must be of this sort even in the most extreme cases. Suppose our interpretation is of brains that have been permanently placed in a vat and hooked up to a computer. Even if the brains are stimulated by the computer in just the ways that our brains are stimulated through our senses when we are in the presence of chairs and tables, our interpretation will not have the brains believing that there are chairs and tables in their immediate environment. The contents of their beliefs must reflect their environment, not ours. And so, our interpretation will assign them beliefs about, say, the inner workings of the computer, since it is with the computer rather than chairs and tables that the brains are causally interacting. Of course, these beliefs may function for them in their vat environment in much the same way that our beliefs about real chairs and tables function for us. If we wish, we can emphasize this point by saying that their beliefs are about chairs-in-the-computer and tables-in-the-computer. But given Davidson's view, the qualification 'in-the-computer' is crucial. Since the brains have not causally interacted in any extensive fashion with ordinary tables and chairs, their beliefs cannot be about ordinary tables and chairs.

According to Davidson, then, we cannot have good reasons to think that even brains in a vat are radically deceived, and thus we cannot have good reasons to think that we might be radically deceived either. Or as Davidson himself puts the conclusion: "What stands in the way of global skepticism of the senses is, in my view, the fact that we must, in the plainest and methodologically most basic cases, take the objects of a belief to be the causes of the belief."[25]

Davidson's is an unlikely conclusion. The nature of belief is itself said to rule out the possibility of extensive error.[26] So, we can know in advance that the beliefs of others are largely true. We need not inquire into their specific origins. Whatever the processes are by which they are acquired, we know that these processes must be in the main reliable. The metaphysics of belief guarantees this, and that same metaphysics guarantees reliability in our own case as well.[27]

But one person's *reductio* is another's welcome result. Davidson declares that one of the advantages of his approach is that it provides us with "a *reason* for supposing most of our beliefs are true that is not a form of *evidence*." Charity, first toward the beliefs of others and then derivatively toward our own beliefs as well, is forced upon us. It is forced upon us by the practice of interpretation. If we are to have any theory at all about what others believe, we have no choice but to look for correlations between their behavior, especially their verbal behavior, and the features of their immediate environment. This is all we have to go on.

But is it? Why aren't other kinds of information also relevant? In particular, if the individuals we are interpreting have brains and sensory equipment structurally identical to ours and if their senses are stimulated in just the way that ours are normally stimulated, why isn't this a relevant piece of data? Or alternatively, if we discovered that their sensory input was significantly different from ours, why wouldn't this be relevant?

Imagine individuals physiologically similar to us who say "gavagai" when in front of rabbits but whose retinae show a pattern of stimulation of just the sort that we have when in front of fish. Shouldn't this make us at least a little reluctant to translate *gavagai* as *rabbit?* Shouldn't we be more reluctant to do so than if their retinae had showed the pattern of stimulation of the sort that we have when in front of rabbits? I think that the answer is yes, and thus I also think that sensory stimulations count for something in interpretation.[28] But of course, sensory stimulations can remain constant while the surrounding environment changes, even while it changes radically. Thus, the more important this evidence is relative to the environmental and behavioral evidence that Davidson restricts himself to, the more leeway there will be for our theory of interpretation to ascribe error to others.

This is not necessarily to give up on charity as a condition of interpretation. After all, there are different ways of being charitable. Even if we don't insist upon making others as verific as possible, we might insist upon making them as egocentrically rational as possible. If so, we will try to see matters from their perspective. We will try to see what they have reasons to believe, given their evidence and training. One way of doing this—indeed, perhaps the only way— is to project ourselves into their situation. We try to imagine what we would have believed, or at least should have believed, were we to have had their evidence and training. We are thus free to ascribe to them the errors that we think it would have been reasonable for us to have made had we been in their situation.[29]

The choice between charity-as-veracity and charity-as-rationality won't make for much of a difference in our interpretations if we simply assume from the start that people must be reliable in order to be rational. But if we don't begin with this assumption, the choice is potentially important. A principle of maximizing rationality might have us preferring the first of two rival interpretations even though the second has people believing more truths. We can prefer the first because it does a better job of making people rational.

In the extreme case, we might even be able to ascribe radical albeit understandable error to them. Suppose that our interpretation is of brains in a vat. Insofar as the brains are structurally identical to ours and insofar as they are stimulated in identical ways to ours, our interpretation might have them believing pretty much what we believe, despite the radical differences between their immediate environment and ours. Our interpretation, then, would have them in widespread error. But even this interpretation can be a charitable one in the sense that it makes most of their beliefs egocentrically rational. This is possible because egocentric rationality does not guarantee reliability. Thus, should the circumstances warrant it, we can interpret the brains as having beliefs that are mostly rational but also mostly false. We can interpret them in this way because from their perspective, there is no indication that they are being greatly deceived. Hence, there is no reason for them to believe other than what they do believe.[30]

Even so, for the moment I will ignore this cluster of ideas concerning interpretation, belief, and rationality, and I will instead grant that the practice of interpretation really is such that if we are to have any theory at all about what others believe, we have no choice but to rely exclusively on the correlations we find between their behavior and their environment. What follows from this? At most, what would seem to follow is a surprising truth about the practice of interpretation, namely, that the practice constrains us in such a way that we cannot have good reasons to accept any interpretation that ascribes what we take to be radically mistaken beliefs to others. However, no antiskeptical conclusion immediately follows. We cannot conclude straightaway that it really is altogether impossible for others to have beliefs that are radically different from ours. We cannot do so until we have assurances that the constraints here are not the result of our own shortcomings as interpreters.

One way of trying to provide the assurances is to presuppose an appropriate conception of truth, one implying that what we cannot possibly have good reasons to believe, cannot possibly be true. But this is just to take a stand on one of the key issues lying in the background of the dispute here. The particular dispute is about whether truth and belief might come drastically apart. The assertion at issue is that they cannot, that beliefs by their very nature are largely true. When we ask why this is so, we are given an argument whose persuasiveness requires us to assume that truths are always in principle accessible to us. To be sure, by itself this assumption does not settle the dispute, and hence making the assumption does not beg the question. Truths might always be in principle accessible to us, even though our actual attempts to find them fail with regularity. Still, the assumption does have the effect of ruling out *a priori* the idea that we might be cognitively ill suited to discover certain sorts of truth, and this in turn makes an argument of the sort that Davidson proposes at least a possibility. But of course, it is also makes the argument controversial. Those who are initially suspicious of the assertion that belief and truth cannot radically diverge are likely to be equally suspicious of any such conception of truth, in part just because it opens the door for arguments such as Davidson's.

Be this as it may, for the sake of pushing these issues as far as possible, let us agree to waive this concern as well. In particular, let us presuppose a conception of truth that precludes there being truths to which we could not possibly have access, not even in the ideal long run. Moreover, let us glide over other complications for Davidson's approach. Let us grant, for example, that on the basis of behavioral evidence, we can reliably distinguish sincere utterances from those that are not, that we can reliably ascertain when sincere utterances are indicators of the utterers' beliefs and when they are not,[31] and so on. In granting all this and granting also that our only evidence is behavioral evidence, we are granting all the essentials of Davidson's approach. In particular, we are granting that the best overall theory of others' beliefs is the one that does the best job of making the content of their beliefs those salient features of the environment with which their behavior is correlated.

Still, even on our best theory, these correlations might not be particularly strong. Given Davidson's approach, we do have to find some correlations if we are to offer an interpretation at all, but by Davidson's own admission the extent of the correlations need be great enough only to ensure that "the plainest and most methodologically basic" of the beliefs that we ascribe to others are not false. Thus, there can still be widespread error among their less basic beliefs. But then, given the symmetry between what we can imagine of others and what we imagine of ourselves, only the most radical kind of skeptical hypotheses are ruled out for us as impossible. If our most fundamental beliefs are those that concern the most general features of our environment, the only skeptical hypotheses ruled out are those that have us mistaken not only about almost all of the details of our environment but also about almost all of its most general features.

Even here, after conceding so much, there are no guarantees that we are not in an extremely hostile intellectual environment, one in which without our realizing it, we are systematically precluded from having beliefs that are both detailed and accurate. Worse yet, since nothing guarantees that we are in a position to pick out which of our beliefs are the most fundamental, there are no particular beliefs or sets of beliefs of whose truth we can be assured. We may think that beliefs of a certain kind are fundamental for us, but we might be wrong. And if we are, it is consistent with Davidson's theory that even these beliefs might be mostly false.

Thus, even if Davidson's theory of belief is accepted in its entirety, it has only limited implications for skepticism. One way of dramatizing these limitations is to imagine that the immediate causes of someone's beliefs change radically over a short span of time. For example, suppose that we remove your brain and briefly envat it, stimulating it through our computer in such a way that you notice nothing even though your immediate environment has changed drastically. We then return the brain to your body and allow it to function in the normal way in your normal environment.

Given Davidson's theory of belief, what do we say about the perceptual beliefs you have during the brief time that your brain is envatted? Are we forced to say that at the onslaught of your envatment the objects of your perceptual beliefs suddenly change? In particular, are we forced to offer an interpretation of these perceptual beliefs that makes most of them true—an interpretation according to which for that brief time you have mostly true beliefs about, say, the inner workings of the computer rather than mostly false beliefs about there being chairs and tables in your immediate environment? And once we return your brain to your body and allow it to function normally in its normal environment, are we then forced to conclude that you just as suddenly revert to believing that there are ordinary physical objects in your immediate environment?

Of course not. Davidson's approach does not require anything this implausible. In general, we must, Davidson says, take the objects of your beliefs to be their environmental causes, but these causes are typically complicated. This is so even for perceptual beliefs. You look out the window and you believe that you see a Mercedes being driven down the street. The Mercedes may be the immediate environmental cause of your belief, but the precise content of the belief is also shaped by various standing beliefs and presuppositions, ones that have accumulated through your causal interaction with your environment over a span of time. And so it is with the perceptual beliefs you have while envatted. The immediate environmental cause of these beliefs is the computer to which your brain is attached, or perhaps more precisely, the inner workings of this computer, but here too the beliefs are produced only in conjunction with various standing beliefs and presuppositions.

So, Davidson is free to say that the causal influences that determine the contents of your beliefs are not just those that are currently operative in the immediate environment but also those that have been operative over an extended period of time. But then, the best Davidsonian interpretation—that is, the interpretation that does the best overall job of making the objects of beliefs their causes—might very well be one that has your envatted brain believing about its immediate environment pretty much the sorts of things that we and you usually believe, even though for the brief time of envatment your immediate environment has been drastically altered.

This is precisely the result that we would expect from a plausible theory of interpretation, but on the other hand it is also a result that shows that even a Davidsonian interpretation is compatible with radical error. To be sure, the interpretation here would ascribe to you an enormous number of true beliefs as well. It would ascribe to you the true general beliefs that there are trees and chairs somewhere in the universe; it also would ascribe to you mostly true beliefs about your past; and so on. However, it is also an interpretation that ascribes to you almost no accurate beliefs about your current immediate environment. According to the interpretation, your beliefs about it are radically mistaken. But then, we cannot be assured that we are not radically mistaken about our current immediate environment either, since the kind of errors we can imagine you making are just the ones that we can imagine us making as well.

It is not hard to concoct variations of this scenario for other subsets of your beliefs. For example, scenarios in which our best interpretation of your beliefs would be one that makes most of what you seem to remember about your immediate environment during the past week false. Imagine, for instance, that your brain was envatted during that week, unbeknownst to you. Likewise, there are scenarios that would make most of what you believe on the basis of testimony false. Imagine that all of your acquaintances have been organized to tell you falsehoods about matters for which you either will not or cannot seek independent verification.[32]

Even if complete and utter error is ruled out by Davidson's views, radical error, even radical perceptual error, is not. Moreover, although his theory, if acceptable, provides us with a guarantee that not every portion of our belief system can be simultaneously in substantial error, it provides no guarantee with respect to any particular subset that it is not in error. It is as if we have been given a map of a number of counties but the mapmakers can assure us only that the general contours of many, but not all, of the counties are accurately represented. The mapmakers may insist that such assurances are better than none, and they may well be right. Even so, with respect to any particular county we have no assurances that the map gives us even a roughly accurate picture of its general contours, and we likewise have no assurances that the map is accurate in any of its details concerning any of the counties.[33]

This is not the strong response to skepticism that Davidson himself seems to want, but for the sake of his metaphysics, this is just as well—the stronger its epistemic pretensions, the less plausible the metaphysics. If Davidson's views about the nature of belief and truth really did imply that we can be assured, say, that most of our current perceptual beliefs are true, his views would strike us as implausible for that very reason.[34] A plausible metaphysics will leave room for epistemology. It will leave room for the possibility of our being in serious error even when, given our own standards, we have no reason to question our reliability. This is just to say that it will leave room for a notion of rationality that brings with it no extensive guarantees of truth.

Notoriously, there are those who disagree, and no one has expressed such a view of the matter more starkly than Brand Blanshard:

> If you place the nature of truth in one sort of character and its test in something quite different, you are pretty certain, sooner or later, to find the two falling apart. In the end, the only test of truth that is not misleading is the special nature or character that is itself constitutive of truth.[35]

Blanshard accordingly felt compelled to identify the conditions of rational belief with the conditions of truth. Since on his view rational belief is a matter of coherence, he concluded that truth must be essentially a matter of coherence as well.

It is possible to sympathize with Blanshard's worry without giving in to the radical view about truth that he uses to dissolve the worry. It might even be possible to ease the worry at least a bit by developing an antirealist conception of truth that is more delicate than Blanshard's, in that it does not threaten to trivialize the distinction between what we think we can establish and what is the case. One general strategy would be to argue that in thinking about the world, it is impossible to separate out our conceptual contributions from what is "objectively there."[36] Another would be to argue that truths are what ideally conducted inquiry would settle on in the long run.[37]

Such views, like Davidson's, can be made compatible with a strong theory of error. They leave room for the possibility of widespread error, and thereby leave room for doubt about even our most firmly held beliefs. Even if we are irremediably enmeshed in our conceptual scheme and even if as a result the nature of reference is such that not all our beliefs can be in error simultaneously, this circumstance provides no guarantees for any particular subset of our beliefs. Similarly, even if the nature of truth is such that ideally conducted inquiry cannot help but lead to the truth eventually, this circumstance provides no guarantees that our present inquiries are on the right track. Moreover, if a metaphysics implied otherwise, it would be suspicious for that very reason. To turn G. E. Moore's position on its head, we are far more sure of our vulnerability to error than we are of any metaphysical speculations to the contrary.

A twentieth-century metaphysics of belief or truth or reference is no more capable of eliminating epistemological problems than a seventeenth- or eighteenth-century metaphysics of God. Descartes, Berkeley, and Reid, for example, all appealed to theology for help in overcoming problems in their epistemologies. They all attempted to use God as an epistemic guarantor of one sort or another. The standard criticism of these attempts is that the proposed solutions are even more problematic than the original problems. In consequence, to contemporary readers of Descartes, it seems astonishing that the man who early in the *Meditations* doubts the existence of his own body asserts only a few pages later that he is able to find nothing at all doubtful in his proof of God's existence. But for now, it is another point that needs emphasizing. Namely, even were we to grant to Descartes his proof, his attempt to use God as an epistemic guarantor would still be problematic. For even granting that there is a God who is by nature benevolent, omnipotent, and omniscient, it does not follow that God would not allow us to be deceived about what is clear and distinct. To get this conclusion, we would need detailed assurances about God's ultimate aims and methods. But of course, it is no simple matter to get such assurances. After all, might not God, for some reason that is beyond our ken, allow us to be deceived for our own good? Might not God even allow us to be regularly deceived? If so, not even an appeal to the nature of God can provide us with strong epistemic guarantees, much less with the guarantees of certainty that Descartes sought. It is presumptuous to think that the nature of belief or reference or truth can do any better.

There is another underappreciated problem to be faced by those who appeal to metaphysics to try to solve the problem of skepticism, and Descartes's system once again provides a good illustration of it. Descartes tried to show that if we reflect carefully enough, we will find it impossible to doubt God's existence and impossible as well to doubt that God would allow us to be deceived about that which we cannot doubt. Perhaps no one other than Descartes has ever thought that these propositions really are impossible to doubt, but even if Descartes had been right about this, it still wouldn't have been enough to provide the guarantees of truth that he sought. There would still be no non-question begging assurances that we might not be psychologically constituted in such a way that we find some falsehoods impossible to doubt. If Descartes's arguments are irresistible, as he asserts, then we will not be able to doubt that the indubitable is true. Or at least, we will not be able to do so as long as we have his proofs clearly in mind. But this does not guarantee that everything that is indubitable for us really is true.[38]

Indeed, regardless of how we marshal our cognitive resources, there can be no non-question-begging assurances that the resulting inquiry is even reliable, much less flawless. This applies to metaphysical inquiry as much as it does to any other kind of inquiry. *A fortiori* it applies to any metaphysical inquiry that purports to rule out the possibility of extensive error. Any such metaphysics is likely to strike us as implausible, but even if it did not, even if we were wholly convinced of its truth, it cannot provide us with a non-question-begging guarantee of its own truth. Nor can it provide us with a non-question-begging guarantee of its likely truth. And nothing else can either.

Thus, the contemporary proponents of metaphysical systems that purport to eliminate the threat of radical skepticism are in a position precisely analogous to the one that Descartes was in with respect to his theistic metaphysics. The indubitability, if that be what it is, of Descartes's metaphysics does not guarantee its truth, and any attempt to use the metaphysics itself to show that the indubitable is true begs the question. As a result, Descartes's method does not and cannot give us non-question-begging protection against the possibility of error. Similarly, the methods used by contemporary metaphysicians do not guarantee the truth or likely truth of their metaphysical systems, and any attempt to use those very systems to guarantee the general reliability of the methods will beg the question. As a result, their metaphysical systems do not and cannot provide us with non-question-begging protection either. They cannot altogether immunize us against skeptical threats.

Our theories of truth, belief, reference, and so on are interesting and debatable as metaphysical positions. They are interesting for what they purport to tell us about the nature of truth, belief, and reference. But for epistemology, they are of only limited interest. They are of only limited interest not only because any such position, if it is to be plausible, must be compatible with a strong theory of error but also because no such position is able to provide us with guarantees of its own truth. Metaphysical inquiry is still inquiry. The conclusions of such inquiry are only as plausible as the method it employs, but no method, no matter how obvious, can bring with it non-question-begging guarantees.

Blanshard argued that if the conditions of rationality and the conditions of truth are different, it will be possible for the two to fall apart dramatically. I agree. Blanshard's proposal was to appeal to metaphysics for a way to deny the antecedent. Mine is to live with the consequent. It is to live with our vulnerability to radical error.

5. *The Epistemological Circle*

The way to respond to skeptical doubts is not to legislate against them metaphysically, and it is not to dismiss them as self-referentially incoherent. It is rather to recognize that what makes epistemology possible also makes skeptical worries inevitable—namely, our ability to turn our methods of inquiry into an object of inquiry. Within the context of such an inquiry, the worry that we might possibly have widely mistaken beliefs is as natural as it is ineradicable. If this illustrates our whimsical condition, then so be it,[39] but it is, after all, not so surprising. We want to be able to defend the reliability of our methods of inquiry, but the only way to do so is within our own system of inquiry. This leaves us vulnerable to the charge that we are begging the question against the skeptic. If the only way to defend our procedures is by using them, then we will not have altogether ruled out the possibility that their products are widely mistaken. This is a generalization of the problem of the Cartesian circle, and it is a circle from which we can no more escape than could Descartes.

But if we too are caught in the Cartesian circle, what's the point of raising questions about the reliability of our methods of inquiry? Why not relax and just assume that at least our most fundamental methods are reliable? Part of the answer is that we cannot help ourselves. Our curiosity urges us on. It urges us not to be complacent. We want to be able to defend or at least explain the reliability of our methods. The other part of the answer is that it is far from pointless to seek such explanations. Not every system of inquiry is capable of begging the question in its own defense, even though this is the least we should expect from it. The least we should expect is that it be self-referentially defensible.

What *self-referentially defensible* means, for beginners, is that a system of inquiry must not undermine itself. It must not be vulnerable to the kind of argument that skeptics are fond of employing. The system's methods, presuppositions, and resources must not generate evidence of its own unreliability. It is no trivial matter to avoid this kind of incoherence.

The avoidance of incoherence is not enough, however. Ideally, a system of inquiry should also be able to defend itself in its own terms. It should be able to provide a positive rationale for itself—a way to defend or explain its own reliability. We want our methods and presuppositions to be capable of generating a story as to why they are to be trusted. The story need not be an altogether complete one, of course. There are degrees in these matters. The point is that it is not just desirable for our methods and presuppositions to avoid self-refutation; to the extent possible, we also want them to be self-authenticating.

Again, it is no trivial matter for our methods and resources to be self-authenticating. On the contrary, an attempt to use our resources in their own defense can produce surprises. For one, it can reveal that our methods are not what they seem to be on the surface. Or it can reveal surprising information about the kind of defense we are capable of giving them. Perhaps the only way to defend them is to take something to be a mark of truth that we otherwise would not have regarded as such—simplicity, for example. Or in the worst case, it can reveal incoherence.

Consider again skeptical challenges of the scientific method. The history of science, it is sometimes argued, is largely a history of error. We look back at the theories of even the best scientists of previous times and find much in those theories that is false and even silly. But there is no reason to think that future scientists won't think the same of our best current theories. In this way, the history of science seems to give us good inductive grounds—grounds that are themselves acceptable, given the methods of science—for thinking that the scientific method is unreliable.

This is a perfectly respectable skeptical strategy. If the scientific method can be shown, in accordance with canons acceptable to that method, to have generated mistaken theories with regularity, then so much the worse for it as a procedure to generate true theories. The least we should expect from a proposed method of inquiry is that it be able to fend off the charge that it undermines itself.

Much of recent philosophy of science can be read as trying to do just that. It tries to provide an interpretation of the scientific method and a reading of the history of science that together constitute a response to this pessimistic induction. Thus, there are those who say that any fair look at the history of science reveals not a history of repudiation of past theories but rather a history in which past theories are largely incorporated into their successor theories. In addition, they say that the immediate aim of scientific theorizing is not to generate theories that are strictly and thoroughly true but rather theories that are at least approximately true. The aim is verisimilitude. They then argue that the history of science, so understood, provides no basis for an induction whose conclusion is that present theories are not even approximately true. On the contrary, the history is marked by ever-increasing predictive success, and the best explanation of this, they say, is that our sciences are getting closer and closer to the truth. So, far from supporting a pessimistic induction, the history of science gives us good empirical reasons to think that the terms of our sciences, especially our more mature ones, typically do refer. Thus, not only is the scientific method not self-refuting, it is self-authenticating.[40]

It can be tempting to dismiss arguments of this sort out of hand on the grounds that the scientific method is itself a method that makes essential use of arguments to the best explanation. Questions about its reliability are in large measure questions about the truth preservingness of such arguments. And yet, this defense of the scientific method itself employs an argument to the best explanation. It is thus presupposing exactly that which it is trying to establish.

But some questions deserve to be begged. Questions about the reliability of our fundamental methods of inquiry are just such questions. Hence, it need not be a fault of the scientific method that its reliability cannot be defended or explained without begging the question. The fault would lie in there being no argument whatsoever for its reliability. If there is no way that the method can be defended, not even a question-begging way, then it would fail even one of the minimum tests for a method of inquiry.

This is only the minimum, of course. There will be many methods, some of them in conflict with one another and some patently silly, that are capable of defending themselves.[41] If a method is to be plausible one, it is not enough that it be self-referentially defensible. On the other hand, this is not an insignificant fact about it either.

Likewise, it is misguided to complain about the Cartesian circle, not because Descartes's attempt to establish the reliability of his method does not beg the question—it does—but rather because this is not the flaw in his strategy. The problem is not that he appeals to what he takes to be indubitable propositions in order to argue that indubitability assures us of truth.[42] If a proposed method of inquiry is fundamental, then it cannot help but be used in its own defense if it is to be defended at all.[43] The problem, rather, is that Descartes thought that his strategy, if successful, could altogether extinguish serious skeptical worries. He was wrong about this.

Suppose that Descartes had in fact provided an indubitable proof of God's existence and also an indubitable proof that God would not allow us to be mistaken about what is indubitable. This still would not have been enough to answer all of the skeptic's questions, although admittedly it perhaps would come as close as possible to doing so. In large part it is this that makes the Cartesian strategy an appealing one. If the arguments work, would-be skeptics are forced to go to some lengths to keep their skeptical concerns alive. But they can do so. They will not be able to do so as long as they have Descartes's proofs clearly in mind, for then the proposition that indubitable propositions are true will itself be indubitable for them. But of course, they need not always keep these proofs clearly in mind. And when they don't, they can suspend belief hypothetically in this proposition. They can distance themselves from the spell of the proofs' irresistibility, and in so doing they can sensibly raise the question of whether indubitability really is sufficient for truth. Descartes can urge them to recall his proofs, since by hypothesis this will dispel all of their doubts. However, and this is the most important point, while not under the influence of the irresistible proofs, the would-be skeptics can grant that recalling the proofs would have this effect upon them and yet still insist that this does not settle the issue of whether indubitability really is sufficient for truth. And they would be right.

Consider an analogy. Suppose you know that when you are in the presence of an oracle, you cannot help but believe what the oracle tells you. Even so, while away from the oracle, you can legitimately doubt whether what it tells you is true. Moreover, these doubts are not ones that can be appropriately settled by once again consulting the oracle. You know full well that if you expressed these doubts to the oracle, it would reassure you that what it tells you is true and that this would have the effect of removing your doubts. But this doesn't help with your present worry. You already know that when in its presence, you find the oracle irresistible. Your worry is that this might not be a good thing. And so it is with the skeptic's worry about Descartes's irresistible proofs.[44]

Inquiry requires a leap of intellectual faith, and the need for such faith cannot be eliminated by further inquiry, whether it be empirical or philosophical or whatever. This has implications for the long-term goal of human inquiry. Since we can never have non-question-begging assurances that our way of viewing things is correct, we can never have assurances that there is no point to further inquiry. The absolute knowledge of the Hegelian system, which requires the knowing mind to be wholly adequate to its objects and to know with utter certainty that it is thus, is not a possibility for us. It cannot be our goal, a human goal. For us there can be no such final resting spot.

Admitting this has its advantages, however. For one, it discourages intellectual smugness and correspondingly encourages a respect for cognitive diversity. If we keep in mind the possibility that our way of looking at things might be seriously mistaken, we will be less inclined to issue easy and self-satisfied dismissals of views and methods that are sharply at odds with ours. We thus open ourselves to the thought that our methods and procedures may not be the best ones, much less the only ones, for those seeking truth.

This thought helps liberate epistemology as well. It encourages us to do epistemology, and egocentric epistemology in particular, nondefensively. The prerequisite of egocentric rationality is not truth or reliability, not even in the long run; it is, rather, the absence of any internal motivation for either retraction or supplementation of our beliefs.[45] Egocentric rationality requires that we have beliefs that are to our own deep intellectual satisfaction—beliefs that do not merely satisfy us in a superficial way but that would do so even with the deepest reflection. To be egocentrically rational is thus to be invulnerable to a certain kind of self-condemnation. It is to have beliefs that in our role as truth-seekers we wouldn't criticize ourselves for having even if we were to be deeply reflective. There are various ways of trying to say what exactly this amounts to, but for the moment the details are unimportant.[46] What is important is that even if we are deeply satisfied with our beliefs, we cannot be assured of avoiding substantial error or even the likelihood of doing so. There are no such assurances. The lack of assurances is built into the nature of our inquiries.

Epistemology itself helps reveal this to us, and in the process illustrates that there is an important sense of rational belief that has invulnerability to self-condemnation as its prerequisite rather than invulnerability to widespread error. In agreeing to this, however, we are also agreeing that it is at least possible for someone with what we regard as wildly mistaken beliefs to be rational in this sense. At the beginning of his *Meditations* Descartes speaks of "those whose cerebella are so troubled or clouded by the violent vapors of black bile, that they constantly assure us that they think they are kings when they are really quite poor, or that they are clothed in purple when they are really without covering, or who imagine that they have an earthenware head, or are nothing but pumpkins or are made out of glass." We will have to admit that it is at least possible even for someone who believes these things to be egocentrically rational.

This may seem shocking, but there are ways of dampening the shock. We can begin by pointing out that if persons lack many of the cognitive abilities that we associate with normally functioning humans, we may be reluctant to make judgments about their rationality or irrationality. We may be inclined to regard them as being more arational than irrational. They lack the capacity for either rationality or irrationality in a full-blooded sense. We will be especially inclined to think this of those who aren't sophisticated enough to have opinions about themselves as inquirers—young children and the severely retarded, for example. They will not be capable of the kind of self-monitoring that we associate with rational beings. But then, we need not feel that we are forced to say that their opinions, however wild, are egocentrically rational by default.

This won't eliminate all the problematic cases, but to ease our minds a bit about the others, we can emphasize how bizarre they are. It is unlikely for those with even roughly normal cognitive abilities to have beliefs that resemble those that Descartes describes, and it is even more unlikely to have such beliefs and yet not have some internal motivation to be suspicious of them. Our cognitive abilities, our environment, the entire fabric of our lives conspire against this.

But suppose the unlikely occurs, and we are confronted by people who have what we regard as drastically mistaken beliefs but who nonetheless have no internal motivation to be suspicious of these beliefs. Are we forced to say that their beliefs are rational? Not without qualification. In many everyday contexts saying this would be misleading, since it would be most naturally taken as an endorsement of these people's beliefs. It would be taken as an endorsement because in some contexts assertions about what it is rational for someone to believe are most naturally given an objective interpretation. This might be so, for example, if we are discussing with our neighbors whether the beliefs of these people should be given any credence by us. But in other contexts this need not be the case. For example, if we are in the midst of a philosophical discussion about our own vulnerability to error, there is a point to saying that in one important sense, an egocentric sense, these people might be as rational as we are.

If our intuitions still balk, we will need to remind ourselves that our intuitions are themselves shaped by the perspective we adopt and that this limits their usefulness in settling such issues. Bare intuitions about what seems rational or irrational mean little. For convincing criticism, we need to do more than simply point out that some of the beliefs that the proposed conditions sanction as rational strike us as irrational. Indeed, for any proposed conditions of rational belief, we will be able to describe a context in which this is so.[47] Convincing criticism requires that we attack the underlying rationale of the conditions. This is done by looking for an interpretation of them in terms of a perspective, a goal, and a set of resources. If we fail to find a plausible interpretation of the conditions or if the only interpretation is an uninteresting one, we will have the criticism we are looking for.

On the other hand, what I have been arguing is that there are plausible and important rationales for an egocentric notion of rational belief. Some of these rationales are nonphilosophical. In evaluating our own past mistakes, we are sometimes inclined to do so in terms of how things then looked to us. Charity toward ourselves pushes us in this direction. Similarly, we are often inclined to be charitable toward the mistakes of others, especially those who live in cultures that we judge to be less advanced than our own. We try to evaluate their beliefs from their own perspectives. Moreover, in each case we may be inclined to report our evaluations using the language of rationality and reason.

In addition, one of the rationales for an egocentric notion of rational belief arises out of epistemological inquiry itself. Such inquiry makes it evident that there can be no non-question-begging assurances of our own reliability. It thus raises the fear that our methods might be radically unreliable even if we don't have any indication of their unreliability. This in turn prompts the question of whether it would be irrational for us to use these methods if contrary to what we think, this fear were true. If we agree that there is some important sense in which they need not be irrational, we are pushed in the direction of a notion of rationality whose prerequisite is invulnerability to self-condemnation rather than invulnerability to widespread error.

Any remaining discomfort must be addressed by lowering expectations. We must not expect too much of the notion of rationality. We need to keep in mind its limitations, especially when doing philosophy. This means keeping in mind that many intellectually undesirable characteristics are compatible with being rational. Consider dogmatism, for example. Some people may be invulnerable to intellectual self-condemnation because they are dogmatic. They have views that effectively protect their beliefs against all possible challenges. They have ready explanations for any conceivable data that would count against their methods or the beliefs that these methods generate.

Take astrology as a case in point. Most contemporary astrologers may be imposters, but suppose some are not. They are deeply convinced of the reliability of their methods, having found ways to explain to their own satisfaction what might seem to be the inadequacies of the methods. Indeed, they have what they would consider to be convincing replies to all possible critiques of their methods, and no amount of disinterested reflection would prompt them to change their minds about the adequacy of these replies. Thus, they have no internal motivation to be critical of their astrological methods or the beliefs that these methods produce. There isn't even any conceivable data that would prompt such criticism. Are their beliefs irrational? In one important sense, no. They are not egocentrically irrational. Are they dogmatic and misguided? Yes.

Most of us are not like this, of course. I assume that not even many astrologers are like this. They are not likely to be dogmatic all the way down. But if so, they aren't altogether invulnerable to self-criticism. There will be at least some conceivable data that they themselves on reflection would take to count against their methods. Indeed, there may be actual data of this sort—that is, data that would make them suspicious of their methods, if only they were sufficiently impartial and sufficiently reflective.

There are those, no doubt, who will think this naive. Perhaps it is. But if so, the alternative is not to make all astrologers irrational by fiat. The impulse to inject every intellectually desirable characteristic into the theory of rationality is one to be resisted. It is not impossible for the radically misguided to be rational.[48] Nor is it impossible for a dogmatist to be rational. It is not even impossible for the insane to be rational.[49]

My approach is to explain as much irrationality as possible egocentrically. It is to rely upon our own characters as inquirers. Thus, for example, I assert that most dogmatists are violating their own deepest standards. If there are some dogmatists left over, some who are not violating even their own deepest standards, they are to be dismissed as dogmatic and that is the end of the matter. It is a mistake to try to construct a theory of dogmatism and then make the avoidance of this kind of dogmatism into a strict prerequisite of rationality. Not every intellectual shortcoming need be one of rationality.

Similarly, it is not impossible for the intellectually unskilled to be rational. Again the strategy is to explain as much as possible internally. If you lack mathematical skills or spatial imagination or even something as mundane as spelling skills, you will normally have clues that this is so. But then, it will be egocentrically irrational for you to place great trust in your own abilities about these matters. On the other hand, we can at least imagine situations in which you have no such clues. We can even imagine that from your perspective, everything points to your being unusually skilled in these matters. Then, to be sure, you are likely to make mistakes, but this need not be due to a failure of rationality. Rather, it is due to a lack of skill and a lack of information about this lack of skill.

The same approach can be used in thinking about other intellectual shortcomings. Think of the gambler's fallacy, for example. It is notorious that many people commit this fallacy in playing games of chance. Moreover, their doing so need not be a symptom of their not having thought about the issue. As anyone who has discussed the matter with students knows, it is often difficult to get people to see what is wrong with the gambler's fallacy. On the contrary, it is easy enough to convince some people that there is nothing wrong with it. Present the issue to them in this way: "If a coin is fair, then in 100 tosses it should come up heads about half the time. I've tossed this fair coin 5 times and each time it has come up tails. So, in the next 95 tosses it should come up heads about 50 times and tails about 45 times. Thus, on the very next toss it's more likely to come up heads than tails."

Students have an easy enough time accepting this argument. Does this then mean that it is egocentrically rational for them to commit the gambler's fallacy? Not necessarily, since egocentric rationality is a matter of being invulnerable to self-criticism even on the most ideally deep reflection.[50] To be sure, many students can be convinced by arguments of the above sort, but it is also the case that with enough tutoring and thought most students will come to see what is wrong with the arguments. What this suggests is that even at the time they are fully convinced by the arguments, it may be irrational for them to commit the gambler's fallacy, since to do so would be be to violate their deepest epistemic standards. It is to suggest, in other words, that even at this point they need not be invulnerable to self-criticism.

Of course, there is no guarantee that this will be so. There is no guarantee that the gambler's fallacy conflicts with everyone's deepest standards, and hence there is no guarantee that it isn't egocentrically rational for some people to commit the fallacy. What do we say of such people? We say that their inferences are egocentrically rational but faulty. And one explanation of this is that they are intellectually unskilled. By hypothesis, no matter how thoroughly and carefully these people thought about the issue, they would continue to think that these inferences are reliable ones. Thus, even with ideal reflection they would be unable to see what the rest of us see. They would be unable to see what's wrong with these inferences. Their inferences are faulty, but from this it doesn't follow that they are irrational. It doesn't follow for us, and it doesn't follow for them either. Suppose that some of our inferences are faulty and that beings more intellectually skilled than we are would see this, but we do not. Even on ideal reflection, we would continue to think that the inferences in question are sound ones. Then our inferences are faulty but not necessarily irrational. And so it is with beings less intellectually skilled than ourselves.

On all these points there are useful analogies between the practical and the intellectual. Our actions are egocentrically rationally insofar as we lack internal motivations to be dissatisfied with them. Much immoral behavior can be criticized as being irrational in just this way. We do what we ourselves could not sincerely endorse on reflection. But of course, this makes the irrationality of immorality a contingent matter. It is possible for there to be fanatics who lack even a deeply internal motivation to detach from their vicious behavior. If so, we must be content with regarding them as fanatics. Their problem, and ours, is that they have vicious characters. They need not be irrational.

Similarly, in prisoner-dilemma situations, we collectively generate an outcome that is unwelcome to each of us despite the fact we each do what we have most reason to do. If the dilemma is genuine, the problem is not one of a lack of rationality. If it were, it wouldn't be a genuine dilemma. At least one of us would be acting irrationally. Nor is the problem necessarily one of improper motivation. Dilemmas of this sort can arise even when we are all motivated by a concern for our loved ones.[51] The problem, rather, is that being rational isn't enough in such situations. Indeed, the distinguishing mark of these situations is that in them we produce results that are unwelcome to all precisely because we are all rational. Thus, it is important for us to prevent such situations from occurring. Once we find ourselves in them, being rational will not help. Hence, prevention rather than cure must be our primary strategy. We must plan our lives and our societies with an eye to avoiding these situations. This is the practical lesson to be learned from such dilemmas. The theoretical lesson is that the rationality of decisions no more guarantees cooperation than the rationality of belief guarantees convergence. As a result, it is possible for there to be situations in which we won't generate even minimally acceptable results by making rational decisions.

None of this is to say that there is not a looser kind of unity between egocentric rationality on the one hand and desirable outcomes on the other. For example, it may be that when we have no internal motivation, not even a deep one, to be dissatisfied with what we are doing, we ordinarily won't be acting in a morally vicious way, and it may be that when we are acting in a morally vicious way, there generally is some internal motivation for detachment that we have ignored or not noticed. Our normal psychological makeup may help ensure that in general this is so, as do the realities of social interaction, which tend to penalize blatant hostility and encourage at least minimal cooperation. If so, egocentric rationality and minimally acceptable moral behavior may go hand in hand except in situations that are bizarre or in people who are deranged.

Similarly for egocentric rationality and intellectually desirable characteristics: it may be that when we have no internal motivations to retract what we believe, then in general we are not thoroughly misguided. Likewise, it may be that when we are thoroughly misguided, there is in general some internal motivation for retraction that we have ignored. Thus, it may be that egocentric rationality and largely accurate beliefs go hand in hand except in situations that are bizarre or in people who are deranged. Our cognitive equipment, our intellectual training, and our environment may combine to make this so.

All this may well be. The mistake is to try to turn this contingent truth into a necessary one. It is a mistake to make it a matter of necessity that those of us who are egocentrically rational will not have fundamentally misguided beliefs. Correspondingly, it is a mistake to make it a matter of necessity that rational people will agree with one another if they have the same information.[52] One of the presuppositions of the Cartesian project was that rationality is what stands between us and error. As a result, it was also supposed to stand between us and "a chaotic disagreement in which anything goes."[53] But this need not be our presupposition. What stands in the way of intellectual chaos is not simply the nature of rationality but also the contingent fact that we are born with broadly similar cognitive equipment and into broadly similar environments.

This may strike some as overly optimistic. After all, even if our intellectual strategies and standards are largely shaped by the forces of natural selection, these forces still leave room for cognitive diversity. Natural selection does not always produce uniform characteristics in a species.[54] And of course, social forces introduce yet further possibilities for intellectual diversity. If these differences are great enough, then the deepest epistemic standards of some of us will be at odds with those of others. But then, intellectual chaos will be a real possibility, and with it skepticism also becomes a real possibility.

The connection between intellectual chaos and skepticism is this: although we need not take seriously the opinions and methods of those we have reason to think are in an epistemically less advantageous position than we, we do have a reason to take seriously the opinions and methods of our intellectual peers. For example, if we have reasons to think that a group of beings are deranged or intellectually unskilled or if we have reasons to think that they, unlike us, haven't had the opportunity to draw upon resources and information that are the products of centuries and centuries of intellectual effort, then we need not be overly concerned if their methods and beliefs conflict in significant ways with ours. But if on the other hand we have no plausible way of explaining away the inferiority of their opinions and methods, we will have reasons to take our differences with them seriously. It won't do simply to say that they are wrong and we are right. On the contrary, this kind of disagreement would give us a good egocentric reason to be suspicious of our own opinions and methods. In this way, facts about cognitive diversity can potentially lead to skepticism. But only potentially.

The situation described is not our situation. Among the cultures that we know anything about, there aren't fundamental disagreements about what kinds of intellectual methods are to be trusted.[55] On the contrary, there is a general agreement about the general reliability of memory and perception, and general agreement as well about the past behavior of physical objects being in general a good guide to their future behavior. There are areas of disagreement, to be sure, but it is important neither to exaggerate them nor to view them as fundamental. Besides, often enough the disagreements can be explained away in terms of some cultures not having access to information that is available to us.

The explanation doesn't altogether rule out the possibility that we may at some future time uncover evidence of beings who are our intellectual peers but who radically disagree with us. But this is only to say once again that our ways of investigating the world might conceivably uncover evidence of their own unreliability. But to say that we might potentially have such reasons to doubt our methods and opinions is not to say we now have them. It is not even to say that we ever will have them. It is only to say that our methods don't close off the possibility of radical self-criticism. But of course, this is hardly a fault.

6. *Rationality and Knowledge*

It is not knowledge but, rather, rational belief that is the central notion for egocentric epistemology.[56] This is yet again a departure from Descartes and his Enlightenment successors. Their aim was to find an intellectual strategy that would guarantee us knowledge, but one of the lessons of skeptical hypotheses is that there is no such strategy. We need the world to cooperate in order to have knowledge. We need some luck.

This would have been an unacceptable conclusion to Descartes, but the conclusion is forced upon us. There are two strains in the Cartesian project. One is that egocentrically rationality is essentially a matter of being sufficiently reflective and cautious in thinking about what to believe. The second and very different strain is that if we are sufficiently reflective and cautious, we can be assured that we won't be led into error. The Cartesian project fails because we cannot have it both ways. There is no method that is at once subjectively convincing and objectively guaranteeing. These two aspects of the Cartesian project cannot cohabit in a single notion of rational belief. The question is how to react to this.

One reaction is to abandon epistemology, to proclaim its death. But of course, this isn't the only option. From the fact that one kind of epistemological project cannot be done, it does not follow that there is no epistemological project that can be done. Indeed, an obvious strategy is to split the Cartesian project into two. One project is to pursue the objective part of the Cartesian enterprise, the part that is predominantly concerned with the conditions of knowledge. Those who pursue this project will be asking how we as inquirers must be related to our environment if we are to have knowledge.

But however we answer this question, whether it be in terms of our using reliable methods[57] or in terms of our cognitive equipment's functioning properly[58] or in terms of our having adequate objective evidence,[59], we will not have given a satisfactory answer to the questions that arise out of the egocentric predicament. Among the questions will be ones such as, What methods are reliable? When is our cognitive equipment functioning properly? and When do we have good evidence? Moreover, the way we answer the questions can be more or less reasonable—more or less reasonable by our own lights. No account of knowledge can capture this egocentric notion of reasonable and the associated egocentric notion of rationality, but it is precisely an interest in these notions that has traditionally prompted much of epistemology.

If we choose to pursue these questions of egocentric rationality, the spirit of our project will be similar to that of the other part of the Cartesian enterprise, the one that associates rationality with the search for subjectively persuasive methods. The project, like Descartes's, will focus upon the egocentric predicament, but unlike Descartes's, it need not assume that by being rational we are thereby assured of having true beliefs. Nor need there be any assurance of reliability, and because of this, there is no assurance that a rational true belief will be a particularly good candidate for knowledge. The reverse need not be so either. You can know something without your belief being egocentrically rational. If your belief is the product of a highly reliable cognitive process, then it might be a good candidate for knowledge even if you yourself would be critical of it on reflection.[60] You might have knowledge in spite of yourself.

An answer to the question, What is required if my beliefs are to be egocentrically rational? will not help answer the question, What is required if I am to have knowledge? Nor will an answer to the latter help answer the former. It can seem otherwise, especially if one accepts the idea that knowledge is something close to rational true belief, for then, it might seem as if an adequate account of knowledge would answer both questions simultaneously. This is an illusion. If knowledge is roughly equivalent to rational true belief, the sense of rationality being invoked cannot be an egocentric one.

Consider the development of Alvin Goldman's reliabilist views. In his early papers on epistemology, Goldman advocated only a causal-reliabilist theory of knowledge. He even suggested that one of the advantages of his approach was its abandonment of an overly intellectualized, justification-driven conception of knowledge.[61] Later, he saw that on the assumption that knowledge involves justified belief, the suggestion could be reversed. His causal-reliabilist account of knowledge, he now asserts, contains the materials for an adequate account of justified belief as well. Justification, like knowledge, is essentially a matter of one's beliefs having been reliably produced.[62]

Or consider Alvin Plantinga, who argues that knowledge is essentially a matter of having true beliefs that are the products of properly functioning cognitive equipment. Since Plantinga defines epistemic warrant as whatever must be added to true belief in order to get knowledge, absent Gettier problems, this account of knowledge also provides an account of epistemic warrant. A warranted belief, Plantinga says, is one that is the product of cognitive equipment that is functioning properly—that is, functioning in the way that it is designed to function.[63]

At first glance, it might seem as if Goldman and Plantinga are appropriating the terms 'justified' and 'warrant' for their own purposes.[64] But if there are problems with such views, they are not terminological. It is not as if Goldman, Plantinga, and other like-minded epistemologists have simply stipulated a new meaning for 'justification' and its cognates, one that is altogether at odds with the historical roots of these terms. On the contrary, the history of these terms indicate that they have both an egocentric and an objective side. This is illustrated, for example, in Descartes's assumption that it is rational to employ the method of doubt precisely because it is both subjectively available to each of us and objectively guaranteed to produce no false beliefs. Descartes saw reason as a bridge between the subjective and the objective, and a permanent one at that; it is supposed to guarantee that the subjectively persuasive and the objectively reliable do not come apart. We see things differently, of course. We see that it is possible for the two to come apart. Thus, for us these egocentric and objective components cannot cohabit in a single notion of rational belief. But this means that in doing epistemology, we must choose between them, and however we choose we will be abandoning a part of the history that the notion of rationality carries with it.

Thus, if we so wish, we can pursue an epistemology of knowledge. There will then be various kinds of accounts—ones that emphasize reliability, ones that emphasize proper cognitive functioning, ones that emphasize adequate objective evidence, and so on. The conditions of knowledge may well include conditions that can be construed as conditions of rational belief as well, albeit not egocentrically rational beliefs. Whether or not this is so depends on whether there is an interpretation of these conditions in terms of an important perspective, goal, and set of resources. Often there will be such an interpretation. For some versions of reliabilism, for example, the interpretation, at least roughly, will be in terms of the perspective of a knowledgeable observer (one who knows the reliability of various cognitive processes), the goal of believing what is true and not believing what is false, and resources consisting of those cognitive processes that are available to the believer.[65]

On the other hand, if there is no such interpretation, the proposed conditions of knowledge cannot be regarded as conditions of rational belief in any important sense. But even here, we can stipulate, if we so wish, some term to designate what must be added to true belief to get knowledge. Plantinga stipulates that he is using 'warrant' in this way, Goldman 'justified', and Alston talks of what 'epistemizes' true belief. If so, then by definition an account of knowledge will also be an account of warranted belief or an account of justified belief or an account of what epistemizes true belief. But whatever notion emerges from this inquiry into the nature of knowledge, it will not be one that provides an answer to the question of what by your own lights it is rational for you to believe. For that, we need an egocentric epistemology.

Nor will it do to try to split the difference between an egocentric epistemology and an epistemology of knowledge by the introduction of a social epistemology. This won't eliminate the need for the two kind of projects that Descartes tried to combine into one. On the one hand, no purely social conception of rationality can provide us with the prerequisites of knowledge, since socially persuasive methods of inquiry are no more guaranteed to be reliable than are egocentrically persuasive ones. So, we still need an epistemology of knowledge. And we will also still need an egocentric epistemology, since whatever the proposed social conditions of rationality might be, they may seem foolish from your point of view. But if so, it won't be egocentrically irrational for you to abide by them.

This is not to deny the obvious truth that we are shaped by our social environment. It is not even to deny that the criticisms we are prone to make of our intellectual environment typically make use of practices, standards and opinions that are largely drawn from that very same environment.[66] It is only to insist that these practices, standards, and opinions are potentially subject to criticism from an egocentric perspective. It is only to insist, in other words, that it might be egocentrically rational for you to repudiate them, no matter how cherished or how taken for granted they may be.

This is part of our Enlightenment inheritance. The picture is one of individuals standing in judgment of the intellectual climate in which they find themselves, and it is a picture that encourages us to worry about 'group think'. Sometimes agreement may be little more than unthinking conformity. Indeed, too much agreement—agreement verging on unanimity—may itself sometimes be a reason for suspicion. It may be a reason to think repressive forces are at work. But even when this is not so, even when the agreement is not enforced agreement, we want to leave room for the possibility of criticism, even radical criticism. It is this that inclines many of us to resist any theory, whether it be political or epistemological, that allows the individual to be swamped by the social. The egocentric approach to epistemology is part of this resistance.

Notes

1. For a discussion of the positive function of doubt within the Cartesian program, see Wolterstorff, "The Emergence of Rationality"; Williams, *Descartes: The Project of Pure Inquiry*, especially chap. 2; and Williams, "Descartes's Use of Skepticism," in M. Burnyeat (ed.), *The Skeptical Tradition* (Berkeley: University of California Press, 1983), 337–52.

2. Descartes apparently thought of revelation as an exception: ". . . above all else we must impress on our memory the overriding rule that whatever God has revealed to us must be accepted as more certain than anything else. And although the light of reason may, with the utmost clarity and evidence, appear to suggest something different, we must still put our entire faith in divine authority rather than in our judgement." From the *Principles*, I, 76, in *The Philosophical Writings of Descartes*, trans. Cottingham, Stoothoff, and Murdoch, vol. 1, 221. Wolterstorff cites this as a reason to regard Locke, and not Descartes, as the first great modern—i.e., the first to argue that all of our judgments whatsoever, including those of religion, must be subjected to the scrutiny of our human reason. See Wolterstorff, "The Emergence of Rationality."

3. What I am asserting here is not at odds with the view that one knows P only if one's belief that P is nonaccidentally true. Even if knowledge does require that belief and truth be nonaccidentally related, we need an element of luck—i.e., we need the world to cooperate—in order for there to be this nonaccidental relationship between the two.

4. See Michael DePaul, "Argument and Perception: The Role of Literature in Moral Inquiry," *Journal of Philosophy*, 85 (1988), 552–65.

5. See Derek Parfit's discussion of practical dilemmas in Parfit, *Reasons and Persons* (New York: Oxford University Press, 1986).

6. I borrow the phrase 'defensive epistemology' from Bas van Fraassen, who uses it in a more restricted way in *Laws and Symmetry* (Oxford: Clarendon Press, 1989).

7. See sec. 3.4.

8. I assume here that probability is to be given some sort of empirical reading, such that if P is probable given Q, P cannot be false in most close situations in which Q is true.

9. Socrates argued that one never acts for the worse by having a virtue. The assertion here is analogous; one never believes for the worse by being rational, where believing for the worse is a matter of believing in a way that is more likely to lead to error. Rationality, it is asserted, guarantees at least this much.

10. Compare with Nagel, *The View from Nowhere*, especially chap. 5.

11. See sec. 1.4.

12. See Stephen Stich, *The Fragmentation of Reason* (Cambridge: MIT Press, 1990), chap. 3.

13. Ibid.

14. See sec. 1.6.

15. Descartes himself emphasized this, insisting that his method of doubt is appropriate for use only in science, not in everyday life. See his *Discourse on Method*, especially Part Four, in Cottingham, Stoothoff, and Murdoch (trans.), *The Philosophical Writings of Descartes*, 111–51.

16. Contrast with Rorty, *Philosophy and the Mirror of Nature*.

17. "I think it is wrong, or at least misleading, to suggest . . . that scepticism here involves taking an 'external' view of our knowledge . . . At least this is wrong if it leaves open a ready way of suggesting that the external viewpoint is optional, or even that it makes no sense . . . it is not as if the philosophical undertaking demands quite different tools or perspectives from the everyday assessments of chance; it just has a different topic. Similarly, our everyday financial standing may be settled by considering the credit we have at the bank; this does not rule out a sensible query about the financial standing of the bank itself." Simon Blackburn, "Knowledge, Truth and Reliability," *Proceedings of the British Academy* (New York: Oxford University Press, 1985), 167–87.

18. In the *Fifth Meditation* Descartes says, ". . . the nature of my mind is such that I cannot but assent to these things [which I clearly and distinctly perceive], at least so long as I clearly perceive them." See Cottingham, Stoothoff, and Murdoch (trans.), *The Philosophical Writings of Descartes*, vol. 2, 45.

19. Compare with Williams, *Descartes: The Project of Pure Inquiry* and "Descartes' Use of Skepticism." See also Kenny's discussion of first-order doubt and second-order doubt in "The Cartesian Circle and the Eternal Truths."

20. Why literary villains and not real-life villains? Why Shakespeare's Richard III but not Eichmann or Charles Manson? Because our moral repugnance at real-life villains, especially recent ones, often overwhelms us, making it difficult for us to appreciate their resourcefulness and ingenuity. Our repugnance tends to swamp everything else. We feel the need to disapprove of them totally. It is a commonplace to point out that literature and art has the power to engage us emotionally and that in large part this accounts for its power to alter us, but it is also true that sometimes literature and art are instructive only because we are able to disengage ourselves from fictional events to a degree that we find difficult for real events.

21. Contrast this with Hume, whose position really does hint of schizophrenia. Hume reported that while engaged in philosophical reflection he found himself forced to give up his ordinary beliefs about material objects, the future, and the self, but that as soon as he left his study these reflections appeared strained and his ordinary beliefs returned. So, according to Hume, his beliefs changed dramatically depending upon which of his personalities was engaged, his philosophical one or his nonphilosophical one.

22. "It [an inquiry into our reliability as inquirers] must be an investigation of a concrete claim if its procedure is to be coherent; it cannot be the investigation of a concrete claim if its conclusion is to be general. Without that coherence it would not have the obviousness it has seemed to have; without that generality its conclusion would not be skeptical." Stanley Cavell, *The Claim of Reason: Wittgenstein, Skepticism, Morality, and Tragedy* (Oxford: Oxford University Press, 1979), 220. See also Norman Malcolm, *Knowledge and Certainty* (Ithaca: Cornell University Press, 1963); Barry Stroud, *The Significance of Philosophical Scepticism* (Oxford: Oxford University Press, 1984), especially chap. 7; and Thompson Clarke, "The Legacy of Skepticism," *Journal of Philosophy*, 69 (1972), 754–69.

23. See Descartes's reply to Boudin: "There may be reasons which are strong enough to compel us to doubt, even though these reasons are themselves doubtful, and hence are not to be retained later on . . ." See Cottingham, Stoothoff, and Murdoch (trans.), *The Philosophical Writings of Descartes* vol. 2, 319. See also Hume on the Pyrrhonian skeptics: ". . . the skeptical reasonings, were it possible for them to exist, and were they not destroy'd by their subtlety, wou'd be successively both strong and weak, according to the successive dispositions of the mind. Reason first appears in possession of the throne, prescribing laws, and imposing maxims, with an absolute sway and authority. Her enemy, therefore, is oblig'd to take shelter under her protection, and by making use of rational arguments to prove the fallaciousness and imbecility of reason, produces in a manner, a patent under her hand and seal. This patent has at first an authority, proportioned to the present and immediate authority of reason, from which it is deriv'd. But as it is suppos'd to be contradictory to reason, it gradually diminishes the force of that governing power, and its own at the same time; til at last they both vanish away into nothing by a regular and just diminution . . ."

24. Donald Davidson, "On the Very Idea of a Conceptual Scheme," *Proceedings and Addresses of the American Philosophical Association* 17 (1973–74), 5–20; and Davidson, "A Coherence Theory of Truth and Knowledge," in E. LePore, (ed.), *The Philosophy of Donald Davidson: Perspectives on Truth and Interpretation* (London: Basil Blackwell, 1986), 307–19.

25. Davidson, "A Coherence Theory of Truth and Knowledge". See also Hilary Putnam, *Reason, Truth, and History* (Cambridge: Cambridge University Press, 1981), chap. 1; and Fred I. Dretske, "The Epistemology of Belief," in G. Ross and M. Roth, (eds.), *Doubting: Contemporary Perspectives on Skepticism* (Dordrecht: Kluwer, 1990).

26. "The question, how do I know that my beliefs are true? thus answers itself, simply because beliefs are by nature generally true." Davidson, "A Coherence Theory of Truth and Knowledge," 319.

27. Notice, moreover, that not just any naturalistic account of belief content imposes significant restrictions on how far we can go wrong (the only question then being exactly what the restrictions are). Only a specific class of theories do so—roughly, those that make the content of a belief heavily dependent on its causal history. By contrast, a nomological approach to content will not impose any such restrictions, since the required nomological relations might hold even if instances of them do not. See Jerry Fodor, "A Theory of Content," in Fodor, *A Theory of Content and Other Essays* (Cambridge: MIT Press, 1990).

28. Contrast with Ernest LePore and Barry Loewer, "Solipsistic Semantics," *Midwest Studies in Philosophy* (1985), 587–606.

29. Compare with David Lewis, "Radical Interpretation," in his *Philosophical Papers*, vol. 1 (New York: Oxford University Press, 1983), 112–13.

30. There would be even fewer obstacles in the way of an interpretation that has others radically deceived if neither truth nor rationality needs to be maximized. And indeed, some philosophers have argued this. They suggest that ascribing too much rationality can actually count against an intepretation—if, for example, it has others avoiding the most common fallacies. See Gibbard, *Wise Choices, Apt Feelings*, 156–60. Also see Richard Grandy, "Reference, Meaning and Belief," *Journal of Philosophy*, 70 (1973), 443ff.

31. Whatever linguistic competence is, it is not a matter of having a flawless understanding of one's own sincere utterances. Thus, the contents of one's beliefs can diverge from the contents of one's sincere utterances, and as a result, one can sincerely say what is true and yet nonetheless believe what is false, or vice versa. This means that an adequate interpretation of someone's sincere utterances is not *ipso facto* an adequate interpretation of that person's beliefs. Contrast with Davidson, "A Coherence Theory of Truth and Knowledge," 315: "Equally obvious is the fact that once an interpretation has been given for a sentence assented to, a belief has been attributed."

32. The variety of such scenarios creates problems for certain theories of interpretation. For example, Martin Hollis says that "the identification of beliefs requires a 'bridgehead' of true and rational beliefs." But he says in addition that the bridgehead is "fixed," in the sense that there are some specific kinds of environment-belief links that must be preserved in any translation. See Hollis, "The Social Destruction of Reality," in Martin Hollis and Steven Lukes (eds.), *Rationality and Relativism* (Cambridge: MIT Press, 1982).

33. Fred Dretske's argument against skepticism is limited in essentially the same way as Davidson's. Dretske's strategy is to argue that "if someone lives in a place where it is impossible to distinguish A-type things from B-type things, hence impossible to know that this particular thing is an A (or a B), then it is likewise impossible, under ordinary learning conditions, to develop a way of representing something as an A (or as a B)." He then goes on to say that this conclusion "completely turns the table on the skeptic," since it shows that in general one cannot believe that which, given the situation, one cannot know. But in fact, even if all the essentials of Dretske's theory are granted, the table is not so completely turned on the skeptic. Dretske admits that his argument is plausible only for "simple or primitive concepts." So, the argument provides no assurances for those beliefs that involve nonprimitive concepts—surely most of our beliefs. Moreover, since we have no surefire way to distinguish primitive from nonprimitive concepts, his argument cannot even give us assurances with respect to any particular portion of our belief system. Again, it is as if we have been given a map by a mapmaker whose only assurance is that at least some of the map's most general features, we know not which, are accurate. See Dretske, "The Epistemology of Belief."

34. See Colin McGinn, "Radical Interpretation and Epistemology," and Peter Klein, "Radical Interpretation and Global Skepticism," both in E. LePore, (ed.), *Truth and Interpretation: Perspectives on the Philosophy of Donald Davidson*, (Oxford: Basil Blackwell, 1986).

35. 35 Brand Blanshard, *The Nature of Thought*, vol. 2 (New York: Macmillan, 1941), 268.

36. The formulation is Hilary Putnam's. See Putnam, *The Many Faces of Realism* (LaSalle, Ill.: Open Court, 1987).

37. ". . . the reality of that which is real does depend on the real fact that investigation is destined to lead, at last, if continued long enough, to a belief in it." C. S. Peirce, *Collected Papers*, vol. 5 (Cambridge: Harvard University Press, 1934), 408.

38. See sec. 2.5.

39. "When [a Pyrrhonian] awakes from his dream, he will be the first to join in the laugh against himself, and to confess, that all his objections are mere amusement, and can have no other tendency than to show the whimsical condition of mankind, who must act and reason and believe; though they are not able, by their most diligent enquiry, to satisfy themselves concerning the foundations of these operations, or to remove the objections, which may be raised against them." David Hume, *An Enquiry Concerning Human Understanding*, ed. L. A. Selby-Bigge, with text revised by P. H. Nidditch (New York: Oxford University Press, 1975), sec. 12, 128.

40. See, e.g., Putnam, *Reason, Truth and History*; Newton-Smith, *The Rationality of Science*; McMullin, "The Fertility of Theory and the Unity of Appraisal in Science."

41. Ernest Sosa gives the following example: "If a rule or principle contains the proposition that the earth is flat, then it is acceptable, as is the proposition that the earth is flat." See Sosa, "Methodology and Apt Belief," *Synthese* 74 (1988), 418.

42. It is at least potentially misleading to refer to this as the problem of the Cartesian circle, since this suggests that Descartes smuggles his conclusion into the premises. In fact, he does nothing of the sort. In his argument, he nowhere asserts the premise that indubitable propositions are true. On the other hand, the propositions that he does use as premises are ones that he takes to be indubitable. This is what makes them eligible to be premises. So, in a broad sense of the expression, he does beg the question even if, strictly speaking, he doesn't argue in a circle. He begs the questions because he makes use of his method in an attempt to defend it.

43. Compare with John Stuart Mill's remarks about first principles in chapter 4 of *Utilitarianism*. Compare also with Alasdair MacIntyre's insistence that although first principles cannot be demonstrated, they need not be devoid of rational support. See MacIntyre, *Whose Justice? Which Rationality?*

44. Contrast with Bernard Williams: "So the believer can always recall the skeptic, unless the skeptic is willfully obstinate, to considering the existence and benevolence of God, and if the skeptic concentrates on those proofs, he will believe not only those propositions themselves but also something that follows from them—namely, that clear and distinct perceptions are reliable, and hence skepticism unjustified." Williams, "Descartes's Use of Skepticism," 349. My point, in turn, is that in this context, where the issue is precisely whether irresistible proofs might be mistaken, it is not mere obstinance to refuse to recall the proofs. The skeptic's refusal to recall them is not unlike the alcoholic's refusal to enter the bar. In each case the refusal is motivated by a fear that one's weaknesses will be exploited.

45. "An ideally rational belief system is one which is in equilibrium under the most acute pressures of internal criticism and discussion." Brian Ellis, *Rational Belief Systems* (Oxford: Basil Blackwell, 1979), 4 .

46. I discuss some of these details in sec. 3.1.

47. See sec. 1.6.

48. "The majority of men follow their passions, which are movements of the sensitive appetite, in which movements of the heavenly bodies can cooperate; but few are wise enough to resist these passions. Consequently astrologers are able to foretell the truth in a

majority of cases, especially in a general way." Thomas Aquinas, *Summa Theologiae* 1, Qu. 115, a.4, ad. Obj. 3.

49. G. K. Chesterton once quipped that madness is not always the absence of reason; sometimes it's the absence of everything else. See also Michel Foucault, who emphasizes that the insane sometime reason impeccably from their delusionary premises. Foucault, *Madness and Civilization*, trans. R. Howard (New York: Pantheon, 1965).

50. For details about what is involved ideally in deep reflection, see sec. 3.1.

51. See Parfit, *Reasons and Persons*.

52. "Let any human being having enough information and exert enough thought upon any question, and the result will be that he will arrive at a certain definite conclusion, which is the same that any other mind will reach . . ." C. S. Peirce, *Collected Papers of Charles Sanders Peirce*, vol. 7, ed. C. Hartshorne, P. Weiss, and A. W. Burks, (Cambridge: Harvard University Press, 1931–58), 319.

53. The phrase is from Bernard Williams. See Williams, "Descartes' Use of Skepticism," 344.

54. See Stich, *The Fragmentation of Reason*, especially chap. 3.

55. For a case study illustrating this, see E. Hutchins, *Culture and Inference: A Trobriand Case Study* (Cambridge: Harvard University Press, 1980).

56. Compare with Mark Kaplan, "It's Not What You Know That Counts," *Journal of Philosophy*, 82 (1985), 350–63; and Isaac Levi, *The Enterprise of Knowledge* (Cambridge: MIT Press, 1980), sec. 1.9.

57. See F. P. Ramsey, "Knowledge," in Ramsey, *Philosophical Papers*, ed. H. Mellor (London: Routledge and Kegan Paul, 1978), 126–27; Goldman, *Epistemology and Cognition*; Fred Dretske, *Knowledge and the Flow of Information* (Cambridge: MIT Press, 1981); D. M. Armstrong, *Belief, Truth, and Knowledge* (Cambridge: Cambridge University Press, 1973).

58. See Alvin Plantinga, "Positive Epistemic Status and Proper Function," in J. Tomberlin (ed.), *Philosophical Perspectives*, vol. 2, (Atascadero, CA: Ridgeview, 1988). See also Lycan, *Judgement and Justification*, especially 144.

59. See Chisholm, *Theory of Knowledge*; William Alston, in Alston, *Epistemic Justification* (Ithaca: Cornell University Press, 1989), 227–48.

60. Think of a student who, when asked, blurts out the precise date of an historical event but who is unsure of her own memory.

61. See Alvin Goldman, "A Causal Theory of Knowing," *Journal of Philosophy* 64 (1967), 355–72; "Discrimination and Perceptual Knowledge," *Journal of Philosophy* 73 (1976), 771–91.

62. See Alvin Goldman "What Is Justified Belief?" in G. Pappas, (ed.), *Justification and Knowledge* (Dordrecht: Reidel, 1979), and *Epistemology and Cognition*.

63. Plantinga, "Positive Epistemic Status and Proper Function."

64. See, e.g., Bonjour, *The Structure of Empirical Knowledge*, especially 37.

65. The notion of a knowledgeable observer is merely shorthand for an observer who has true beliefs of the relevant kind—e.g., true beliefs about the objective probabilities or the reliability of the relevant processes or whatever. So, as I intend it, this interpretation doesn't violate the requirement that an interpretation not make use of the notion of rationality or any of its cognates. See sec. 1.6.

66. "One cannot think for oneself if one thinks entirely by oneself." Alasdair MacIntyre, *Whose Justice? Which Rationality?* 296.

3

Egocentric Rationality

1. The Subject Matter of Egocentric Epistemology

Egocentric epistemology is concerned with the perspectives of individual believers and the goal of having an accurate and comprehensive belief system. This characterizes at least in a rough way its subject matter, but more needs to be said about the exact nature of both the goal and the perspective.

Begin with the goal. It is an intellectual goal but a synchronic one. The concern is with what it is rational for individuals to believe at a given moment insofar as their goal is to have an accurate and comprehensive belief system at that moment. If the moment is the present one and the believer is you, the concern is with what it is rational for you to believe, given your current perspective and given your goal of now having an accurate and comprehensive belief system.

By contrast, nonintellectual and nonsynchronic goals are beside the point. A dramatic way to illustrate this is to imagine situations in which you yourself realize that goals of this sort are best promoted by your believing an obviously false proposition. You might realize, for example, that if you were to believe that the intellectual prospects of the entire human race were dependent solely on you, you would conduct your intellectual life with significantly more care and precision, and this over time would result in a significant improvement of your beliefs.[1] If so, then you may have a reason to believe this obviously false proposition, but it is not the kind of reason in which epistemologists have traditionally been interested.

This is not to say that nonintellectual and nonsynchronic goals are not important for the way we conduct our intellectual lives. They obviously are important. Whenever the concern is with intellectual progress and epistemic improvement, it will be our long-term intellectual goals that are at issue. We will want to know what strategies are likely to promote these goals. We need temporally extended strategies in the theoretical realm just as much as we do in the practical realm. It is important, for example, that we have stable, dependable strategies governing the gathering and processing of information. We need to know when to do so and how to go about it. And since we need these strategies to be feasible ones—we cannot spend all of our time and energy on epistemic pursuits at the expense of our other goals—our nonintellectual goals will also have to be taken into account. If for no other reason, they will be relevant as practical constraints on inquiry.[2]

So, nonsynchronic and nonintellectual goals are important, but they don't eliminate the need for a notion of rational belief that is concerned with a purely synchronic intellectual goal. Even when we are in the midst of gathering more information about a topic or processing the information that we already have in a different way, we can and sometimes do wonder what it is rational for us to believe in the interim. Our having reasons to continue our inquiries on a topic does not mean that it is rational to withhold judgment until we complete the inquiries. We often have good reasons to believe a proposition even though for safety's sake we also have good reasons to gather additional information about it.[3]

Besides, whether we have good reasons to gather more information about a topic is itself a function of what it is rational for us to believe, as are all questions about what intellectual strategies and procedures it is rational for us to follow. There may be procedures that would dramatically improve the quality of our beliefs, but we won't have a good egocentric reason to adopt these procedures unless we have a good egocentric reason to believe that this is so.[4] Accordingly, as important as questions of epistemic improvement are, questions of the synchronic rationality of our beliefs have at least a theoretical priority.

There are two other issues about the nature of the goal that also need clarification. The first is whether the goal is to be understood in terms of beliefs *simpliciter* or in terms of degrees of belief. If the former, then having an accurate and comprehensive belief system is essentially a matter of believing those propositions that are true and not believing those propositions that are false. If the latter, things are not quite so simple. Since degrees of belief are not straightforwardly true or false, we will need to find some other way to characterize their accuracy. One natural way to do so is in terms of objective probabilities, the rough idea being that these probabilities can play a role analogous to the one that truth plays for beliefs *simpliciter*. On this view, accuracy is essentially a matter of having a strong degree of belief in propositions that are highly probable and a low degree of belief in those that are highly improbable. For convenience, however, I am going to put this issue aside, at least for the time being,[5] and simply assume that the epistemic goal is to be understood in terms of beliefs rather than degrees of belief.

The second issue arises because the goal has two aspects, accuracy and comprehensiveness, that pull against each other. Something must be said about the relative weight that is to be given to each. What Descartes said was that accuracy is always to take precedence over comprehensiveness. The Cartesian goal is to make one's belief system as comprehensive as possible subject to the constraint that it be risk-free. So for Descartes, risk-taking is never justified by the prospect of having a more comprehensive belief system. Roderick Chisholm, by contrast, has often emphasized the value of comprehensiveness, insisting that "playing it safe" is not always the most reasonable intellectual course. Most of us will be sympathetic with this suggestion,[6] but even so there are likely to be differences among us as to just how much relative weight is to be given to accuracy and comprehensiveness. Should the two be given equal weight, or should accuracy be weighted somewhat more heavily, or perhaps should comprehensiveness be weighted more?

The answer is that none of these should be a strict prerequisite of egocentric rationality. Whatever one's favored attitude toward epistemic risk, one should refrain from imposing it upon others in the name of rationality.[7] Insofar as the issue is egocentric rationality, the attitudes that matter are your own, not Chisholm's and not Descartes's and not anyone else's. What matters is what from your own perspective would seem to be an acceptable risk, insofar as your goal is to have accurate and comprehensive beliefs.

There is more to be said about the issue of one's attitude toward epistemic risk, but for now I am going to postpone the discussion[8] and concentrate instead on the more general question of what a perspective is. It is essentially a set of beliefs, a body of opinion. However, there are a number of such bodies of opinion that can plausibly be regarded as your own, ranging from one that consists simply of your uncorrected opinions to one that consists of deeper and presumably more stable opinions. It is this last body of opinion that is the measure of egocentric rationality. Indeed, were egocentric rationality simply a matter of having beliefs that, given your uncorrected state of opinion, you were satisfied with, it would border on the trivial that your beliefs about any given topic are egocentrically rational. There would be little or no sorting of your beliefs, and hence little or no point to our declaring them to be rational by your own lights. What matters is your reflective opinion. It is egocentrically rational for you to believe a proposition only if you would think on deep reflection that believing it is part of what is involved in your having an accurate and comprehensive belief system. Your belief must be able to stand up to your own critical reflection. It must meet your own deep standards and in this sense be invulnerable to criticism.[9]

On the other hand, it need not be invulnerable to criticism come what may. There may be data that would provide you with grounds for criticism, were you to have it. This doesn't matter. Egocentric rationality requires only that you have no grounds for dissatisfaction, given your current personal resources. Your current resources consist of the data and information represented in your current beliefs, plus any additional data or information that you would acquire were you to be more introspective. For example, there can be sense experiences of various sorts that aren't currently represented in your beliefs but that would be represented were you to be appropriately introspective.

These resources can be thought of as your starting point. The idea is to imagine you reflecting and to imagine the reflection's being grounded in your current resources, without new data being gathered. To be sure, the reflection itself might prompt new ideas or new ways of looking at things. Indeed, this is the point of it: to determine whether something would occur to you on reflection that would cause you to be dissatisfied with what you now believe about a topic. If it would, then your belief is not egocentrically rational.

So, the standards you must meet if you are to be egocentrically rational are not timeless, objective rules of thought that are out there somewhere, waiting to be discovered if only you are clever enough. They are internal standards. But it is not as if the internal standards are always there waiting to be discovered either. You cannot simply peer inward and read off what your standards are. You cannot do so even if you are skilled at introspection, since these standards are not always present in fully developed form. They are based on your own deep dispositions, but often enough the relevant dispositions will be activated only with hard thought—and not so much by hard thought on the question of what your standards are but rather by hard thought on the issues at hand, whatever these may be. In the process of grapppling with the issues, the standards emerge. Indeed, in many cases it may be less misleading to think of them as being created rather than emerging. Despite the impression one might get from much of epistemology, dealing with hard intellectual issues is almost never a matter of first discovering what your standards are and then applying them to the issue at hand. More often it is a matter of making a number of tiny, specific decisions about the best way to think about the issue, and these decisions, without too much exaggeration, can be thought of as creating your standards. Even so, for convenience I will continue to say that your beliefs are egocentrically rational if they meet your epistemic standards, and I will say this even if you haven't been reflective and hence even if those standards are merely implicit in your dispositions, waiting to be activated by the proper sort of reflection.

But suppose you happen to distrust reflection. Is egocentric rationality still a matter of what you would think on reflection? In particular, suppose you think that reflection usually just confuses you, causing you to be less reliable in your judgments than you would be otherwise. As a result, you avoid reflection. You think it is better to believe the first thing that pops into your head about an issue. Moreover, you aren't incoherent. This belief, the belief that reflection is not to be trusted, is itself the first thing that popped into your head about the issue of belief acquisition. Nevertheless, on reflection you would be critical of this belief. You would think that this is a silly way to conduct your intellectual life. Then according to what I have said, it isn't egocentrically rational for you to believe what first pops into your head. This might seem counterintuitive. After all, you now think that your reflective views are less reliable than your unreflective ones. Doesn't this suggest that by your own lights it is unreasonable for you to be reflective? And more generally, doesn't it also suggest that egocentric rationality is not always a matter of what you would think on reflection?

This much is right: from your present unreflective perspective, you have no reason to be reflective, since you think that this would make you less reliable. But this is just to say that there is one sense of reason, a radically subjective sense, that is to be understood in terms of your current beliefs, whatever they happen to be. Whenever you believe that a policy or decision is a sensible one, it is reasonable in this radically subjective sense for you to follow it. Consider an analogy. Two horses are racing each other, and the betting odds on the two are equal. You have overwhelming evidence that horse A will win the race, evidence that you yourself would acknowledge were you to reflect for even a moment. Nevertheless, you haven't been reflective and you instead believe that B will win. If so, it is unreasonable in one sense, a radically subjective sense, for you to bet on A. After all, to do so would be to bet on a horse that you now believe is less likely to win. And what, we might rhetorically ask, could be more unreasonable than that?

But of course, it is also the case that we often criticize decisions as irrational, even when the decision-maker believes that the decision is a good one. Such criticisms must be presupposing a less radically subjective notion of rationality, one that allows us to say that betting on A may be the most reasonable alternative for you even if you believe otherwise. Indeed, an especially forceful way to make such criticisms is to point out that were you to be reflective, you yourself would admit that it would be foolish to bet on anything other than A.

And so it is with the above case involving reflection. Although your current unreflective opinion is that it is best to believe the first thing that pops into your head, on reflection you would regard such a policy as a foolish one. You yourself would be critical of it. Thus, in one important sense, a reflective sense, this is not a reasonable policy for you. It is a policy that violates your own deep standards.

If it is reflective opinion that is the measure of egocentric rationality, we need to have some idea about the amount of reflection and the kind of reflection that is required. For a belief to be egocentrically rational, is it enough that a few moments of reflection would give you no motivation for retraction? Or must it be the case that you wouldn't be dissatisfied with your belief even if you were to engage in lengthy and careful reflection? And if so, how lengthy and how careful must the reflection be?

Descartes thought that he had a straightforward answer to these questions. He thought that there was a natural stopping point to reflection. You reflect until you perceive the truth of the proposition in question with such clarity and distinctness that you are no longer able to doubt its truth. At this point you can terminate your reflection and be assured of not making a mistake. So, additional reflection would be gratuitous.[10] However, Descartes was wrong about there being such a stopping point. There is no point at which we can terminate reflection and be altogether assured of not making a mistake. We need another way to specify the point at which opinion is rational if reflection up to that point leaves you satisfied with it.

Suppose we say that the stopping point is reached when you have reflected in a reasonably careful fashion for a reasonably lengthy amount of time. This is sensible advice. Indeed, in one sense, a sense that I will later try to explicate, it is obviously the right advice.[11] Nevertheless, for the epistemologist it has a devastating drawback. Like much advice that smacks of common sense, it is itself reason-saturated. It thus leaves us within the circle of terms that are at issue. We now need to say what is involved in your reflections' being reasonably lengthy and careful, but, and here is the rub, this will inevitably involve reference to what it is rational for you to believe. The time and care that it is reasonable for you to devote to such reflections will itself be a function of what it is reasonable for you to believe about the potential benefits and costs of reflection. So, we find ourselves back where we started, confronted once again with questions of rational belief.

Thus, contrary to the familiar saying, this is advice that may work well enough in practice but not in theory. For our theoretical concerns, we need to look elsewhere for a solution. We need to ask, as Descartes in effect did, when it is gratuitous for you to reflect further on a topic. When we think of the matter in this way, there is a natural fallibilistic counterpart to Descartes's proposed stopping point. Further reflection is gratuitous when it would not alter your opinion of the topic at issue. This is the point of stability, the point at which you become invulnerable to self-criticism. Further reflection wouldn't cause you to change your mind. Of course, stable opinion is not the same as true opinion. There is no guarantee of truth here. Even so, there is nothing to be gained from further reflection.[12]

Descartes thought that his stopping point could sometimes be reached easily and sometimes not so easily. He thought that you could clearly and distinctly perceive the truth of some propositions with relatively little reflection, but for other propositions you could do so only with a considerable amount of reflection. Similarly for this notion. Certain topics will be such that even the most casual reflection would produce the relevant kind of stability. Your opinions need not be unrevisable in the face of new information in order to be stable in this sense. They need to be only reflectively stable, and presumably many of your opinions, even those to which you have given little thought, are stable in this sense.

On the other hand, with certain complicated topics, a considerable amount of reflection might be required to reach the point of reflective stability. With respect to these topics, it won't be easy for you or for anyone else to tell whether further reflection would motivate you to retract your current opinion. This is exactly as it should be. After all, the topics are complicated. If it were easy to determine at what point your opinions of them are stable, it would be easy to determine what it is egocentrically rational for you to believe about them, but this shouldn't be easy.

With yet other topics, it may be the case that no amount of reflection would produce stability. On reflection your opinion of them would simply continue to vacillate. If so, it is rational for you to withhold judgment. Thus, there are two ways in which it can be rational for you to withhold judgment on a proposition, theory, or whatever. If reflection would lead to the stable opinion that withholding is your best option, it is rational for you to withhold. Think, for example, of the proposition that the fair coin you are about toss will land heads. But in addition, it is rational for you to withhold if reflection would lead you to no stable opinion whatsoever. Perhaps this is the case for the proposition that there is intelligent life elsewhere in the universe. Sometimes it may seem to you that the available data point to this being true, other times to its being false, and still other times it may not seem to point strongly in either direction. And it may be that no matter how much you reflected on the data, you would continue to vacillate.

Of course, you need not have actually engaged in lengthy reflection in order to rationally believe (or rationally withhold on) a proposition. It is enough for your current opinion to conform with what your stable opinion would be (or as the case may be, conform to the absence of any stable opinion). So, even if the point of stability is one that could be reached only with unfeasibly lengthy reflection, you can still be egocentrically rational.

But if it would take deep reflection to arrive at a stable opinion and if as a result of this, your stable opinion is not in any interesting sense represented in your current beliefs, can it really be relevant for questions of egocentric rationality? Consider an example. Imagine a man and woman who believe a proposition on exactly the same evidence. There is no difference in their current beliefs toward the proposition, but there is a difference between the two. He but not she would come to the conclusion, given appropriate reflection, that what they now take to be good evidence for the proposition is not in the final analysis adequate. Since this counterfactual difference, by hypothesis, is not reflected in any of their current beliefs, it might be tempting to think that if her current belief in the proposition is rational, then so too must be his, the counterfactual difference between them not withstanding.[13]

This much should be admitted: for there to be a relevant difference between the two, it is not enough that on reflection he would alter his opinion of the proposition but she would not. After all, it might be that he but not she has had a restless night's sleep. So, if he were to reflect, he would become drowsy and lose his train of thought, whereas she would not. Counterfactual differences of this sort are not relevant. Not just any kind of reflection under any kind of conditions is indicative of an individual's deepest epistemic standards. In imagining these two people reflecting upon their evidence, we need to ignore potentially distorting features of their current psychological states. We are to imagine that neither their drowsiness nor their crankiness nor any other such feature affects their deliberations.

There are problems here, to be sure, the most pressing of which is that there may be no precise way to determine whether or not something is a distortion of an individual's outlook. Still, there is a distinction to be made. Some of an individual's psychological features are in the normal course of things relatively fixed and deep, while others are either temporary or abnormal. If the former, we are to imagine the individual reflecting with the feature intact, and accordingly it will play a role in shaping the individual's deepest epistemic standards. If the latter, the feature is to be regarded as a distorting one. Accordingly, it is to be treated more like, say, the state of drunkenness. Even while drunk, individuals have deep epistemic standards, but to determine what they are, we are not to imagine the individuals reflecting in their present drunken condition. Rather, we are to imagine them reflecting in a sober state.[14]

Suppose we put all of these distorting factors to one side and grant that were the above two people to be ideally reflective, they would come to different conclusions. He but not she would come to think that their evidence for the proposition in question is not adequate. Then this counterfactual difference between them is epistemically relevant. It does not matter that this difference is not reflected in their current beliefs. Not everything that is epistemically relevant needs to be captured in the contents of their current beliefs.[15] Their dispositions and their inclinations also count for something, and by hypothesis their dispositions are different. Something in his current state would result in his being critical of his belief were he to be appropriately reflective, but nothing in her current state would result in her being critical of her belief. This is enough to warrant an epistemic difference between the two. It is enough to make the proposition that they both believe egocentrically rational for her but not for him.

This, then, is the way to understand the primary subject matter of egocentric epistemology. Like the subject matter of any proposed epistemology, it is identified by reference to the point of view it adopts, where the point of view consists of a goal, a perspective, and a set of resources. For egocentric epistemology, the goal is a synchronic, intellectual one, that of having an accurate and comprehensive belief system. The perspective is an egocentric one, that of individual believers who reflect, free from distorting influences, on the topic at issue to the point of stability, if there is one. And the set of resources is a personal one, the data and information represented in the individual's beliefs. So, to say that it is egocentrically rational for you to believe something is just to say that it is appropriate for you to believe it, given this point of view. It is to say that your beliefs and your intellectual character are such that if you were sufficiently reflective, you would think that this is an appropriate belief for you to have insofar as your end is now to have an accurate and comprehensive belief system. Moreover, further reflection wouldn't prompt you to change your mind. You are in this sense invulnerable to self-criticism.

Since according to this view the crucial conditions of rational belief are ones having to do with your own perspective, the view can be regarded as a version of epistemic internalism. But it is not a version of internalism that implies you always have ready access to the conditions that make your beliefs rational or irrational. On the contrary, I have emphasized that you cannot always simply peer inward and read off what your deepest epistemic standards are. Thus, it can be easy to make mistakes about what it is egocentrically rational for you to believe. You can make such mistakes even if you are reasonably careful and sophisticated about epistemic matters.

It is useful to distinguish epistemic varieties of internalism from metaphysical varieties. The former insist that the conditions of rational belief be ones to which we have ready access, while the latter insist only that the conditions of rational belief be internal—roughly expressed, they must be conditions that take place from the skin in. I am recommending an account of egocentrically rational belief that is internalist in this latter sense but not in the strong epistemic sense.

2. *Responsible Belief*

Egocentrically rational belief is explicated without recourse to the notion of rationality or any of its cognates. This makes it suitable as a theoretical anchor. It can be used to explicate related but less basic notions.

Indeed, there is a schema for introducing such notions. It is egocentrically rational for you to _____ just if it is egocentrically rational for you to believe that _____ would be an acceptably effective means to your goals, where the blanks here can be filled with an action, a decision, a strategy, a plan, or whatever. This is merely a schema. It glides over many complications, ones concerning the relative values of your ends, ones about what would constitute an acceptably good overal job of satisfying these ends,[16] and ones concerning the relative amount of confidence with which it is rational for us to believe that _____ will satisfy them. Moreover, there is at least one derivative notion that is anchored to epistemically rational belief in a negative manner. More on it in a moment. For now the simplicity of the schema has the advantage of highlighting the idea that, in one importance sense, the rationality of an action, decision, or strategy is not a matter of whether in fact it will do an acceptably good overall job of satisfying your ends—after all, it might do so even though from your perspective there is no indication of this. Nor is it a matter of your simply believing that it will do an acceptable job of satisfying your ends—after all, you might believe this despite your having strong evidence to the contrary, evidence that you yourself would find convincing were you to think about it for a moment. Rather, the rationality of an action, decision, or strategy is a matter of its being egocentrically rational for you to believe that it will acceptably satisfy your ends.

This same schema can be applied to belief itself, and this creates an opportunity for confusion. You have adequate egocentric reasons to believe a proposition, all things considered, if it is egocentrically rational for you to believe that believing this proposition would be an effective means to your goals. There are two notions of rational belief at work here. One is the anchoring notion. It presupposes a purely epistemic goal, the goal of having accurate and comprehensive beliefs. The other is a derivative notion, defined in terms of the anchoring notion. It is rational in this derivative sense for you to believe a proposition just in case it is rational in the anchoring sense for you to believe that believing the proposition is acceptable, given all your goals.

Since having accurate and comprehensive beliefs is ordinarily a good way to promote your nonepistemic goals, these two notions tend not to come apart.[17] But they can come apart. It can be egocentrically rational for you to believe that the overall benefits of believing a falsehood outweigh the overall costs of doing so. If so, then what it is egocentrically rational for you to believe, all things considered, is different from what it is egocentrically rational for you to believe in the basic, anchoring sense. To avoid confusion, I will reserve the expression 'egocentrically rational belief' for the basic sense. The derivative sense can then be identified by adding the phrase, 'all things considered'.

Whether a proposition is egocentrically rational for you to believe is a matter of what your attitude toward it would be were you to be reflective. But of course, what you would think of a proposition on reflection depends in part upon what intellectual abilities and skills you have. A logically omniscient being might be able to see that proposition P has some unacceptable implication, but if your abilities and skills are such that you would not notice this implication regardless of how you reflected, P might very well be egocentrically rational for you.

So, the notion of egocentric rationality doesn't idealize your intellectual abilities. But it does idealize the conditions under which you employ these abilities. In thinking about whether a proposition is egocentrically rational for you, we are to imagine you reflecting on the proposition to the point of stability, but we are also to imagine the reflection's being carried out free from various distorting conditions. We imagine, for example, that you are not overly tired or drunk or in severe pain. In addition, we imagine you reflecting with only one concern in mind, that of having an accurate and comprehensive belief system.

But in reality, you have many concerns, and these concerns sharply curtail the amount of time it is reasonable for you to spend reflecting on epistemic matters. Besides, even if your sole concern were to have an accurate and comprehensive belief system, you would still lack the time to reflect upon all topics to the point of stability. But none of this matters when it is egocentric rationality that is at issue. Questions of resource allocation do not arise for it. What attitude it is egocentrically rational for you to take toward proposition P is a matter of what your attitude toward P would be were you to reflect on it; similarly, the attitude that it is egocentrically rational for you to take toward proposition Q is a matter of what your attitude toward Q would be were you to reflect on it; and so on for every other proposition. It is irrelevant that you don't have sufficient time to reflect on all of these propositions.

This is not a criticism. It is only to say that the notion is idealized in a certain way. But this has its advantages for our theoretical purposes. In particular, it makes the notion suitable as a theoretical anchor. What it is egocentrically rational for you to believe is not a matter of what you would believe were you to be reasonably reflective. If it were, we would be left with the problem of saying what it is to be reasonably reflective. Rather, egocentric rationality is a matter of what you would believe, were you to be ideally reflective.

On the other hand, its idealized character makes the notion generally unsuitable for our everyday purposes. Our everyday evaluations of belief tend to be reason-saturated. We tend to be interested, for example, in whether you have been *unreasonably* careless in gathering evidence or *unreasonably* hasty in drawing conclusions from this evidence, where the standards of reasonability here are realistic ones. They are sensitive to the fact that you have interests other than epistemic ones and that you have only a limited amount of time and resources for pursuing these interests.

Similarly, in legal contexts we are often required to make reason-saturated evaluations. Think of negligence cases, in which the issue is liability for unintended harm. The defendants may have failed to foresee that their activities would produce the harm, but the issue of their liability is decided by asking what a *reasonably* prudent individual would have foreseen in their situation.

If we want a notion that is capable of capturing the spirit of these kinds of evaluations, it will have to be a non-idealized notion. In particular, it will have to be one that is sensitive to questions of resource allocation and the like. Indeed, perhaps more than one such notion will be needed. We evaluate one another's beliefs in a variety of contexts for a variety of purposes, and it may be that no single notion will be able to do justice to this variety. Still, at least many of our everyday evaluations can be understood in terms of a notion that I will call 'responsible belief'. As I use the term, your responsibly believing a proposition is essentially a matter of its not being unreasonable for you to have this belief. Imagine that you have spent a reasonable amount of time and care in investigating and reflecting on a proposition. On the basis of these investigations and reflections, you have come to believe the proposition. Nonetheless, the proposition might not be egocentrically rational for you, since it might be the case that if you had been still more reflective, you would have changed your mind. Still, there is something to be said for your belief. What there is to be said, roughly expressed, is that it is not unreasonable for you to have it.

Of course, this statement itself appeals to a cognate of rationality. But with the primary notion of egocentrically rational belief in hand, this need not be a problem, since we can use it as a theoretical anchor. We can use it to explicate the relevant sense of unreasonable. The result will be a theoretically respectable account of responsible belief—that is, one that makes no ineliminable use of a notion of rationality or any of its cognates.

In particular, my proposal, subject to a qualification that I will discuss in a moment, is that you responsibly believe a proposition just in case the belief is not an unreasonable one for you to have, where this in turn is a matter of its not being egocentrically rational for you to believe that your procedures with respect to it have been unacceptably sloppy or thin, given all your goals.[18] Thus, just as egocentrically rational belief anchors egocentrically rational decisions, plans, strategies, and so on—a plan, for example, is egocentrically rational if it is egocentrically rational for you to believe that it will acceptably satisfy your goals—so too egocentrically rational belief anchors responsible belief, albeit in a negative way. Your belief is a responsible one only if it is not egocentrically rational for you to believe that you have spent an unacceptably small amount of time in gathering evidence or in thinking about this evidence, and if it is not egocentrically rational for you to believe that you have used unacceptably sloppy or flimsy procedures in gathering and processing this evidence.

It is also possible for you to use unacceptably thorough procedures in coming to believe something. The topic may not be worth the effort you have expended on it. You had better things to do. But of course, this doesn't result in irresponsible belief; only unacceptable sloppiness does. The kind of unacceptability that matters here is one that takes into account all your goals, not just your epistemic ones. Your nonepistemic goals impose constraints on how much time and resources it is acceptable to expend on epistemic pursuits. An intellectual procedure that would be unacceptable if you had only epistemic goals might nonetheless be perfectly acceptable, given that you have a range of goals and only a limited amount of time and resources to devote to them.

Thus, as I am using the notion, responsible belief is to be understood negatively. It is, to borrow van Fraassen's phrase, bridled irrationality.[19] Often you don't have a very good idea of how it is that you came to believe what you do. You may not remember or perhaps you never knew. This doesn't matter. Such beliefs can still be responsible ones. What matters is your not having reasons for thinking that your procedures, whatever they may be, are unacceptable. Similarly for your withholdings. Your withholding judgment on a proposition is a responsible attitude for you to take unless you have reasons for thinking that the procedures leading you to withhold are unacceptable ones.

This notion of responsible belief is to be applied only to those who are capable of having a rich stock of egocentrically rational beliefs. In particular, it does not apply to beings who are sophisticated enough to have beliefs but not sophisticated enough to have egocentrically rational beliefs—for example, young children.[20] Otherwise, it would be trivial that all of their beliefs are responsible ones. It is better to say of them that their beliefs are neither responsible nor irresponsible.

As an initial characterization, I have said that you responsibly believe P just in case it is not egocentrically rational for you to believe that your procedures with respect to P have been unacceptable—that is, unacceptable, given that you have wide variety of ends that impose limitations of how much time and resources you can devote to any subset of these ends. A qualification is needed, however. If you responsibly believe that your procedures with respect to P have been unacceptable, then you cannot responsibly believe P, even if it is not egocentrically rational for you to believe that these procedures have been unacceptable.

Situations of this sort are a possibility because you can responsibly believe a proposition that isn't egocentrically rational for you. Suppose that it isn't egocentrically rational for you to believe P', where P' is the proposition that your procedures with respect to P have been unacceptable. This creates a presumption that your belief P is a responsible one, but the presumption can be overridden.

Suppose, for example, that you have been reasonably reflective and thorough in thinking about P', and that as a result you have concluded that P' is true. Then this belief is a responsible one for you to have, even if P' is not egocentrically rational for you. Perhaps you would have changed your mind about P' if you had reflected still more. Nevertheless, if you have been reasonably reflective and

thorough, your belief is still a responsible one. But if you responsibly believe P'—
that is, if you responsibly believe the proposition that your procedures with respect
to P have been unacceptable—then it is not responsible for you to believe P.

Analogous sorts of considerations suggest that your belief Q need not be
irresponsible even if it is egocentrically rational for you to believe that your
procedures with respect to Q have been unacceptable. There is a presumption
here that your belief Q is not a responsible one, but once again the presumption
can be overridden. Let Q' be the proposition that your procedures with respect to
Q have been unacceptable. Suppose that the evidence that makes Q' rational for
you is complicated and that you have not reflected enough to see why this
evidence makes it likely that Q' is true. Nonetheless, given all of your ends and
needs, you have been reasonably reflective, and on the basis of this reflection
you may have concluded that not-Q' is true—that is, you have concluded that
your procedures with respect to Q were acceptably careful. Then this belief Q' is
a responsible one for you to have, despite your evidence to the contrary. But if
you believe that your procedures with respect to Q have been acceptable and if
this belief is a responsible one for you to have, then your belief Q is also a
responsible one for you to have.

Having made these qualifications, I will for the most part ignore them, so that
the main idea is not obscured. And the main idea is that responsible belief is a
much less idealized notion than egocentrically rational belief. Given the scarcity
of time and the relative unimportance of some topics, it is reasonable for you not
to spend much time gathering information about these topics and thinking about
them. Indeed, you acquire many beliefs with little or no thought. You believe
that there is a table in front of you because you see it. You don't deliberate about
whether or not to trust your senses. You simply believe. Most of your beliefs are
acquired in an unthinking way, and in general this is an acceptable way for you to
proceed intellectually. Unless there are concrete reasons for suspicion, it is
foolish to spend time and effort deliberating about what you are inclined to
believe spontaneously. It is better to keep yourself on a kind of automatic pilot
and to make adjustments only when a problem manifests itself.[21] The old saw,
don't try to fix what isn't broken, is good intellectual advice as well.

This is not an endorsement of intellectual passivity. On the contrary, we
ordinarily have good reasons, both intellectual and otherwise, to be intellectually
aggressive. We have reasons to seek out people, situations, and experiences that
will challenge our existing opinions, and we likewise have reasons to be aggressive in building and then maintaining a repertoire of reliable intellectual habits
and skills.

The point, rather, is that any intellectual project will make use of an enormous number of opinions, skills, and habits, most of which we are forced to rely
on without much thought. The brunt of our intellectual proceedings must be
conducted in an automatic fashion. We have no choice in this matter. Only a tiny
fraction of our intellectual lives can be subject to careful scrutiny. Our real
difficulty, then, is to identify that which is the most deserving of our attention.

Epistemology cannot help us much with this. We must instead look at the details of our lives. We are constantly confronted with intellectual problems. Indeed, every new situation presents us with new intellectual challenges, if only because we will want to know the best way for us to react to this situation. We are thus swamped with potential intellectual projects. But some of these projects are more important than others, and likewise some are more pressing than others. These are the ones that are the most deserving of attention.

The notion of responsible belief takes all this into account. It is sensitive to the fact that you have no alternative but to rely heavily and unthinkingly on your preexisting skills and habits, and it is also sensitive to the fact that some intellectual questions are not particularly important for us to settle.

Consider, for example, the logical implications of a proposition P that is egocentrically rational for you. Perhaps not all of the implications of P will themselves be egocentrically rational for you. Some may be too complicated for you even to understand. Still, a huge number of these implications will be egocentrically rational for you, since a huge number will be such that were you to be sufficiently reflective about them, you would see how they are implied by P. But of course, ordinarily it won't be reasonable for you to try to identify and hence believe all these propositions. After all, many of the implications of P will be unimportant ones. But if so, this is one of the ways in which responsible belief and egocentrically rational belief can come apart. You can responsibly not believe these propositions even though they are egocentrically rational for you.[22]

This is a welcome consequence. It amounts to an acknowledgment that it is unreasonable for you to be fanatical in your epistemic pursuits. Of course, it isn't reasonable for you to be lackadaisical either. You normally have good reasons, intellectual and otherwise, to try to make your belief system accurate and comprehensive. It's just that you shouldn't get carried away with this. You shouldn't spend most of your time in epistemic reflection. The unreflective life may not be worth living, but neither is the overly reflective one. Life is too short, and you have too many other worthwhile goals.

The result, then, is a rationale for moderation, which is just what one would expect. Being a responsible believer requires you not to be noticeably slovenly in your intellectual pursuits, but it doesn't normally require you to exercise extraordinary care either.

More exactly, it doesn't require this unless the issue at hand is itself extraordinarily important. The standards that you must meet if your belief is to be a responsible one vary with the importance of the issue. If nothing much hangs on the issue, there won't be much point in going to great lengths to discover the truth about it. Accordingly, the standards that you must meet in order to have a responsible opinion about the issue are likely to be low. On the other hand, if an issue is extraordinarily important, the standards will be correspondingly high. The more important the issue, the more important it will be to reduce the risk of error.

Moreover, it is not just intellectual importance that matters. If people's lives are at issue, it ordinarily will be unreasonable for you not to conduct an investigation that is more thorough than normal. If you fail to do so, your resulting beliefs about the issue at hand are likely to be irresponsible ones. They will be irresponsible even if they are egocentrically rational. This is possible because egocentric rationality doesn't require certainty, not even moral certainty. You need only to have evidence that reduces the risks of error to an acceptable theoretical level. They have to be acceptable insofar as your concern is to have accurate and comprehensive beliefs. But then, the risks might be acceptable in this theoretical sense even if your procedures have been unacceptably sloppy, given that people's lives are hanging in the balance. If so, these beliefs are irresponsible ones for you to have despite the fact that they are egocentrically rational for you.

Thus, your nonepistemic ends shape what it is responsible for you to believe. But they don't do so in the way that Pascal envisioned. The idea is not so much that your nonepistemic ends give you a good reason to believe a proposition for which you lack good evidence. Rather, the idea is that your nonepistemic ends help determine the extent of evidence gathering and processing that it is reasonable for you to engage in for a particular issue. They thus shape what it is responsible for you to believe in an indirect way rather than in a direct Pascalian way. They do so by imposing constraints on inquiry, but subject to these constraints your aim will normally be to determine what beliefs would be true, not what beliefs would be useful.[23]

These constraints are reflected in our actual intellectual practices. It is relatively rare for us to engage in Pascalian deliberations. We don't very often weigh the practical costs and benefits of believing as opposed to not believing some proposition. On the other hand, it is anything but rare for us to weigh the costs and benefits of spending additional time and resources in investigating a topic. In buying a used car, for example, I will want to investigate whether the car is in good condition, but I need to make a decision about how thoroughly to do so. Should I merely drive the car? Should I look up the frequency of repair record for the model? Should I go over the car with a mechanic, or perhaps even with more than one mechanic? Similarly, if I am interested in how serious a threat global warming is, I need to decide how much time to spend investigating the issue. Should I be content with looking at the accounts given in newspapers, or should I take the time to read the piece in *Scientific American*, or should I even go to the trouble of looking up some articles in the relevant technical journals? And if it turns out that in order to understand the models discussed in these articles, I need to brush up on my statistics, should I do that?

The reasonable answer to such questions is in large part a function of how important the issue is. As the stakes of being right go up, so too should your standards. Thus, the standards of responsible belief will be significantly different for different issues. They can even be different for a proposition and its negation. If you are picking wild mushrooms for tonight's dinner, the costs associated with falsely believing that this mushroom is poisonous are relatively insignificant.

After all, there are other mushrooms to pick. On the other hand, the costs associated with falsely believing that this mushroom is nonpoisonous may be disastrous: you may be poisoned. So, the standards for responsibly believing that the mushroom is not poisonous are higher than the standards for responsibly believing that the mushroom is poisonous. They are higher because in this case, there are heavy costs associated with a false negative while only relatively light ones associated with a false positive.

The intellectual standards it is reasonable for you to meet vary not just with the importance of the topic but also with your social role.[24] If it is your obligation but not mine to keep some piece of safety equipment in good working order, this will ordinarily place special intellectual demands upon you. My belief that the equipment is in good working order might be responsible even if I have done little if any investigation of the matter. I need not have tested the equipment. A quick look might do. But this presumably won't do for you. It will be unreasonable for you not to run the tests. The standards of responsible belief are higher for you. You need to do more than I in order to have a responsible belief about this matter.

One's social role can be relevant even when the issue at hand is primarily of theoretical interest. What is involved in my responsibly believing that the principle of conservation of energy is not violated in the beta decay of atomic nuclei is very different from what is involved in theoretical physicists' responsibly believing this. My familiarity with this issue derives mainly from Lakatos's brief discussion of it,[25] but this kind of appeal to authority is presumably enough to make my belief a responsible one. No more can be reasonably expected of me. On the other hand, more can be reasonably expected of the authorities themselves. They are part of a community of inquirers with special knowledge and special standards, and as a result they may be required to be able to explain away the apparent violations in a relatively detailed way. Besides, the rest of us tend to defer to the authorities in these matters, and this in itself imposes extra requirements of care upon them.

The notion of responsible belief is also able to give easy expression to the importance of stability in our belief systems. If you responsibly acquired a belief and if at no time subsequent to its acquisition was it irrational of you not to reconsider it, then the belief is still a responsible one for you to have.[26] Thus, there is a presumption that what it is responsible for you to believe is transferred from one moment to the next.

One way to appreciate this feature of responsible belief is to consider cases in which you have lost or forgotten the evidence that originally made a belief rational for you. If you no longer have this evidence, the belief may not be defensible, given your current situation. It may no longer be egocentrically rational for you. Still, you might not have a good reason to reconsider the proposition or to try to reconstruct your evidence for it, especially if your believing it hasn't led to any noticeable problems. Indeed, you may not even realize that you have lost your original evidence, and in any event, it is unrealistic to expect you to keep track of your evidence for everything you believe.[27] To be sure, some issues are so important or so subject to public debate that you should try to keep track of your evidence. It may even be part of your job to keep track of the evidence with respect to some issues. But in a great many other cases, you can responsibly continue to believe a proposition, despite the fact that you no longer have positive evidence for it.

Of course, it will often be the case that even if you have lost or forgotten your original evidence for a proposition, you will not have forgotten the fact that you once did have this evidence, and this itself may be enough to make your current belief egocentrically rational. Think, for example, of a theorem that you remember having proved long ago. Even if you are not now able to reconstruct the proof, you nonetheless do have indirect evidence for its truth.

Thus, in practice, this difference between egocentrically rational belief and responsible belief may not be quite as dramatic as first appearances would suggest. Even so, there is a difference, and it is theoretically important. It helps explain, for example, a divergence in intuitions about the doctrine of epistemic conservatism. On the one hand, there are those who claim that the mere fact that you believe a proposition gives you a reason, albeit perhaps a weak one, to continue believing it,[28] while there are others who cannot understand why this should be so.[29] Why, they ask, should the mere fact that you believe a proposition always give you a reason to think that it is true?

The distinction between responsible and rational belief suggests that each side may be on to something. The opponents of conservatism are right if the issue is one about egocentrically rational belief. It is not conservative. The fact that you believe a proposition is not in itself enough to give you an egocentric reason, even a weak one, to think that what you believe is true. After all, you can believe strange propositions, ones that even you would regard as having nothing to recommend them were you to reflect for even a moment.

On the other hand, responsible belief is conservative, or at least it is more conservative than egocentrically rational belief. It is not conservative in as strong a way as some would wish. Believing a proposition is not enough in itself to make your belief a responsible one, all else being equal. But something close to this often is the case. Most of our beliefs are ones that we acquire without thought. We simply believe. And most of the time, these beliefs will be responsible ones for us to have. Moreover, it is responsible for us to continue holding such beliefs unless there are positive reasons for not doing so.

There is another way in which the notion of responsible belief reflects the importance of having stable beliefs. Suppose you irresponsibly believe a proposition. Perhaps it is rational for you to think that you have not gathered enough evidence or not the right kind of evidence, or alternatively it may be rational for you to think that you have been sloppy in processing your evidence. Whatever the exact problem, how does your irresponsibility affect subsequent belief, both in the proposition at issue and in other propositions that you might believe as a result of it? Are they also irresponsible? Is the irresponsibility passed on from one generation of belief to another until you have done something concrete to correct the original difficulty—say, gather new evidence or process more adequately the old evidence?

Not necessarily. Once again it depends upon your situation and the proposition in question. The key is whether or not it continues to be egocentrically rational for you to think that you have dealt with the proposition inadequately. Sometimes this will continue to be the case until you have reconsidered or reinvestigated the proposition. But often enough, this won't be necessary. Instead, the passage of time will do the work. With time it may no longer be rational for you to think that your treatment of the proposition has been inadequate. This might be so simply because you no longer have evidence of your original sloppiness. It may have been lost with time.

Thus, the notion of responsible belief, as I am understanding it, is not equivalent to the notion of having responsibly acquired a belief. If the procedures that originally led you to believe P were unreasonably sloppy, then you acquired the belief in an irresponsible manner. Still, your current situation might be such that you can no longer reasonably be expected to see (or remember) that these procedures were sloppy. If so, it can be responsible for you to go on believing P even though the belief was originally acquired irresponsibly. As I have said, this can be so because the evidence of your original sloppiness has been lost with time. But it also might be so because your overall treatment of P has begun to look more respectable in light of the fact that your belief P apparently has not led to any significant problems, theoretical or otherwise.

Consider an analogy. Despite having heard that the magnets in telephones sometimes interfere with the proper functioning of computers, I placed my computer close to my telephone. This may well have been an irrational decision. Yet as time goes by without there being any difficulty, my overall history with respect to the placement of the computer begins to look better and better. It's not that this history makes the original decision any more rational. Given my perspective at that time, it probably was an irrational decision. On the other hand, from my present perspective, my overall treatment of this issue, which includes not only my original decision but also my subsequent refusals to move the computer, looks increasingly respectable. It looks as if it will have acceptable consequences. As far as I can tell, the placement has not yet led to any problems, and this increases my confidence that it is not likely to do so in the future either.

Something similar is the case for irresponsible belief. You may have been sloppy in acquiring a belief, but if the belief leads to no significant difficulties or anomalies, the importance of the original sloppy treatment tends to be diluted with time. It may be diluted not because you have done anything positive to correct the original sloppiness but simply because the sloppiness seems less and less problematic when viewed in the context of your overall history with the belief. Irresponsible beliefs tend to become respectable with age as long as they behave themselves and don't cause problems.

Often enough there will be something of a self-fulfilling prophecy about this,

since the irresponsible belief might influence your other opinions in such a way
as to remove your original qualms about it. This isn't surprising, however.
Phenomena of this sort are common enough whenever issues of rationality are
involved. For example, even if you have irrationally opted for a plan, you can
sometimes turn it into a rational one simply by sticking with it. It originally may
have been rational for you to move to New York rather than California, but if the
irrational decision has already been made and you are now driving toward
California, it may now be rational for you to continue on your way rather than
turn around. Plans often have a snowballing effect. They require you to make
arrangements for carrying them out, and these arrangements foster still other
plans and arrangements, ones that are often complicated and costly to undo.
Thus, the further you are along on a plan, the greater will be the pressures for not
abandoning it.[30]

In an analogous way, beliefs can have snowballing effects. Just as plans tend
to engender yet other plans, so beliefs tend to engender yet other beliefs, the
collective weight of which may make it increasingly unreasonable for you to
reconsider the original beliefs, even if they were sloppily acquired. This is
especially likely to be unreasonable if the original beliefs and the ones they
engendered seem to be serving you well enough.

The advantages, theoretical and otherwise, of having a stable belief system
are thus built into the notion of responsible belief. Not only does responsible
belief tend to be transferred from one moment to the next but, in addition,
irresponsibility tends to dissipate with time.

Related considerations can be used to illustrate the relevance for epistemology of the so-called theoretical virtues: simplicity, fertility, problem-solving
effectiveness, and the like. Consider simplicity, for example. Suppose that simplicity is not a mark of truth, and that as such it cannot give you an objective
reason to believe a hypothesis.[31] Suppose also that on reflection you wouldn't
take simplicity to be a mark of truth and that, accordingly, it does not give you an
egocentric reason to believe a hypothesis either.

Even so, considerations of simplicity are likely to play a significant role in
shaping what you believe. They may not have the important positive role in
theorizing that some philosophers have ascribed to them. If you have limited the
number of hypotheses you are seriously considering to just two and if neither is
terribly complex, then considerations of simplicity may not play much of a role
in your deliberations about the respective merits of these two hypotheses, even if
one is somewhat more simple than the other. On the other hand, considerations
of simplicity inevitably do play a role in your theorizing, albeit a less fine-
grained one. They do so because you have only limited cognitive abilities and
only a limited amount of time to exercise these abilities. Indeed, if a hypothesis
is complex enough, it may not be possible for you even to understand it. So, it
won't even be a candidate for belief; it will be filtered out automatically. But
even among those hypotheses that you are able to understand, some will be so
complex that it would be impractical for you to take them seriously. It would take

far too much of your time even to deliberate about them, much less to use them in making predictions and constructing other hypotheses. They are so complex that they would be of little value to you or anyone else even if they were true. In consequence, they too will be filtered out. You won't take them seriously. You will simply ignore them.

Ignoring complex hypotheses need not be a conscious policy on your part. You need not have made a decision to follow such a procedure. It is more likely to be a matter of your dispositions and practices, ones to which you may have given little thought. But the result of these dispositions and practices is that simple hypotheses as a group tend to get a preferential treatment over complex hypotheses as a group. You are disposed to take them, as a group, more seriously than complex ones, and often enough the result may be that you are more disposed to believe them as well. You are disposed to believe them even though, we are assuming, their simplicity does not give you a reason to believe, insofar as your aims are purely epistemic. Nor need you have good reasons to believe these hypotheses, all things considered—for example, when all of your ends, both epistemic and nonepistemic, are taken into consideration. It may be rational, all things considered, for you to commit yourself to their truth rather than believe them. Nevertheless, these beliefs might still be responsible ones for you to have.

This is so because it need not be unreasonable for you to have dispositions or engage in practices or adopt procedures that produce irrational beliefs. This may have the sound of paradox, but in fact it is merely an acknowledgment that you are operating under various constraints—constraints imposed by the kind of cognitive equipment you have and the kinds of situation in which you find yourself, as well as constraints imposed by the fact you have many goals and only a limited amount of time and resources to pursue them.

Let me make the point in terms of dispositions, although it can be made for practices and procedures as well. Your being disposed to use simplicity as an initial filter may result in your also being disposed to believe some hypotheses that are not egocentrically rational for you. Even so, you might not have good egocentric reasons to try to rid yourself of this disposition. It may not be worth the effort, especially if the disposition is a deeply seated one. Besides, believing as opposed to committing yourself to these hypotheses may have few if any disadvantages beyond the purely epistemic ones. The irrationality here may not adversely affect your life in any major way, and thus it may not be that big a deal. It may be analogous to your believing that the tie that has just been given to you really is your favorite color rather than merely acting as if this were the case. You believe this because you are touched by the gift, and this causes you, at least temporarily, to ignore the fact you never buy ties of this color for yourself. This belief may be irrational, but you probably don't have reasons to try to change the elements of your character that are responsible for this irrationality. It's not worth the effort.

Moreover, it's not just that you don't have good reasons to rid yourself of the disposition to believe simple hypotheses. You may not have good reasons to worry about the resulting beliefs either, even if they are irrational. Once again, it may not be worth the effort. It may be too difficult and too costly to reconsider these hypotheses and evaluate your evidence for them, especially if your believing them hasn't led to any apparent difficulties. But this is just to say that you can responsibly continue to believe these hypotheses. It is responsible for you to do so despite the fact that you didn't have adequate evidence for them when you first came to believe them and despite the fact that you still don't.

An even stronger result may be possible. It may be positively rational for you to have a disposition to believe rather than commit yourself to simple hypotheses. This may be rational for you in an objective sense and an egocentric sense as well. It may be rational for you to have this disposition even though the beliefs themselves tend to be irrational, and not just irrational with respect to your epistemic goals but also irrational, all things considered—that is, when all your goals are taken into account.

This again may have the sound of paradox, but consider an analogy. The love you have for your family may sometimes cause you to act wrongly. It may cause you to go too far in your efforts to do what is best for them. The result may be that sometimes your actions cause undue hardships for others. You excessively favor your family's interests over the interests of others. Still, it might be worse if you did not have this strong love for your family. If you loved them less, you perhaps wouldn't be disposed to favor them excessively. So, it would correct this problem, but on the other hand it might be far worse for your family. If you loved them any less, you might carry out your responsibilities toward them less well, and this might lead to results that overall are much worse than those that are produced by your being too zealous in favoring them. Thus, it might be best for you to have this strong love for your family. This might be best even though, given the kind of person you are, it sometimes inclines you to act wrongly.[32]

Similarly, given the kind of cognitive creature you are, it might be positively desirable for you to have a disposition to believe simple hypotheses. It might be part of the best set of cognitive dispositions for you to have. Any other set, or at least any other set that you are capable of, might be worse. If you didn't have this disposition, you wouldn't be as inclined to believe simple hypotheses and, thus, you would avoid one kind of irrational belief. But it might have other drawbacks. Were you to lack this disposition, you might have to spend more time in deliberations over whether to believe or merely commit yourself to hypotheses, and this might divert your attention from other, more important matters, causing you to make errors of judgment about them. Besides, committing yourself to a hypothesis, as opposed to believing it, may not be easy. It may require more effort and more monitoring than belief.[33] The difference may not amount to much with respect to any given hypothesis, but when a large number of hypotheses are involved, the costs of committing yourself to them may be considerable. If so, it is objectively rational for you to have the disposition to believe simple hypotheses, despite the fact that it inclines you toward objectively irrational beliefs.[34]

Analogous points hold for egocentric rationality. It might be egocentrically rational for you to have this disposition, despite the fact that it often inclines you to have egocentrically irrational beliefs.

Points of this general sort are enormously important for epistemology. They mark the path toward a more realistic epistemology, one that pays something more than lip service to the idea that our intellectual lives are constrained by the kind of cognitive creatures we are. In doing so, points of this sort also provide a useful framework for thinking about the significance of recent empirical work that has been done on irrational belief. Much of this work seems to show that we have disturbingly stubborn tendencies to make certain kinds of faulty inferences—for example, even well-educated subjects tend not to seek out relevant and readily available base rate information.[35] But points of the above sort hold out at least a sliver of hope that the cognitive dispositions that tend to produce these faulty inferences might nonetheless be rational ones for us to have. They might be rational because they might serve us well enough on most occasions. Indeed, they might even be part of the best set of cognitive dispositions available to us. Any other available set might have even worse failings. Or short of this, they at least may be dispositions that it is not rational for us to go to the trouble of extinguishing. In our normal everyday affairs, they may not do enough harm to make it rational for us to try to rid ourselves of them. This is not to say that we shouldn't correct faulty inferences when they are pointed out to us. But it is to say it may be rational for us to put up with the dispositions that tend to produce these faulty inferences.

But whether this is so is a side issue. For the discussion here, the main importance of such points is that they constitute the beginnnings of a possible defense for simplicity. And similar defenses may be available for many of the other theoretical virtues—fertility and problem-solving effectiveness, for example. It is not a defense that tries to argue that simplicity really is a mark of truth or that all of us at least implicitly treat it as such. Nor is it a defense that ignores the difference between belief and commitment. On the contrary, it acknowledges that it may very well be irrational for you to believe as opposed to commit yourself to a hypothesis if simplicity has played a significant role in selecting it. This may be irrational not only in an epistemic sense but also all things considered.

The defense instead consists of arguing that the irrationality here is of a very weak kind. A mark of its weakness is that ordinarily you won't have adequate reasons, objective or egocentric, to rid yourself of the belief in the hypothesis, and likewise you ordinarily won't have adequate reasons to rid yourself of the disposition to acquire such beliefs. It may even be positively rational for you to have such a disposition, despite the fact that it often inclines you to have irrational beliefs. It may rational for you to be irrational in this way.

The notion of responsible beliefs provides us with a way to recognize all of these points. Your disposition to use simplicity as a filter and your corresponding disposition to believe simple hypotheses can produce responsible beliefs even if they don't produce rational beliefs. They can do so even if you are aware of the influence of these dispositions, for despite this, you need not have good egocentric reasons to believe that these are unacceptable dispositions for you to have, given all your goals and given all the constraints you are operating under. But if not, the beliefs you acquire as the result of these dispositions are ones that it can be responsible for you to have.

Three characteristics of responsible belief combine to account for this and the other features I have been cataloguing. First, the emphasis is upon the intellectual procedures that led to and sustain our believing what we do. Second, the evaluation takes into consideration not just our epistemic ends but our other ends as well. Third, the evaluations are negatively anchored; what matters is its not being egocentrically rational for us to think that the procedures, habits, decisions, and so on that led to or sustain our beliefs are unacceptable in the light of all our goals and all of the constraints we are operating under.

The belief system it is responsible for us to have is thus determined by our lives in all of their fullness. It is not a matter of what would be unacceptable were we purely intellectual creatures, ones who had only intellectual ends, and it is not a matter of what would be unacceptable were we creatures who had unlimited time and resources to pursue our ends. We are not such creatures. We have all sorts of ends, some simply by virtue of being human and others by virtue of our special circumstances. Moreover, there are strong constraints on the time and resources we have to pursue these ends. Choices have to be made. The notion of responsible belief recognizes the inevitability of such choices. In doing so, it begins to give us what we wanted all along: a general and theoretically respectable but nonetheless realistic way of evaluating our beliefs. It is the beginnings of an epistemology that matters, one that takes into account the constraints of our intellectual lives and the roles that we actually play in our societies and one that thus has application to the intellectual pursuits of real human beings.

Although the notion of responsible belief captures many of the concerns that are present in our everyday evaluations of beliefs, it does not capture them all. No single notion is capable of doing that. We make such evaluations in a number of different contexts and for a number of different purposes, but we nonetheless tend to express them all using the language of rationality. Doing so might seem to preclude a theoretically unified treatment of rational belief, but part of my purpose has been to illustrate this need not be.

My strategy has been to introduce a general way of thinking about questions of rationality of whatever sort. All such questions concern a perspective, a set of goals, and a set of resources. Questions of rational belief are no different. To say that it is rational for you to believe _____ is essentially to say that from the presupposed perspective, believing _____ seems to be an effective way for someone with your resources to satisfy some important goal that you have. Different senses of rational belief result from the fact that different goals and different perspectives can be adopted. These constitute the basic notions of rational belief, but once these basic notions are in hand, they can anchor other related notions, such as the one that I have called 'responsible belief'.

The terminology is not important, however. What is important is that this general approach to questions of rationality provides a framework for under-standing an especially important kind of evaluation. It is an evaluation that results in a favorable assessment of your beliefs just in case it is not unreasonable by your own lights for you to have these beliefs, where this is essentially a matter of the three characteristics listed above.

This notion of responsible belief, in turn, can be of use in helping us to understand our everyday evaluations of decisions and actions. As with our every-day evaluations of belief, the evaluations are frequently shaped by considerations of resource allocation. They reflect the fact that we do not have time to deliberate over each of our actions and decisions. Here too we have no choice but to operate in a largely automatic fashion. We deliberate only when there is a special reason to do so—for example, when the issues are especially important or when our accustomed ways of acting have led to difficulties.

However sensible such a procedure may be, it will sometimes result in our doing things that we ourselves would regard as unwise, were we to take more time to think about them. Even so, we may be acting responsibly. After all, we might responsibly believe that our action won't have unacceptable results. Or short of having this positive belief, we may at least fail to believe that the action will have unacceptable consequences, and our not believing this may be perfectly responsible, given the constraints on our time and given the importance of other needs and goals. There may be no reason for us to think that special care is needed. In this way, responsible belief helps us understand responsible action.

The importance of this notion of responsible belief for our everyday purposes does not detract from the importance of the more idealized notion of ego-centrically rational belief. On the contrary, it puts us in a position to appreciate the latter's importance. Our everyday evaluations tend to be reason-saturated. They themselves make use of the notion of rationality or one of its cognates. They thus leave us within the circle of terms for which we want a philosophical account. This is why the idealized notion is important. Its importance is pri-marily theoretical, which is what we should have expected all along. It provides a theoretical anchor for our egocentric but everyday notions. Egocentric rationality is important because it is indispensable for understanding these notions. It is indispensable for a complete theory of rationality.

3. What Am I to Believe?

The central issue of Descartes's *Meditations* is an intensely personal one. Des-cartes asks a simple question of himself, one that each of us can also ask of himself or herself, What am I to believe? One way of construing this question—indeed, the way Descartes himself construed it—is as a methodological one. The immediate aim is not so much to generate a specific list of propositions for me to believe. Rather, I want to formulate for myself some general advice about how to proceed intellectually.

If general advice is what I want, I am not likely to be content with telling myself that I am to use reliable methods of inquiry. Nor will I be content with telling myself to believe only that which is likely to be true, given my evidence. It is not as if this advice is mistaken; it's just unhelpful. I knew all along that it is better for me to use reliable methods rather than unreliable ones, and I also knew that it is better for me to believe that which is likely to be true rather than that which is not. Besides, I cannot simply read off from the world what methods are reliable ones, nor can I read off when something is likely to be true, given my evidence. These are just the sorts of things about which I want advice.

An appeal to the prevailing intellectual standards won't provide me with what I am looking for either. For example, I won't be satisfied with a recommendation that tells me to conduct my inquiries in accordance with the standards of my community, or alternatively in accordance with the standards of those recognized in my community as experts. I will want to know whether these standards are desirable ones. The dominant standards in a community are not always to be trusted, and those of the recognized experts aren't either.

My question is a more fundamental one and also a more egocentric one. It is not that I think that the task of working out intellectual guidelines is one that is best conducted by me in solitude. If I do think this, I am being foolish. Tasks of this sort are best done in full public view, with results being shared. Openness increases the chances of correction and decreases the chances of self-deception. Still, in the end, I must make up my own mind. I must make up my own mind about what is true and who is reliable and what is worth respecting in my intellectual tradition. It is this that prompts the question, What am I to believe? The question is one of how I am to go about making up my own mind.

At first glance, the notion of egocentric rationality would seem well suited to provide an answer to this question, since it does seem to tell me something about how to go about making up my own mind. It tells me that I am to do so by marshaling my intellectual resources in a way that conforms to my own deepest epistemic standards. If I conduct my inquiries in such a way that on reflection I myself would not be critical of the resulting beliefs insofar as my ends are epistemic, then these beliefs are rational for me in an important sense, an egocentric sense.

This may tell me how I am to go about making up my own mind insofar as my ends are epistemic, but suppose my question is, How am I to do so insofar as I have a wide range of ends? Once again, the notion of egocentric rationality might seem to be of help, this time by serving as a theoretical anchor. The recommendation is that I am to proceed in a way such that it is egocentrically rational for me to believe that my intellectual conduct is acceptable, given all of my goals. This means, roughly, that I am to use procedures that it is egocentrically rational for me to believe are appropriately reliable and appropriately efficient, given the importance of the issues at stake. Or short of this, I am at least to proceed in such a way that it will not be egocentrically rational for me to believe that my procedures have been unacceptable, given all of my goals. Otherwise my beliefs will be ones that it is irresponsible for me to have.

Unfortunately, neither of the recommendations is very satisfying. At least they aren't very satisfying insofar as what I want is advice. They do have the right egocentric flavor. There's that much to be said for them. But the latter recommendation, the one that takes into consideration all of my goals, isn't very helpful, since it makes use of the notion of egocentric rationality. It merely pushes the problem back a step. On the other hand, the former recommendation seems misdirected. When I am trying to formulate some intellectual advice for myself, or more generally when I am deliberating about what to believe and how to proceed intellectually, my concern is not with my own standards. The point of my deliberations is not to find out what I think or would think on deep reflection about the reliability of various methods. My concern is with what methods are in fact reliable; it is with the objective realities, not my subjective perceptions.

Be this as it may, the recommendation that I conform to my own standards is an appropriate answer to the egocentric question, What am I to believe? More precisely, it is an appropriate answer if the question is interpreted as one about what I am to believe insofar as my ends are epistemic. Even more precisely, it is an appropriate philosophical answer to the question, the one that should be given if the question is pushed to its limit. To be sure, the reflection prompted by the egocentric question initially has an outward focus. The object of my concern is the world. I wonder whether this or that is true. If pushed hard enough, however, the reflection ultimately curls back upon me. I become concerned with my place in the world, especially my place as an inquirer. I want to know what methods of inquiry are suitable for me insofar as I am trying to determine whether this or that is true. Should I trust the evidence of my senses? Should I use scientific methods? Should I rely on sacred texts? Should I have confidence in my intuitions?

These questions can lead to still others. They can make me wonder about the criteria that I am presupposing in evaluating various methods. Meta-issues thus begin to occupy me. My primary concern is no longer with whether it would be more reliable for me to use this method rather than that one. Nor is it with what each would have me believe. Rather, it is with my criteria for evaluating these various methods and in turn with the criteria for these criteria, and so on. This is the point at which the egocentric question can be appropriately answered by talking about me. What am I to believe? Ultimately, I am to believe that which is licensed by my own deepest epistemic standards. An answer of this sort is the appropriate one for epistemologists. It is the appropriate answer for those whose concern is with purely epistemic goals and whose reflections on the egocentric question take them to this meta-level.

Insofar as nonepistemologists raise the question of what they are to believe, they are principally interested in a different kind of answer. They want an answer that gives them marks of truth and reliability. Epistemologists also want such marks, but once their deliberations reach the meta-level that is characteristic of epistemology, they are forced to admit that regardless of how they marshal their intellectual resources, there are no non-question-begging guarantees that the way that they are marshaling them is reliable. Vulnerability to error cannot be avoided. It is built into us and our methods. However, vulnerability to self-condemnation is not, and it is essentially this that egocentric rationality demands. It demands that we have beliefs that we as truth-seekers wouldn't condemn ourselves for having even if we were to be deeply reflective. This is the post-Cartesian answer to the Cartesian question.

It is also an answer that is bound to be disappointing to anyone who thinks that an essential part of the epistemologist's job is that of providing intellectual guidance. Much of the attractiveness of the Cartesian method of doubt is that it purports to do just this. It purports to provide us with a way of proceeding intellectually, and a concrete one at that. The proposed method tends to strike the contemporary reader as overly demanding, but it would nonetheless seem to be to Descartes's credit, indeed part of his greatness, that he at least attempted to provide such guidance. Contemporary epistemology is apt to seem barren by comparison. Concrete intellectual advice has all but disappeared from it. Of course, no one expects epistemologists to provide advice about local intellectual concerns. The specialist is better placed to give us that—the physicist, the mathematician, the meteorologist, whoever the relevant expert happens to be. What we might like from epistemologists, however, is useful advice about the most basic matters of intellectual inquiry, but it is just this that contemporary epistemology fails to provide.

This is to be regretted, however, only if epistemologists are in a privileged position to give such advice, but they are not. They may be in a privileged position to say something about the general conditions of rational belief. Likewise, they may be able to say interesting things about the conditions of knowledge and other related notions. The mistake is to assume that these conditions should provide us with useful guidelines for the most basic matters of intellectual inquiry. They can't. The conditions will either be misdirected or not fundamental enough or both.

Consider the proposal that, at least in one sense, being rational is essentially a matter of using methods that are reliable. Perhaps this is so, but if a proposal of this sort is meant to provide me with intellectual guidance, I must be able to distinguish reliable from unreliable methods. However, this is precisely one of the matters about which I will want advice. It is also a matter about which epistemologists are not in a privileged position to give advice, except indirectly. They may have useful and even surprising things to say about what reliability is, but once these things are said, it will be up to the rest of us to apply what they say. We will have to determine what methods and procedures are in fact reliable. So, no condition of this sort will be able to provide me with fundamental intellectual advice. On the contrary, if such conditions are to help guide inquiry, I must already be able to make the kind of determinations that they themselves imply are fundamental for me to make if I am to be rational. I reliably must be able to pick out which methods are reliable.

The same is true of other proposals. One proposal, for instance, is that I am rational only if I conform to the standards of the acknowledged experts.[36] If I am to use this to guide inquiry, I once again must be able to make determinations of just the sort that are said to be fundamental to my being rational. How am I to determine what the relevant expert standards are? Presumably by conducting an inquiry that itself conforms to the standards of the experts. But which standards are these? I want to know.

Consider, then, a proposal that is more inward looking. In particular, consider the proposal that it is rational in an important sense, an egocentric sense, for me to believe only that which I would not be motivated to retract even on deep reflection. If what I want is advice, this proposal is a nonstarter. It is misdirected. I want guidance about what is likely to be true. Besides, I don't have the time to be deeply reflective about everything that I believe. Hence, even here I am confronted with the problem of figuring out how to apply the recommendation. How am I to determine whether my practices and my resulting beliefs conform to my own epistemic standards, the ones that would emerge on reflection? Presumably by conforming to those very standards. But what I want to know, and what is often by no means obvious, is how I am to do this, short of being deeply reflective about all of these practices and beliefs?

There would be a solution to problems of this sort if the conditions of rationality were ones to which we have immediate and unproblematic access. But this has a familiar and unpromising ring to it. Recall Bertrand Russell's epistemology, for example. He asserted that we are directly acquainted with certain truths and that these truths make various other propositions probable for us. If this kind of epistemology is to provide us with fundamental intellectual advice, we must be capable of determining immediately and unproblematically when we are directly acquainted with something and when we are not. Likewise, we must be capable of determining immediately and unproblematically what propositions are made probable by the truths with which we are directly acquainted. Otherwise we will want advice about how to make these kinds of determinations. Russell's epistemology leaves room for the possibility that we do have these capabilities. Being directly acquainted with something is itself the sort of phenomenon with which we can be directly acquainted. Similarly, according to Russell's epistemology, we can be directly acquainted with the truth that one thing makes another thing probable.[37]

An epistemology of direct acquaintance or something closely resembling it is our only alternative if we expect the conditions of rationality to give us fundamental advice—that is, advice about those matters that the conditions themselves imply are fundamental to our being rational. It is also a kind of epistemology that few are willing to take seriously anymore. But if not, we must give up the idea that epistemology is in the business of giving fundamental intellectual advice. For that matter, we must give up the whole idea that there is such advice to be had. There can be no general recipe for the conduct of our intellectual lives, if for no other reason than that questions can always arise about how to follow the recipe, questions to which the recipe itself can give no useful answer.

By contrast, consider the kind of advice that logic professors sometimes give their students. They sometimes tell them to try to solve difficult proofs from both

ends, working alternatively down from the premises and up from the desired
conclusion. This is advice that is often useful for students, but it is also advice
that has no pretenses of being about the most fundamental issues of inquiry. It is
not even about the most fundamental matters of logical inference. This is no
accident. It is useful precisely because it is embedded in a prior intellectual
enterprise, one in which certain skills and abilities are taken for granted.

This is an obvious enough point once it is made explicit, but it is nonetheless
a point that is easy enough to overlook. It is overlooked, for instance, by those
internalists who argue against externalist conditions of rational belief on the
grounds that they are unhelpful insofar as we are interested in advice about how
to go about improving our beliefs systems. As a complaint against externalism,
this won't do, but not because externalist conditions of rational belief provide us
with useful advice. They don't. It's not especially useful to be told that we are to
have beliefs that are products of reliable cognitive processes, for example. The
problem, rather, is that internalist conditions of rational belief don't provide us
with genuinely useful advice either.

Of course, internalists have often thought otherwise. One of Descartes's
conceits, for example, was that the method of doubt provides advice to inquirers
that is at once both useful and fundamental. By this I do not mean that Descartes
intended his method to be used by everyone, even the fishmonger and the
butcher. He didn't. He intended it to be used only by philosopher-scientists, and
he intended that even they use it only for a special purpose. It was not to be used
in their everyday lives. It was to be used only for the purpose of conducting
secure theoretical inquiry. However, the method was intended to provide advice
at the most fundamental level about how to conduct such inquiry. But in fact, it
fails to do this. It faces the same difficulties as other attempts to give intellectual
advice that is both fundamental and useful. Either it presupposes that
philosopher-scientists can make determinations of a sort that the recommendation
itself says is fundamental or it is misdirected advice or perhaps both. Which of
these difficulties Descartes's advice is subject to depends on how we interpret
Descartes.

If we interpret Descartes as telling philosopher-scientists to believe just those
propositions whose truth they cannot doubt when they bring them clearly to
mind, then the advice faces both difficulties. First, it is not fundamental enough.
It need not be immediately obvious to philosopher-scientists just what is indubitable for them in this sense and what isn't. They thus can have questions about
that which the advice says is fundamental to their being rational, and these will
be questions that the advice cannot help them answer. Second, the advice is
misdirected. It is advice that looks inward rather than outward. Insofar as the
goal of philosopher-scientists is to conduct theoretical inquiry in an absolutely
secure manner, their interest is to find propositions that cannot be false rather
than ones cannot be doubted. Of course, Descartes thought that there was a
linkage between the two. He thought that what cannot be subjectively doubted
cannot be objectively false, but there is no reason to think that he was right about
this.

Suppose, then, that we interpret Descartes as offering more objective advice. He is telling philosopher-scientists to believe just those propositions that are clear and distinct for them, and he is stipulating from the very beginning that only truths can be genuinely clear and distinct. Then this exacerbates the first difficulty. If philosopher-scientists try to take the advice to heart, the question of whether something really is clear and distinct in this sense becomes one of the fundamental issues about which they will want advice.[38]

So, contrary to his hopes, Descartes did not succeed in providing advice that is both useful and fundamental. More precisely, he did not succeed in providing advice about the conduct of inquiry as opposed to its goals, for despite the above difficulties, we can still view Descartes as making a recommendation about what our intellectual goal should be. He is advising us to make certainty our goal, at least for theoretical purposes. We should try to believe as much as possible without encountering the risk of error. Of course, even this is advice that few of us would be willing to take seriously. The goal is far too demanding. Almost all of us are willing to put up with some risks of error in our theoretical pursuits.

But the important point here is that even if you do have this as your intellectual goal, Descartes has no good, substantive advice for you about how to achieve it. The advice he gives is either misdirected or not fundamental enough. If the advice is to believe what is clear and distinct, where by definition only truths are clear and distinct, it is not fundamental enough. If the advice is to believe what you cannot doubt, it is misdirected. At best, it is a piece of meta-advice. Indeed, when stripped of its spurious guarantees of truth, the advice amounts only to this: insofar as your goal is to believe as much as possible without risk, then from your perspective the way to go about trying to achieve the goal is to believe just that which strikes you as being risk-free and then hope for the best.

The recommendation is sensible enough but also altogether safe. After all, I can give you this kind of advice even if I have no convictions one way or the other about whether you are constituted in such a way that what you find impossible to doubt is in fact true. It is not much different from telling you to do what you think is best about the problem you have confided to me, even when I have no idea whether what you think best really is best.

Of course, if I am presumptuous enough, I can go on to advise you about what you yourself deep down really think is the best way to deal with the problem. Indeed, this would be the counterpart of Descartes's strategy. He first recommends that you believe just those propositions that you cannot doubt, and he then tries to tell you, albeit with a notorious lack of success, which propositions these are. On the other hand, if I am not presumptuous, if I simply tell you to do what you think is best and then leave matters at that, this is not so much genuine advice as a substitute for it. I am not trying to tell you what is best for you. I leave this to you to figure out for yourself.

The recommendation that you have beliefs that you as a truth-seeker wouldn't condemn yourself for having, even if you were to be deeply reflective, has a similar status. This recommendation is internalist in character, since it emphasizes matters of perspective. But insofar as it is conceived as a piece of advice, it is at best meta-advice. If it were interpreted as an attempt to provide you with something more than this—if it were interpreted, for example, as an attempt to provide you with serious, substantive intellectual guidance—it would be clearly inadequate.

Nor does it help to rephrase the recommendation, by saying, as I have sometimes done, that egocentric rationality is essentially a matter of living up to your own deepest epistemic standards. This way of putting the matter might suggest that there is advice to be had about fundamental matters of intellectual inquiry, only the advice is to be sought by peering inward. If you could introspect your deepest standards, you could then use them to guide inquiry.

But in fact, the recommendation faces all the familiar problems. First, it is misdirected. Insofar as you are seeking advice about how to conduct inquiry reliably, you won't be interested in being told that you are live up to your own deepest epistemic standards. Instead, you want to know what standards would be reliable ones. In addition, the recommendation is not fundamental enough. Introspection is not always a simple matter. There are better and worse ways of going about it. Unless you are supposed to have direct and altogether unproblematic access to your deepest epistemic standards, questions will inevitably arise about how you are to go about introspectively determining what your standards are, and these questions cannot be usefully answered by telling you to do so in a way that conforms to the standards.

Besides, there is another and in some ways even more fundamental problem with the recommendation. Your deep epistemic standards, the ones that measure the rationality of your beliefs, are not always to be found within you in fully developed form. But then, it is not even a possibility for you to discover what these standards are simply by peering inward. On the contrary, often enough these standards emerge only with deliberation. The standards may be grounded in your current intellectual dispositions, but the dispositions are activated only with the relevant kind of deliberation. Moreover, the relevant kind of deliberation is not deliberation about what these standards are but rather deliberation about whatever issue is at hand. But if the standards that measure the rationality of your beliefs about an issue emerge only in the course of deliberating about the issue, they can hardly guide your deliberations about that issue.

In this respect, the rational conduct of our intellectual lives is not much different from the rational conduct of the nonintellectual aspects of our lives. In neither case does self-discovery play as important a role in guiding conduct as is sometimes thought. With nonintellectual matters, it is appealing to think that the strategy should be first to discover what we truly value, since only then will we be in a position to deliberate about how we might best secure these things. As appealing as this picture may be, it is far too simple. We cannot always peer inward and discover what we genuinely value. Often enough, our values are vague and half-formed, and it is only in the very conduct of our lives that they begin to emerge with definite shape. It is not as if they are always there inside us in fully developed form, waiting to guide us if only we could discover what they were. Our true values may emerge only after the choice has been made, and we have lived with it for a while. The result is that we are frequently forced to act without even our own values to guide us. Indeed, in some cases it can even seem appropriate to think of our choices as themselves creating our values, the very values that are then used to measure the rationality of these choices. The conduct of every life involves elements of self-invention as well as self-discovery.

And so it is with our intellectual lives. Having egocentrically rational beliefs is a matter of having beliefs that make us invulnerable to certain kinds of self-criticism. This can be expressed by saying that egocentric rationality is a matter of conforming to our deepest epistemic standards. But if we do express the point this way, we need to guard against the idea that these deep standards are always available to us as guides for our intellectual lives. They aren't. On the contrary, they often emerge only in the course of inquiry. So, however we interpret the recommendation that you believe all and only those propositions that you would have no motivation to retract on reflection, it cannot be charitably thought of as an attempt to provide you with serious, substantive intellectual guidance. It must instead be conceived as a different kind of recommendation. But what kind of recommendation?

First and foremost, it is a recommendation about the conditions of rational belief—more precisely, the conditions for a certain kind of rational belief, egocentrically rational belief. The goal is to provide a notion of rational belief that is both enlightening and recognizable. It should help us think more clearly about related notions—truth, knowledge, skepticism, dogmatism, and intellectual disagreement, to name a few. And it should also help us understand the claims of rationality that we make in all of their variety, the ones we are inclined to make in our everyday lives but also the ones we are inclined to make when doing epistemology. This will require our admitting that there are different senses of rational belief, egocentrically rational belief being only one. It will also require our using some of these senses as anchors to introduce still other notions, notions such as that of responsible belief, for example.

This conception takes epistemology, even internalist epistemology, out of the business of giving intellectual advice. The primary epistemological project is to offer an account of the conditions of rational belief, and there is no reason that this project must generate useful advice. Indeed, epistemology is not even the part of philosophy that is most closely tied to the giving of intellectual advice. Studies in logic and probability are more likely to generate useful advice than is epistemology proper. But even here, expectations should not be too high. Nothing extensive in the way of advice can come out of these studies either. In part, this is so because nothing in logic or probability theory tells us how to react when we discover logical inconsistency and probabilistic incoherence. There will be any number of ways for us to restore consistency or coherency. Similarly, when inconsistency or incoherency threatens, there will be any number of ways for us to avoid them. In neither case does logic or probability theory have anything to tell us about which of these many ways is preferable.[39]

Not much in the way of concrete positive advice, then, can come out of either logic or probability theory. In addition, there are limits even to the usefulness of the negative advice they are able to generate. Part of this is because of a familiar problem. If the advice is always to avoid inconsistency and incoherency, the advice is often difficult to follow. To do so, we need to be able to determine whether a set of opinions is inconsistent or incoherent, but the original advice cannot help with this. For help with this problem, we will need new advice: in effect, advice about how to apply the original advice.

There is, moreover, an even more basic limitation on the original advice. It is not always good advice. It is not always and everywhere desirable to avoid inconsistency and incoherency. Doing so might make your situation worse. It might even make it intellectually worse. If you recognize that your opinions are inconsistent or incoherent, you know that they cannot possibly all be accurate. Hence, you know that your opinions are less than ideal. But from this it does not follow that it is irrational for you to have these opinions. What is rational for you in such situations depends on what realistic alternatives you have.[40] In betting situations, it is often rational to adopt a strategy that you know in advance is less than ideal, one in which you are sure to lose at least some of your bets. This can be rational even when other strategies available to you hold out at least some possibility of a flawless outcome. The other strategies may be unduly daring or unduly cautious. The same is true of beliefs. Sometimes it is rational for you to have beliefs that you know cannot possibly all be accurate. Indeed, this is the real lesson of the lottery and the preface paradoxes.[41]

This is not to say that logic and probability theory don't have a special role to play in intellectual guidance. They obviously do. Logical inconsistency and probabilistic incoherence indicate that your opinions are less than ideal. They thus put you on guard about the opinions. What they do not tell you is how to react to the situation. From the fact that your opinions are less than ideal, it does not automatically follow that you must on pains of irrationality change any of these opinions. And even in the cases where you do have to change something, nothing in logic or probability theory tells you which opinions to change. They give you no concrete advice about this.[42]

Of course, things are different when issues of logic and probability theory are themselves being debated. Similarly, they are different when other specifically philosophical issues are being debated. The relevant philosophical experts will then be in a special position to give you substantive advice. But when it is not philosophical matters that are at issue, advice will have to come from other sources. Fortunately, there is no shortage of such sources. Most are relatively specific in nature. You are confronted with an intellectual problem. So, you go to an expert on the topic in question or you consult a reference work or perhaps you simply ask a knowledgeable friend.

There are also sources that hold out the hope of more general advice, and it is no accident that among the richest of these are those in which philosophers have become increasingly interested: cognitive science and the history of science. Of course, there are other philosophical motives for interest in these fields. Nevertheless, there is a story to be told here, one whose rough outlines are that as it became increasingly obvious that epistemology could not be expected to give fundamental intellectual advice, philosophers were more and more taken with empirical disciplines that have human intellectual inquiry as part of their subject matter.

It is not as if these disciplines can be expected to provide the kind of fundamental advice that epistemology fails to provide. If this were their aim, they would encounter all the familiar problems, how to apply the advice, for example. But with these disciplines, unlike epistemology, there is not even a pretense of their being able to provide fundamental advice. This is so not just because we can have questions about the way inquiry is conducted within these disciplines themselves, although this is true enough. It is also because the kind of information that these disciplines are in a position to provide itself calls for epistemic interpretation. The fact that scientists have historically used procedures of a certain kind or the fact that we are disposed to make inferences of a certain kind are themselves facts that need to be evaluated before they can provide us with intellectual advice. We will especially want to know whether these procedures and inferences are reliable. But to answer the question, we will need to appeal to something more than the history of science and cognitive science.

On the other hand, if what we seek is not advice about the most fundamental matters of inquiry but rather some useful rules of thumb, these disciplines can be of help. At their best, they are able to provide a rich supply of data from which, with persistence and the help of still other disciplines, we may be able to tease out some useful advice.

Sometimes it may not even take much teasing, especially for negative advice. Recent cognitive science is filled with studies that purport to show recurrent patterns of error in the way that we make inferences. The errors arise, for example, from an insensitivity to sample size, or an underutilization of known prior probabilities in making predictions, or an inclination in certain kinds of situations to assign a higher probability to a conjunction than one of its conjuncts.[43] These are data from which we can fashion intellectual advice for ourselves, advice that alerts us to our tendency to make these kinds of errors.

Extracting intellectual advice from the history of science will seldom be so straightforward a matter, but it too can sometimes provide us with useful data.[44] It does so in part because historical examples are less easily manipulable than purely hypothetical ones. This is not to say that dreamed up examples cannot instruct. They obviously can, and indeed they are often more convenient, since they are neater than real-life examples. They can be designed to our purposes, with extraneous features deleted. But this is just the danger as well. It is sometimes all too easy to tailor them to suit our purposes. Actual cases in all of their detail are not so malleable.[45]

Suppose, then, that you have looked at the history of science and at the findings of cognitive science and at various other studies that provide data about human inquiry. How are you to go about using the data to generate some rules of thumb for the conduct of inquiry? Sometimes, as I have said, it will be obvious, since sometimes the data will reveal that you have a tendency to make what you yourself readily concede to be errors. But matters won't always be this obvious, and besides, you want positive as well negative advice. Is there any general advice to be had about this, the process of using the available data to generate intellectual advice?

Those who have been influenced by contemporary moral theory might advise you to employ something akin to the method of wide reflective equilibrium. The rough idea would be that you are to begin with your initial intuitions about what constitute sound methods of inquiry. You are then to test these intuitions against all the data and all the cases that strike you as relevant: data from psychology about our cognitive abilities and our characteristic patterns of inference, cases from the history of science, imaginary cases, and anything else that you deem to be germane. Finally, you are to use your best judgment to resolve any conflicts among these intuitions, data, and cases. Sometimes you will judge that your original intuitions are sound. Other times the data or the cases will convince you to alter your original intuitions, and still other times you will be disposed to alter both by a process of give-and-take.

The problem with this recommendation is familiar. It is not so much mistaken as unhelpful. At best, it is meta-advice. Indeed, it is essentially the same meta-advice that is implicit in the notion of egocentric rationality. It tells you essentially this: take into account all the data that you think to be relevant and then reflect on the data, solving conflicts in the way that you judge best. On the other hand, it does not tell you what kinds of data are relevant, nor does it tell you what is the best way to resolve conflicts among the data. It leaves you to muck about on these questions as best you can.

And muck you must, for this is part of the human intellectual predicament. It's not that there is no useful intellectual advice to be had. There clearly is. It is just that philosophy is not in a particularly privileged position to provide it. The kind of intellectual advice that philosophy has sometimes been thought to be in a privileged position to give—namely, general advice about the most fundamental issues of intellectual inquiry—is precisely the kind of advice that cannot be usefully given. Attempts to provide this kind of advice are inevitably misdirected or not sufficiently fundamental.

On the other hand, philosophy in general and epistemology in particular has no special claim on more modest kinds of advice—for example, specific advice on local intellectual concerns or general rules of thumb about the conduct of inquiry. The relevant expert is better positioned for the former; the latter is best produced by reflection upon all of the available data. We can potentially use anything to fashion intellectual rules of thumb, from the findings of cognitive science to studies in the history of science to mnemonic devices and other intellectual tricks, even relatively trivial ones, such as carrying nines, for example.

Philosophers can make important and diverse contributions to the project of fashioning intellectual rules of thumb. They can help us to appreciate that there are various ends at which inquiry might be aimed, for example. Some of the ends are epistemic in nature, in that they are concerned with the accuracy and comprehensiveness of our belief systems. Others are more pragmatic. Moreover, there are distinctions to be made even among the ends that are epistemic. Some are synchronic (roughly, getting things as right as we can for the moment); others are diachronic (roughly, getting things right eventually). Such distinctions can be important when we are trying to provide ourselves with intellectual advice, since certain kinds of recommendations—for example, the recommendation that we prefer the simplest of otherwise equal hypotheses—will seem plausible relative to some of these aims and not so plausible relative to others.

Philosophers can tell us much else of relevance. They can tell us what it is to have an explanation of something, or what it is to have a merely verbal disagreement as opposed to a substantive one. They can distinguish different sorts of arguments for us, emphasizing that different criteria are appropriate for evaluating these arguments. More generally, they can act as intellectual gadflies, examining and criticizing the developments in other intellectual disciplines. And of course, they can also try to describe the conditions under which inquiry is conducted rationally, only these conditions will not be of a sort that provide us with much useful intellectual guidance.

Some people will insist that this will not do. They will insist that one of our most important intellectual projects is that of generating sound intellectual advice and that we need guidance about how to conduct this project. There are better and worse ways of doing so, and it is epistemology's special role to instruct us. Nothing else is positioned to do so. Science, for example, cannot because what we need is advice that is prior to inquiry rather than the result of inquiry. It is only epistemology that can provide us with this kind of fundamental guidance.

This is a view that sees epistemology as the arbiter of intellectual procedures. The presupposition is that epistemology can be prior to other inquiries and that as such it is capable of providing us with a non-question-begging rationale for using one set of intellectual procedures rather than another. Just the reverse is true. Epistemology begins at a late stage of inquiry. It builds on preexisting inquiry and without that inquiry it would be subjectless. One consequence is that there is no alternative to using antecedent opinion and methods in thinking about our intellectual procedures. There is no way of doing epistemology *ex niholo*, and hence it is no more capable of giving us non-question-begging advice about basic issues of intellectual procedure than is anything else.

A deeper presupposition must also be abandoned: that it is important for us to have such advice. Descartes and the Enlightenment figures who followed him—Locke, for example—thought that this was important, since they thought that the alternative was intellectual anarchy, and perhaps as a result religious and political anarchy as well. Their assumptions seemed to be that there are countless ways of proceeding intellectually, that we are pretty much free to choose among them as we please, and that there must be a non-question-begging rationale for preferring one of these ways over the others if chaos is to be avoided. Descartes and Locke saw it as their task, the task of the epistemologist, to provide such a rationale.

If these assumptions accurately depicted our intellectual situation, they might have been right. But in fact, the assumptions don't accurately depict our situation. It is not as if we are each given a menu of basic intellectual procedures and that our task is to find a non-question-begging way of choosing among them or face intellectual anarchy. Our problem tends to be the opposite one. By the time we reach the point at which it occurs to us that there might be fundamentally different kinds of intellectual procedures, we are largely shaped intellectually. We come to this point equipped not only with a battery of assumptions about the world but also a battery of intellectual skills and habits. All of our intellectual inquiries are grounded in these resources, and the bulk of our intellectual lives must be conducted using them in largely automatic fashion. We have no choice about this. Fundamental rules for the direction of the mind would do us little good even if we had them. We wouldn't have the time or resources to make proper use of them. Insofar as our goal is intellectual improvement, the emphasis is better placed on the development of skills and habits that we think will help make us more reliable inquirers.

The project of building up such skills and habits lacks the drama of the Cartesian project. It is inevitably a piecemeal project. To engage in it, we must draw upon an enormous number of background assumptions, skills, and habits, ones that for the time being we are content to use rather than reform. Questions can still arise about this background. We may realize that had we been born with significantly different cognitive equipment or into a significantly different environment, these assumptions, skills, and habits might have been considerably different. Such possibilities are mainly of theoretical interest, however; they are of interest for epistemology. They can be used to discuss skeptical worries, for instance. On the other hand, they normally will not be of much interest insofar as our purpose is epistemic improvement. After all, most of these fundamentally different ways of proceeding will not be real options for us. It is not as if we are radically free to reconstitute ourselves intellectually in any way that we see fit and that we need some guidance about whether to do so or how to do so.

Of course, we are not entirely without options. We cannot alter our fundamental intellectual procedures by a simple act of will, but by making incremental changes over a long enough period of time, we perhaps could train ourselves to use procedures that are very different from those that we currently employ. There may even be ways of bringing about the changes more immediately. Drugs might do the trick, for instance. There are those who have recommended peyote or LSD as a way to truth. But even here, insofar as our worry is intellectual chaos, the search need not be for a non-question-begging way of deciding which procedures, our present ones or the drug-induced ones, are the more reliable. It is enough to point out that from our present undrugged perspective, most of us have no reason to think that the drugged perspective is the more reliable one. Quite the contrary; from our current perspective it seems far less reliable. Thus, insofar as our ends are epistemic, most of us will have no motivation to drug ourselves.

Descartes and Locke notwithstanding, our primary intellectual threat is not that of chaos, and our primary intellectual need is not for advice about the most fundamental matters of intellectual outlook. We cannot help but be largely guided by our intellectual inheritance on these matters. The primary threat is rather that of intellectual conformity, and our primary need is for intellectual autonomy. There is little in life that is more difficult than resisting domination by one's intellectual environment. It is all too easy for us to be intellectual lemmings. We do not have the ability to cast off wholesale the effects of our environment and adopt a radically new intellectual outlook. So, our having this ability cannot be the basis of our intellectual autonomy. Our intellectual autonomy is instead based upon our ability to use our existing opinions and existing methods to examine our opinions and methods. It resides in our ability to make ourselves into an object of study, to evaluate and monitor ourselves, and moreover to do so not so much in terms of the prevailing standards as in terms of our own standards. This ability creates a space for intellectual autonomy. But it is only a space.

Self-monitoring in terms of our own personal standards does not altogether eliminate the threat of intellectual domination. As Foucault argued recently and as Marx argued earlier, the most effective and therefore most chilling kind of control is that which is internalized.[46] We accept as our own the very norms by which we are controlled. Be this as it may, our only alternative is to monitor ourselves for this as well, to try as best we can to make ourselves aware of the possibility and thereby prevent it. Of course, there is no guarantee that we will be successful. If the domination is thorough enough, leaving no trace of its influence, then no amount of self-monitoring will do much good.

But in this respect, the possibility of complete and utter domination is not much different from the possibility of complete and utter deception. Just as a powerful enough demon could use our own experiences to deceive us thoroughly without our being aware of it, so too a powerful enough dominating force could use our own standards to control us thoroughly without our being aware of it. But neither of these gives us a rationale to be dismissive of our intellectual projects. The possibility of radical error does not mean that knowledge is altogether impossible for us, and the possibility of radical domination does not mean that intellectual autonomy is altogether impossible for us.

Our intellectual standards cannot help but show the effects of our intellectual environment, but they need not be swallowed up by it. My standards can and presumably sometimes do differ from the standards of the people who surround me. And when they do, intellectual autonomy as well as egocentric rationality requires that I conform to my standards rather than the prevailing ones.

4. Why Be Egocentrically Rational?

Why should you care whether your beliefs are egocentrically rational? Part of the difficulty in answering this question is that different kinds of worries might be prompting it. For example, the concern might be with the purely epistemic goal.

By definition, egocentric rationality is a matter of what you have reasons to believe insofar as your goal is to have accurate and comprehensive beliefs. But is this really one of your goals? Do you or should you care whether or not your beliefs are accurate and comprehensive?

Most of us do care about this, and perhaps even care about it intrinsically. We tend to be curious about our world. We are curious about its origins, its history and its future. We want to have true and comprehensive beliefs about these matters, and we want this independently of whether or not these beliefs are useful. But of course, we also think that they are useful. They may not be useful in each and every case. There are plenty of examples where the discovery of a truth does more harm than good. But in general, this isn't so. Having accurate and comprehensive beliefs is ordinarily helpful in our attempts to secure those things that we value. Or at least so we think. And insofar as we do think this, we value having accurate and comprehensive beliefs. We value them as a means.[47]

But there may be other worries that are prompting the above question. One has to do with the restricted nature of egocentric rationality. Your egocentric reasons to believe something are the reasons you have to believe it insofar as your goal is to have accurate and comprehensive beliefs. But in fact, you have many goals, not just epistemic ones. But then, why should you be especially interested in being rational in this restricted, epistemic sense?

If this is the worry, it should be granted. Epistemic goals are only one kind of goal, and they need not be overriding goals. Thus, it need not be rational, all things considered—that is, when all of your goals are taken into consideration— for you to have egocentrically rational beliefs. To be sure, there are pressures that tend to keep these two notions from falling too far apart.[48] But the two can diverge, and when they do, it is not particularly important for you to have egocentrically rational beliefs. On the contrary, it will be important for you not to have them. If someone threatens to kill your children unless you come to believe P, then you had better find some way of getting yourself to believe P regardless of what your current evidence for P is.[49] But this is not to say that being egocentrically rational isn't valuable. It's only to say that its value can be over- ridden.

There is also a more radical worry that may be prompting the above question. Egocentric rationality is concerned with purely epistemic goals. Even so, there is no guaranteed connection between egocentric rationality and truth or likely truth. Being egocentrically rational does not ensure that most of your beliefs are true. It does not even ensure that this is likely. But if not, why should you care whether or not your beliefs are egocentrically rational? Why should you care about this even if your only concerns are epistemic ones?

It is not altogether clear what the above question is asking. One natural way to interpret it is as a request for reasons. In asking why you should be ego- centrically rational, you are asking what reasons you have to believe the proposi- tions that are egocentrically rational for you. But if this is your question, there is a straightforward answer to it. By hypothesis there are considerations that from your perspective seem to indicate that these propositions are true. Hence, you have egocentric reasons to believe these propositions. You have such reasons insofar as your goal is to have accurate beliefs.

The ease of this answer suggests that if you are tempted to ask the question, Why be egocentrically rational? you must have something else in mind. But what else? Perhaps your question is not best construed as a request for reasons, since this invites an uninteresting response. The question, rather, is one about egocentric rationality itself. You want to know what there is to be said for it. You want to know why it should be valued.

But again, there is a straightforward answer. You want or need to have accurate and comprehensive beliefs, and insofar as you are egocentrically rational, you are by your own lights effectively satisfying this end. This is what can be said for being egocentrically rational. Perhaps this still does not strike you as enough. You grant that you are interested in having true beliefs. That's not the issue. What you cannot see is why you should value having beliefs that by your lights seem to be an effective means to this goal. There is something to this. In your deliberations about what to believe, your primary interest is not to determine what is egocentrically rational for you. Your interest is not you and your own deep epistemic standards. It's the world that you are interested in. You want to determine what's true of it.

So, if determining what's true of the world is what you have in mind when you insist that you cannot see why you should be interested in egocentric rationality, you may be right. Your primary intellectual goal, presumably, is not to have egocentrically rational beliefs. It's to have accurate and comprehensive beliefs. Considered in itself, it may not be all that important for you to be egocentrically rational. On the other hand, this doesn't mean that being egocentrically rational is of no value whatsoever to you. After all, in believing propositions that are egocentrically rational for you, you are believing propositions that on reflection you would think effectively satisfy the goal of having an accurate and comprehensive belief system. But this is one of the ways in which a thing can have value for you. It can have value for you because you think it would effectively promote something else that is of value. Valuing something as a means is still a way of valuing it.

In addition, egocentric rationality is something that can be valued for its own sake as well. Being egocentrically rational is essentially a matter of being invulnerable to a certain kind of intellectual self-condemnation, and there is nothing especially implausible about the idea of this kind of invulnerability's being intrinsically valuable to you. It may be important to you, important for its own sake, that you not to be intellectually at odds with yourself. You want to be beyond self-reproach in intellectual matters. Being so, you may realize, gives you no guarantee that you won't make mistakes. It doesn't even give you a guarantee that you are not a brain in a vat, being radically deceived. But your reaction may be, "Perhaps so, but if I am a brain in a vat, I can at least be a good brain in a vat, one with no motivation for intellectual self-reproach."

So, being egocentrically rational is the sort of thing that you might very well intrinsically value. Still, it would be at least a little peculiar for this to be your primary source, much less your only source, of intellectual motivation. To see why, consider two inquirers. The first is motivated by a desire to know the truth. This prompts her to be thorough and careful in her inquiries, and as a result she believes that which is egocentrically rational for her. The second is motivated by a desire to avoid intellectual self-condemnation. This prompts him to be thorough and careful in his inquiries, and as a result he believes that which is ego-centrically rational for him. The result is the same in each case: each is ego-centrically rational. Nevertheless, we are more likely to look askance at his intellectual motivation than hers. His motivation seems shallower, more self-indulgent.

There is an analogy here with at least some views about moral motivation. Suppose one person acts in the morally required way because she feels genuine sympathy for the suffering of others and she believes that suffering is bad, and a second person acts in the morally required way because he wants to be a morally good person.[50] Her motivation does not involve any particular thoughts of herself, but his does involve thoughts of himself. Indeed, this is his primary motivation. Once again, her motivation seems more morally advanced and hence more admirable than his. This is so precisely because doing the morally right thing is for her merely a means, while for him it is an end in itself, one that is intrinsically valuable. This makes his motivation seem shallow, perhaps even narcissistic.[51]

And so it is with matters of rationality, including those of egocentric rationality. To be sure, you might intrinsically value being rational, but there would be something misdirected, something narcissistic, about this rather than a desire for the truth to be your primary source of intellectual motivation.

Besides, even if being rational were your principal intellectual goal, it is a goal that is best sought indirectly. It is like happiness in this respect. Trying to be happy ordinarily won't make you happy. Happiness is best won as a by-product. You engage in activities and projects that you regard as worthwhile, and happiness is the result. The same goes for rationality. Trying very hard to be rational ordinarily isn't a good way to become rational. A better way is to try very hard to believe truths and not to believe falsehoods.

Suppose, then, that the desire to be rational isn't the principal source of intellectual motivation for you and that, hence, the value you attach to being egocentrically rational is for the most part a derivative value. It has value for you because insofar as you are egocentrically rational, you have beliefs that by your own lights seem to be an effective means to the goal of having an accurate and comprehensive belief system. But this still might not seem to be enough to answer your questions about the value of egocentric rationality. After all, ego-centric rationality may not help get you to the truth. What by your own lights seems to be an effective means to the truth may in fact not be an effective means to it. What then? What is there to be said for egocentric rationality in this kind of situation, where you are rational but misguided?

But notice, you are not aware that you are misguided. On the contrary, your beliefs are such that even on deep reflection you would be satisfied with them. Even on reflection you would continue to think that they are highly likely to be true. Of course, it might be obvious to the rest of us that you are misguided. We might even be in a position to see that you would do better by being egocentrically irrational than rational. But if it is this possibility that is worrying you and causing you to wonder why you should care about being egocentrically rational, you are merely raising the issue of guarantees once again. What you are saying is that egocentric rationality is valuable only if there are assurances that egocentric reasons to believe something are reliable indicators of truths. Or at the very least you are demanding assurances that you will do better by being rational than irrational. But there are no such guarantees. So, if in asking the question, Why be egocentrically rational? you are demanding assurances of this sort, there is little to be said to you.

The most we can do is to point out to you that the reality of your intellectual life is that like the rest of us, you are working without a net. Regardless of how you marshal your cognitive resources, you are not going to have non-question-begging guarantees of truth or reliability. No procedure, no amount of reflection, no amount of evidence gathering can guarantee that you won't fall into error and perhaps even great error. As a result, all of your intellectual projects require at least an element of intellectual faith in yourself.

If you cannot accommodate yourself to the reality of your intellectual life, if on reflection you would not be satisfied with anything short of guarantees, then you are something rare: a genuine skeptic. Your deep epistemic standards are such that little if anything can possibly satisfy them.

Notes

1. For the sake of the argument, I'm assuming here that committing yourself to the proposition wouldn't be sufficient to produce these benefits. Only genuine belief will do. See sec. 1.4.

2. See sec. 3.2, where these issues are discussed in more detail.

3. See Richard Feldman, "Foley's Subjective Foundationalism," *Philosophy and Phenomenological Research* (1989), 149–58.

4. See sec. 3.2.

5. I return to the issue in Chapter 4.

6. Roderick Chisholm's attempts to make this suggestion precise have their problems, however. In *The Foundations of Knowing* (Minneapolis: University of Minnesota Press, 1982), 7, Chisholm says that "epistemic reasonability could be understood in terms of the general requirement to try to have the largest possible set of logically independent beliefs that is such that the true beliefs outnumber the false ones." But this implies that a belief system of size $n + \mu$, where μ is as small as one likes, that has just one more true belief than false belief is always epistemically preferable to a belief system of size n that has only true beliefs. Later, in the third edition of *Theory of Knowledge*, 13, Chisholm tries to emphasize the value of comprehensiveness by committing himself to the following principle: if P is beyond reasonable doubt and if Q is beyond reasonable doubt, then the conjunction (P & Q)

is beyond reasonable doubt. But this principle also has its problems; see the discussion of conjunction rules in sec. 4.5.

7. "He who says 'Better go without belief forever than believe a lie!' merely shows his own preponderant private horror of becoming a dupe." William James, *Essays in Pragmatism* (New York: Hafner, 1948), 100.

8. I return to it in sec. 4.9.

9. Those who are sophisticated enough cognitively to have beliefs but not sophisticated enough to have beliefs about their beliefs—young children, for example—will not be able to meet these conditions. Their beliefs will be neither egocentrically rational nor irrational; they will be arational.

10. In the negative case, things are not quite so simple. If after reflection you fail to reach a clear and distinct perception about the proposition, you are to refrain from believing it. Unfortunately, even if the reflection has been lengthy, there is no assurance that further reflection wouldn't produce clarity. Thus, even for Descartes, there is no natural negative stopping point for reflection, a point at which further reflection on the topic at issue is gratuitous because we can be assured that clarity about it is beyond us.

11. See sec. 3.2.

12. There are analogies in psychiatric theory about the proper end of analysis. Freud's position is a counterpart to the one Descartes held about reflection. Patients are to continue in analysis until they are cured, and according to Freud, there are relatively clear indications when this has occurred, although it is to the analyst and not necessarily the patient to whom these indications are clear. But Freud, like Descartes, was wrong. In many and perhaps even most cases it is anything but clear whether a patient has been cured. Indeed, it is often far from clear what it would even mean to say that there has been a cure. This suggests that the only sensible policy is for patient and analyst to discuss between themselves whether the potential gains of further therapy warrant its continuation. But like the recommendation that in epistemic matters we be reasonably careful and thorough, this advice is theoretically unsatisfying. It doesn't even purport to say when there is no point to further therapy. But if this is what we want, there is a natural fallibilistic alternative to Freud's recommendation, just as there is a natural fallibilistic alternative to Descartes's recommendation. Namely, therapy becomes gratuitous when it no longer has a significant effect on the therapeutic goal, whether this goal is a cure or insight or stability or whatever. There is no guarantee that this is the point in analysis at which the therapeutic goal has been reached, just as there is no guarantee in epistemology that our stable reflective opinion will be a true one. However, it is a point at which further therapy becomes pointless.

13. The case is Richard Feldman's. See Feldman, "Foley's Subjective Foundationalism."

14. Compare with Richard Foley, *The Theory of Epistemic Rationality*, (Cambridge: Harvard University Press, 1987), sec. 1.3, especially n. 27, and Foley, "Reply to Alston, Feldman, and Swain," *Philosophy and Phenomenological Research* L(1989), 169–88.

15. See John Pollock's attack on what he calls 'the doxastic assumption', which is the assumption "that the justifiability of a belief is a function exclusively of what beliefs one holds—of one's doxastic state." Pollock, *Contemporary Theories of Knowledge* (Totowa, N.J.: Rowman and Littefield, 1986).

16. See the discussion at the beginning of sec. 1.2.

17. Compare with secs. 1.3 and 1.4.

18. I continue to be neutral about the theory of goals. On some accounts, your goals

will consist of the things that you significantly value (or perhaps the things you would value were you acquainted with all of the relevant facts). On other accounts, your goals will include things that are valuable, whether or not you are disposed to value them. See sec. 1.1. For the sake of simplifying the discussion here, I will glide over such differences by simply assuming that those things that are the best candidates for being objectively valuable (e.g., the saving of human lives, the diminishing of human suffering, etc.) are also valued by you. Hence, on either view, they are among your goals.

19. See van Fraassen, *Laws And Symmetry*, especially chap. 7.

20. See n. 9 in sec. 3.1.

21. Compare with Kent Bach, "Default Reasoning," *Pacific Philosophical Quarterly* 65 (1984), 37–58.

22. "An inference may be sound, but it may not be reasonable to make it, because it has no foreseeable value at the time and prevents the agent from using his limited cognitive resources to do other things that are obviously valuable at the time." Christopher Cherniak, *Minimal Rationality*, (Cambridge: MIT Press, 1986), 24

23. Similarly, in thinking about what intellectual methods we have reason to use, we will regard pragmatic considerations mainly as constraints. Some methods will be too awkward or too complex for us to use; we won't take them seriously. But once we have used pragmatic considerations to filter out unworkable methods, we will be inclined to evaluate the remaining set of methods in terms of their reliability, not in terms of their usefulness. Compare with the discussion of simplicity below. For a defense of the view that pragmatic considerations should enter more directly into the evaluation of intellectual methods, see Stich, *The Fragmentation of Reason*, especially chap. 6.

24. This point is forcefully made by Phillip Quinn in "Epistemic Parity and Religious Argument," *Philosophical Perspectives* 5(1991), 317–41.

25. I. Lakatos, "The Methodology of Scientific Research Programmes," in I. Lakatos and A. Musgrave (eds.), *Criticism and the Growth of Knowledge* (Cambridge: Cambridge University Press, 1970), 91–196, see especially 168–73.

26. Compare with Michael Bratman, who makes an analogous claim about intentions; see his *Intentions, Plans, and Practical Reasons*, especially chap. 6.

27. See Gilbert Harman, *Change in View* (Cambridge: MIT Press, 1988), especially chap. 4.

28. Chisholm, *The Theory of Knowledge*, especially 63–64; Harman, *Change in View*, Lycan, *Judgement and Justification*, especially chap. 8; D. Goldstick, "Methodological Conservatism," *American Philosophical Quarterly* 8 (1971), 186, 191; and Lawrence Sklar, "Methodological Conservatism," *Philosophical Review* 84 (1975), 398.

29. Richard Foley, "Epistemic Conservatism," *Philosophical Studies* 43 (1983), 163–82.

30. See Bratman, *Intentions, Plans, and Practical Reasons*.

31. See sec. 1.4.

32. See Parfit, *Reasons and Persons*, especially chap. 1.

33. Harman emphasizes this in *Change in View*, 47–50

34. Similarly, if your preference for simple hypotheses is a matter of deliberate policy, this policy might be a rational one for you to follow, even though beliefs in accordance with it are often irrational. This is so because it might nonetheless be part of your best set of policies. Any other set of policies, or at least any other that you are capable of following, might leave you worse off.

35. For an overview of some of this work, see Stich, *The Fragmentation of Reason*.

36. ". . . when we judge someone's inference to be normatively inappropriate, we are comparing it to (what we take to be) the applicable principles of inference sanctioned by expert reflective equilibrium.' Stich, "Could Man Be an Irrational Animal?"

37. Bertrand Russell, *The Problems of Philosophy* (New York: Oxford University Press, 1959). See also Richard Fumerton, *Metaphysical and Epistemological Problems of Perception* (Lincoln: University of Nebraska Press, 1985), especially 57–58.

38. Roderick Chisholm's epistemology faces analogous problems. Like Descartes, Chisholm thinks that our "purpose in raising [epistemological] questions is to correct and improve our own epistemic situation; . . . we want to do our best to improve our set of beliefs—to replace those that are unjustified by others that are justified and to replace those that have a lesser degree of justification with others that have a greater degree of justification." See Chisholm, *The Theory of Knowledge*, 1. He takes this to show that the notion of epistemic justification cannot be explicated in an externalist manner. Instead, the conditions of epistemic justification must be both *"internal* and *immediate* in that one can find out directly, by reflection, what one is justified in believing at any time" (p. 7) However, the conditions that Chisholm himself defends, as expressed in his principles of epistemic justification, are often very complicated. They are difficult enough to understand and even more difficult to apply, especially since many of them make reference to the believer's total evidence and total set of beliefs. Thus, even if you thoroughly understand Chisholm's principles, it is unlikely that you will always be able to determine by reflection on your state of mind whether or not a belief is justified according to them. Moreover, even if this always were at least theoretically possible, it need not always be obvious to you how you are to go about making these determinations. You won't always be able to look inward and simply read off whether Chisholm's conditions are met. So, not just any kind of reflection will do. But if not, you will want to know how to conduct these reflections, and Chisholm's principles do not provide you with any helpful advice about this.

39. Compare with Harman, *Change in View*.

40. Again, see Harman, *Change in View*. Also see Cherniak, *Minimal Rationality*.

41. I argue this in Chapter 4.

42. This is one of the reasons that treatises on informal logic and critical reasoning tend to be either unhelpful or theoretically unsatisfying. Insofar as the project is seen to be one of deriving useful advice for our everyday intellectual lives from the rules of logic and the axioms of the probability calculus, there simply isn't a lot of useful advice to be had. On the other hand, insofar as the treatise does contain useful rules of thumb, these rules must have extralogical sources. But then, we will want to have information about these sources, information that these treatises rarely give us.

43. See, e.g., Richard Nisbet and Lee Ross, *Human Inference: Strategies and Shortcomings of Social Judgement* (Englewood Cliffs, N.J.: Prentice-Hall, 1980).

44. See, e.g, Pat Langley, Herbert A. Simon, Gary L. Bradshaw, and Jan M. Zytgow, *Scientific Discovery: Computational Explorations of the Creative Process* (Cambridge: MIT Press, 1987).

45. The detail is important, however. Without it, real cases and real arguments can be manipulated just as easily as hypothetical ones. Witness textbook examples of the so-called informal fallacies. The examples are often arguments from real sources that have been taken out of context and then uncharitably interpreted as deductive.

46. Karl Marx, *The German Idealogy* (London: Lawrence and Wishart, 1938); Michel Foucault, *The History of Sexuality*, trans. R. Hurley (New York: Vintage Books, 1980).

See also Gary Gutting's discussion of Foucault's views on these matters in his *Michel Foucault's Archaeology of Scientific Reason* (Cambridge: Cambridge University Press, 1989).

47. For a different view, see Stephen Stich's pragmatist attack on the value of truth in *The Fragmentation of Reason*, especially chaps. 5 and 6.

48. See sec. 1.3.

49. Again see sec. 1.3

50. This will not be possible on every view of moral motivation. On some views, if someone acts out of a mere desire to be moral rather than out of a concern for the suffering of others, she cannot be acting in the morally required way, since this requires that she act for the right kind of reasons. I owe this point to Alasdair MacIntyre.

51. Compare Bernard Williams, *Moral Luck* (Cambridge: Cambridge University Press, 1981), chap. 3.

4

The Epistemology of Beliefs and the Epistemology of Degrees of Belief

1. The Lockean Thesis

Consider two questions. What propositions are egocentrically rational for you to believe? With what confidence is it egocentrically rational for you to believe a proposition? Each concerns a question of egocentric epistemology. Answering the first requires an epistemology for beliefs, answering the second an epistemology for degrees of belief.

The two kinds of account seem to be close cousins, the problems they encounter and the range of options for solving them being essentially the same. An account of rational degrees of belief simply adopts a more fine-grained approach to doxastic attitudes than does an account of rational beliefs. The latter classifies these attitudes with a simple threefold scheme: you believe a proposition, you disbelieve it, or you withhold judgment on it. By contrast, the former introduces as many distinctions as are needed to talk about the levels of confidence you might have in various propositions—that is, your degrees of belief in them. Nevertheless, each account has a similar aim, that of describing what is required if your doxastic attitudes are to conform to your evidence.

Indeed, a natural first impression is that the two kinds of accounts complement each other. Begin with the assumption that it is rational for your confidence in the truth of a proposition to be proportionate to the strength of your evidence.[1] Add the idea that belief-talk is a simple way of categorizing degrees of confidence: to say that you believe a proposition is just to say that you are sufficiently confident of its truth for your attitude to be one of belief. Then it is rational for you to believe a proposition just in case it is rational for you to have sufficiently high degree of confidence in it, sufficiently high to make your attitude toward it one of belief.

I will call this way of thinking about the relationship between the rationality of beliefs and the rationality of degrees of belief 'the Lockean thesis'. John Locke hinted at the idea that belief-talk is but a general way of classifying an individual's confidence in a proposition,[2] and he explicitly endorsed the idea that one's degree of belief in a proposition ought to be proportionate to the strength of one's evidence for it:

The mind, if it will proceed rationally, ought to examine all the grounds of probability, and see how they make more or less, for or against any probable proposition, before it assents to or dissents from it, and upon a due balancing the whole, reject or receive it, with a more or less firm assent, proportionably to the preponderance of the greater grounds of probability on one side or the other.[3]

Locke also endorsed a strong foundationalist thesis about what he calls 'the grounds of probability', what we would more naturally call 'evidence'. For Locke, the hallmark of knowledge is certitude. You know a proposition just in case it is certain for you. These propositions constitute your evidence, and you are rational in your opinions just to the extent that they conform to what you know—that is, just to the extent that the firmness of your opinions is proportionate to the strength with which your knowledge supports them.[4]

However, what I am calling 'the Lockean thesis' does not require this kind of strong foundationalism. All it says is that insofar as your goals are purely epistemic ones, it is rational for your degree of belief in a proposition to conform to your evidence. It then goes on to say that it is rational for you to believe a proposition just in case it is rational for you to have a degree of confidence in it that is sufficient for belief. To be sure, those who endorse the Lockean thesis need to say something about evidence, but they need not say what Locke said. More on this later.[5]

One immediate benefit of the Lockean thesis is that it allows us to finesse the worry that accounts of rational degrees of belief are apt to be overly demanding. After all, perhaps it is too much to expect you to believe very many propositions with exactly the degree of confidence that your evidence warrants. But even if this is so, the Lockean thesis implies that accounts of rational degrees of belief have an important theoretical function, for according to the thesis, it is egocentrically rational for you to believe a proposition P just in case it is egocentrically rational for you to have a degree of confidence in P that is sufficient for belief. Hence, you can rationally believe P even if your specific degree of belief in it is somewhat higher or lower than it should be, given your evidence. The Lockean thesis thus leaves room for the possibility of your believing precisely the propositions that are rational for you, even when few if any of these propositions are believed by you with precisely the appropriate degree of confidence. This is a tidy result. It makes the theory of rational degrees of belief important, even if it is only rarely the case that our degrees of belief are precisely what the theory says they should be.

2. Two Paradoxes for the Lockean Thesis

According to the Lockean thesis, it is rational for you to believe a proposition just in case it is rational for you to have a degree of confidence in it that is sufficient for belief. What degree is sufficient? It is not easy to say. There doesn't seem to be any principled way to identify a precise threshold.

Even so, in itself this isn't a serious objection to the Lockean thesis. It only illustrates what should have been obvious from the start—namely, the vagueness of belief-talk. According to the Lockean, belief-talk and degree-of-belief-talk are not fundamentally different. Both categorize your confidence in the truth of a proposition. Belief-talk does so more vaguely, but on the other hand vagueness is often just what is needed, since we are generally not able to specify in a precise way the degree of confidence that you have in a proposition. There are perhaps a few exceptions. We may be able to do so for propositions that concern games of chance (for example, that either 1 or 2 will come up on the first roll of the die) and propositions whose likelihoods can be measured in terms of well-established statistical frequencies (for example, that a randomly selected American male will have a heart attack before the age of forty). But these are the exceptions. For other propositions, the vagueness of belief may be just what is needed.[6]

Still, we will want to be able to say something, even if vague, about the threshold above which your level of confidence must rise if you are to believe a proposition. What to say is not obvious, however, since there doesn't seem to be a nonarbitrary way of identifying even a vague threshold. But perhaps we don't need a nonarbitrary way. Perhaps we can just stipulate a threshold. We deal with other kinds of vagueness by stipulation. Why not do the same here?

To be sure, stipulating a threshold may do some violence to our everyday way of talking about beliefs, but violence may be what is called for. The benefits of increased precision would seem to warrant our discounting sensitivities about ordinary usage. It warrants our simply stipulating, at least for the purpose of doing epistemology, that belief is an attitude of confidence greater than some degree x. This will still leave us with the problem of measurement, of course. Often enough, we will have difficulty determining whether or not you have a degree of confidence x in a proposition, and as a result, we won't be sure whether or not your attitude toward it is one of belief. Moreover, if the difficulty here is not simply one of measurement, if it is sometimes the case that there just isn't any numerically precise degree of confidence that you have in a proposition, then the degree x will itself have to be vague.

In either case, however, the stipulation is likely to be useful when we are discussing issues of rational belief. Indeed, it might not even matter much where we set the threshold, as long as we are forthright about what we are doing. There are some restrictions, of course. We won't want to require subjective certainty for belief; the threshold shouldn't be that high. On the other hand, we will want the threshold to be high enough so that you don't end up believing almost everything whatsoever. At a minimum, we will want to stipulate that for belief you need to have more confidence in a proposition than its negation. But except for these two restrictions, we might seem to be pretty much on our own. What matters, at least for the theory of rational belief, is that some threshold be chosen, for once such a threshold x is stipulated, we can use the Lockean thesis to say what is required for rational belief: It is rational for you to believe P just in case it is rational for you to have degree of confidence y in P, where $y \geq x$.

Or can we? Although at first glance this seems to be an elegant way to think about the relationship between rational belief and rational degrees of belief, a second glance suggests it leads to paradoxes, the most well known of which are those of the lottery and preface. More precisely, it leads to paradoxes, if we make two assumptions about rational belief.

The first assumption is that of noncontradiction: explicitly contradictory propositions cannot be rational. If it is rational for you to believe P, it cannot be rational for you to believe notP. *A fortiori* it is impossible for the proposition (P and notP) to be rational for you. This follows from noncontradiction via simplification: if it is rational for you believe (P & Q), then it is also rational for you to believe each conjunct. Thus, if it is impossible for P and notP both to be rational for you at the same time, it is also impossible for (P & notP) to be rational for you. The second assumption is that rational belief is closed under conjunction: if it is rational for you to believe P and rational for you to believe Q, then it is also rational for you to believe their conjunction, (P & Q).

I will later argue that the second assumption should be rejected. But for now the relevant point is that if both assumptions are granted, the Lockean thesis must be abandoned. The argument is simple. Suppose that degrees of belief can be measured on a scale from 0 to 1, with 1 representing subjective certainty. Nothing in the argument requires this assumption, but it does help clarify the argument's force. So, for the moment at least, grant the assumption. Let the threshold x required for belief be any real number less than 1. For example, let $x = 0.99$. Now imagine a lottery with 100 tickets, and suppose that it is rational for you to believe with full confidence that the lottery is fair and that as such there will be only one winning ticket. More exactly, assume that it is rational for you to believe that (either ticket #1 will win or ticket #2 will win . . . or ticket #100 will win). This proposition is logically equivalent to the proposition that it's not the case that (ticket #1 will not win and ticket #2 will not win . . . and ticket #100 will not win). Assume that you realize this and that as a result, it is also rational for you to believe this proposition.

Suppose finally that you have no reason to distinguish among the tickets concerning their chances of winning. So, it is rational for you to have 0.99 confidence that ticket #1 will not win, 0.99 confidence that ticket #2 will not win, and so on for each of the other tickets. According to the Lockean thesis, it is rational for you to believe each of these propositions, since it is rational for you to have a degree of confidence in each that is sufficient for belief. But given that rational belief is closed under conjunction, it is also rational for you to believe that (ticket #1 will not win and ticket #2 will not win . . . and ticket #100 will not win). However, we have already assumed that it is rational for you to believe the denial of this proposition, since it is rational for you to believe that the lottery is fair. But according to the assumption of noncontradiction, it is impossible for contradictory propositions to be rational for you. So, contrary to the initial hypothesis, x cannot be 0.99.

A little reflection indicates that x cannot be anything other than 1, since the same problem can arise with respect to a lottery of any size whatsoever, no matter how large. However, we have already agreed that x need not be 1.

Subjective certainty is not required for belief. The conclusion, then, is that despite its initial attractiveness, the Lockean thesis cannot be the correct way to think about the relationship between beliefs and degrees of belief. Or more precisely, this is the conclusion if we continue to grant the above two assumptions.

To make matters worse, another argument, similar in form, seems equally devastating to the Lockean thesis from the opposite direction: the preface argument. It seems to show that a degree of confidence greater than 0.5 is not even necessary for belief.

Here is a version of the preface. You write a book, say, a history book. In it you make many assertions, each of which you can adequately defend. In particular, suppose that it is rational for you to have a degree of confidence x or greater in each of these propositions, where x is sufficient for belief but less than 1.0.[7] Even so, you admit in the preface that you are not so naive as to think that your book contains no mistakes. You understand that any book as ambitious as yours is likely to contain at least a few errors. So, it is highly likely that at least one of the propositions that you assert in the book, you know not which, is false. Indeed, if you were to add appendices with propositions whose truth is independent of those you have defended previously, the chances of there being an error somewhere in your book becomes greater and greater. Thus, it looks as if it might be rational for you to believe the proposition that at least one of the claims in your book, you know not which, is false. And insofar as you realize that this proposition is equivalent to the denial of the conjunction of the assertions in your book, it looks as if it might also be rational for you to believe this denial. But given conjunctivity and noncontradiction, it cannot be rational for you to believe this. On the contrary, it must be rational for you to believe the conjunction of the claims in your book. This is so despite the fact that it is rational for you to have a low degree of confidence in this conjunction—a degree of confidence significantly less than 0.5, for example.

These two arguments create a pincer movement on the Lockean thesis. The lottery argument seems to show that no rational degree of confidence less than 1 can be sufficient for rational belief, and the preface argument seems to show that a rational degree of confidence greater than 0.5 is not even necessary for rational belief. Despite being similar in form, the two arguments are able to move against the Lockean thesis from opposite directions because the controlling intuitions about them are different.

The controlling intuition in the lottery case is that it is rational for you to believe that the lottery is fair and that exactly one ticket will win. Unfortunately, the only remotely plausible way to satisfy this intuition without violating either the noncontradiction assumption or the conjunctivity assumption is to insist that 0.99 confidence in a proposition is not sufficient for belief.

On the other hand, the controlling intuition in the preface case is just the opposite. The intuition is that it is rational for you to believe each of the individual propositions in your book. Unfortunately, if we grant this intuition, then given the conjunctivity assumption, we must also admit that it is rational for you to believe the conjunction of the propositions you assert in your book, despite the fact that it is rational for you to have less than 0.5 confidence in it.

Thus, the lottery and the preface might seem to show that the most serious problem for the Lockean thesis has nothing to do with the vagueness of belief. If that were the only problem, it could be dealt with by simply stipulating some degree of belief as the threshold. The problem, rather, is that there doesn't seem to be any threshold, not even a vague one, that we can sensibly stipulate. Anything less than 1.0 is not sufficient for belief and something greater than 0.5 is not even necessary for belief.

Of course, this conclusion follows only if we grant the above two assumptions. A natural reaction, then, is to wonder whether the problems of the lottery and the preface are caused by one or the other of these assumptions rather than the Lockean thesis. This is precisely what I will be arguing, but before doing so, I want to look at another kind of diagnosis of these problems.

The diagnosis is that the problems are the result of our thinking about the lottery and the preface in terms of beliefs *simpliciter* rather than degrees of belief. There is also a recommendation that arises out of this diagnosis. It is that we altogether abandon the epistemology of belief and replace it with an epistemology of degrees of belief. The problems of the lottery and the preface are then easily avoided. We simply observe that it is rational for you to have a high degree of confidence in the individual propositions—in the lottery, the proposition that ticket #1 will lose, that ticket #2 will lose, and so on; and in the preface, the propositions that constitute the body of the book—but a low degree of confidence in their conjunctions. We leave the matter at that, without trying to decide whether it is rational to believe *simpliciter* these propositions. We don't even try to stipulate a threshold of belief. We just quit talking about what it is rational for you believe.

This is exactly what a number of epistemologists have done. They have abandoned the epistemology of belief. They thereby avoid the problem of setting a threshold for belief, and thus make the problems of the lottery and the preface disappear. Moreover, and this is part of the beauty of their strategy, it is not immediately obvious that anything is lost in doing so. After all, what reasons would we have to be interested in a theory of rational belief if we had an adequate theory of rational degrees of belief? Would the former tell us anything useful above and beyond the latter?[8] Is it really needed for anything? It doesn't seem to be needed for the theory of rational decision making, for example. That theory seems to require something more fine-grained than beliefs *simpliciter*. It requires rational degrees of belief. Whether or not it is rational for you to bring about x is a function of its estimated desirability in comparison with your other alternatives, where estimated desirability is roughly a matter of the confidence it is rational for you to have that x will obtain your ends. So, for the general theory of rationality, we seem to be able to get along without a theory of rational belief but not without a theory of rational degrees of belief. But then, why have two theories when one will do just as well?

There are good answers to all these questions, and I will try to give them. I will argue that we do lose something in abandoning the epistemology of belief. For the time being, however, I will simply help myself, without argument, to the assumption that it is not to be altogether abandoned. Doing so will allow me to develop some analogies between the epistemology of belief and the epistemology of degrees of belief, and these analogies in turn will prepare the way for answers to the above questions. Before pursuing these matters, however, it will be helpful to say something about one way of constructing an epistemology of degrees of belief—an approach that can be called 'probabilism'.

3. *Degrees of Belief*

According to probabilists, the central normative requirement governing your degrees of belief is that they be coherent. Assume for the moment that your degrees of belief can be precisely measured on a scale from 0 to 1, with 1 representing maximum confidence in a proposition and 0 minimum confidence. Your degrees of belief are coherent, then, just if they can be construed as subjective probabilities. They must obey the axioms of at least the finitely additive probability calculus.[9] In this way, the probability calculus is used as a logic of opinion.

Consider some simple cases. Since a proposition can be no more probable than a proposition it implies, it is irrational for you to believe a proposition with degree of confidence $x + n$ (where n is positive) if you believe some proposition it implies with degree of confidence x. Similarly, since a proposition must be equiprobable with a proposition that is logically equivalent to it, it is irrational for you to believe a proposition with degree of confidence x if you believe some logically equivalent proposition with degree of confidence y where $x \neq y$. And since the probability of the disjunction of two mutually exclusive propositions is equal to the probability of the first plus the probability of the second, it is irrational for you to believe a disjunction of mutually exclusive propositions with a degree of confidence x if you believe the first disjunct with degree of confidence y and the second with degree of confidence z and $x \neq y + z$.

Examples such as these are potentially misleading, however, since according to probabilists, the primary unit of rational assessment is a system of doxastic attitudes, not the individual attitudes that constitute the system. The individual attitudes themselves are rational (or irrational) only in a derivative sense, by virtue of belonging to a system of attitudes that conform (or do not conform) to the probability calculus. Does this mean that either all or none of your degrees of belief are irrational? Strictly speaking, yes. Still, there may be ways of making this seem less odd. One way is to ask what is rationally required of you if your current degrees of belief are incoherent. Suppose, for example, that you are required to make the minimal alterations necessary in order to restore coherence and that the minimal alterations would involve your altering your degree of belief in P while keeping all of your other degrees of belief stable. Then your degree of belief in P can be singled out as being particularly irrational. Unfortunately, this way of handling the difficulty generates its own questions. Is it always and

everywhere unreasonable for you to make anything less than the minimal alterations necessary to restore coherence? And what makes an alteration a minimal
one?

For purposes here, I will set aside these questions about what is rationally
required of persons whose opinions are irrational. Such questions are difficult to
answer on any view. And in any event, there are other difficulties for probabilism. One immediate difficulty, for example, is that probabilism might seem to
make it too easy for you to be rational. Mere coherence might not seem enough.
Moreover, this worry will be all the more serious if, contrary to the above
assumption, you typically don't have precise degrees of belief in a wide variety
of propositions, for the less comprehensive and the less precise your degrees of
belief, the less exacting is the requirement that they not be incoherent. So, it
would be convenient for probabilists to be able to declare that you have a precise
degree of belief in every proposition that you understand, or at the very least in a
wide variety of propositions.

This doesn't seem to be the case, however. There are many propositions that
you can understand but have never explicitly considered. At least at first glance,
you don't seem to have a precise degree of belief in each of them. But in
addition, you don't seem to have precise degrees of belief in all the propositions
that you have explicitly considered either. You may be significantly more sure
than not that I will be on time for dinner, but your attitude might not be any more
fine-grained than it is. It is important to resist the idea that this possibility can be
safely ruled out from the start. It is perhaps true that you cannot help but have
some degree of belief or other in the propositions that you are explicitly considering, but it is something else again to say that these degrees of belief must be
numerically precise.

Compare belief with love, patience, jealousy, aesthetic pleasure, intellectual
understanding, hope, and other such phenomena. They too come in varying
degrees, but their strengths cannot be measured with numerical precision. And
the problem isn't simply one of our lacking adequate techniques of measurement
at present. The problem is with the phenomena themselves. They lack the requisite kind of richness. The distinctions among them with respect to strength aren't
fine enough.

Of course, we might try to force the issue. We might force you to make very
fine distinctions about how strongly you love various people. But then we are
likely to encounter another kind of problem, a problem of orderliness. The
distinctions you make might not even be transitive, for example. But if not, the
distinctions, albeit fine, won't admit of numerical measurement. They will lack
the requisite orderliness.

Consider an analogy. Your subjective perceptions of sweetness in a beverage
cannot be calibrated in anything like the fine-grained way that the quantity of
sugar in a beverage can be calibrated. Suppose we nonetheless force you to make
fine distinctions among your perceptions of sweetness; this can lead to problems
with orderliness. If we put minutely increasing amounts of sugar in, say, twenty

cups of a beverage, we can set up a sequence that in a blind tasting will tend to produce intransitive perceptions of sweetness. You may perceive cups 1 and 2 as equally sweet, cups 2 and 3 as equally sweet, and so on for each of the other adjacent cups but nonetheless perceive cup 20 as more sweet than cup 1.

Similarly, you ordinarily won't be inclined to make extremely fine distinctions about the strengths of your loves, jealousies, aesthetic pleasures, and the like. On the other hand, if we forced you to do so, these too might turn out to lack the kind of orderliness that is needed for us to assign a numerical measure to them. We must make allowances for a lack of orderliness in whatever view we take of the nature of these phenomena. For example, suppose we think of love in phenomenological terms: it is essentially a feeling that is distinguished from other feelings not so much by its behavioral products as by its special phenomenological character. Maybe this is the right approach, but if so, we need to admit that the feelings are diffuse in a way that precludes there being fine distinctions among them with respect to strength. On the other hand, if we think of love as a disposition of some complicated sort, we will need to admit that this disposition is sufficiently embedded in a network of other, related dispositions as to preclude once again fine distinctions with respect to strength.

It is undeniable that some loves, some jealousies, and some aesthetic pleasures are stronger than others, but it's a mistake to think that they have numerically precise strengths. No doubt we could devise tests—for example, questionnaires, skin stimulation readings, and so on—that would measure numerically the relative strength of your reaction to a person or a situation or whatever, but the problem would be to find a rationale for thinking that it is the strength of your love or jealousy or aesthetic pleasure that we are measuring. This is not to say that loves aren't subtly different from one another, nor that jealousies and aesthetic pleasures are not. On the contrary, these phenomena admit of endlessly fine distinctions. It's just that the distinctions are not primarily ones of strength. Their subtlety is more a matter of the ways in which they can interact with comparable phenomena. Think, for example, of how love can be mixed with resentment, or even hate, of the very same person.

Something similar may be true of beliefs. Subtle distinctions can be made among them, but it may be that the distinctions are not primarily ones of strength. Indeed, this is just what first appearances would suggest. They would suggest, in particular, that the fine distinctions are ones of content, not strength. Neither casual introspection nor casual observation indicates that the strengths of our beliefs are finely distinct from one another. You may be more confident that I will be on time for dinner tonight than that I will remember the book you lent me, but at first glance there wouldn't seem to be a numerically precise way to represent the relative strengths of these two beliefs. Indeed, if we were to request such numbers of you, you ordinarily would be reluctant to supply them, and if we ourselves were to tell you what we think the numbers are, you would be skeptical. You would think that we are mistakenly assuming that your degrees of belief are more precise than they in fact are.

These kinds of considerations don't settle the issue, of course. The point is only that it is a mistake to assume from the start that your degrees of belief cannot help but have precise strengths, the difficulty merely being one of finding out what they are. The assumption may be right, but it is not obviously right. An argument is needed. Moreover, the best argument would be one that described how, contrary to first appearances, your degrees of beliefs can be precisely measured.

Probabilists have tried to supply such arguments. Their basic assumption is that both casual introspection and casual observation are misdirected. Your feelings of conviction are the natural objects of the former, but the strength with which you believe something is not the same as the strength of these feelings. As Ramsey remarked, "The beliefs we hold most strongly are often accompanied by practically no feeling at all; no one feels strongly about things he takes for granted."[10] On the other hand, your everyday actions are the natural objects of casual observation, but they are enmeshed in contexts that make it impossible to see them as the products of some particular degree of belief rather than another.

Nevertheless, according to many probabilists, there is something right about this latter approach. Beliefs, they say, are dispositions that in combination with desires produce behavior. Thus, the right way to determine how strongly you believe something is to determine how strongly you are disposed to act on it, but this, they say, is something best discovered in tests specifically designed to reveal strength of belief. The trick is to find test situations in which your actions can be interpreted, or at least are best interpreted, only as the products of specific degrees of belief.

Various tests have been proposed, some of which are meant to determine both strengths of belief and strengths of desire simultaneously; others are meant to determine only strengths of belief, with minimal assumptions about value lurking in the background. For example, a simple test of the latter sort is one in which you are asked to post odds on the truth of propositions, with your opponent then being free to determine all the other details of the bets, including which side of the bet to take and its size. The odds that you would be willing to post are said to represent your degrees of confidence in these propositions. If the odds you would post on a proposition are x:y, your degree of confidence in it $= x/x + y$.[11]

The most obvious drawback to this suggestion is that if you are like most other individuals, you would volunteer to post precise odds only on a very few propositions, perhaps only on those that concern games of chance and the like. On most others you would be unwilling to do so. Of course, we might force you to set odds, but then the question is whether you chose a particular set of odds rather than another simply because you were forced to choose something. Other odds might be equally agreeable to you. So, why think that the odds you would post reflect your preexisting degrees of confidence in these propositions? Why even think that they reflect your existing degrees of confidence—that is, the degrees of confidence you have, given that you have been forced to post odds? By way of analogy, suppose I tell a bank teller that I do not care whether I am paid in tens or in twenties but that the teller nonetheless insists that I make a choice. I say, "Give me twenties then." Does this show that I was not telling the truth when I said that I was indifferent, that I really preferred the twenties all along? Does it even show that I now prefer the twenties?

Moreover, the odds you would choose to post will vary with what you take to be the nature of the betting situation, including what you take to be the knowledge and skill of your opponent. If you are convinced that your opponent is more knowledgeable than you, the conviction will typically cause you to adopt a more conservative betting strategy than otherwise, which in turn can affect the odds you are willing to post. For example, if you believe that your betting opponent is a perfect calculator of probabilities, you may be disposed to go to great lengths to avoid posting incoherent odds. On the other hand, if you believe that your opponent is a poor calculator, you may not worry as much about avoiding incoherence.[12]

Suppose we attempt to deal with the problem by specifying in detail what you take to be the nature of the betting situation, including your views about the knowledge and skill of your opponent. Then other problems arise. We have now used your beliefs about the betting situation to specify the relevant test, but this was supposed to be a test that we could use to measure your beliefs. Besides, which beliefs are the relevant ones? Should we assume you believe with full confidence that your opponent is more knowledgeable than you? Or should we assume instead that you believe with full confidence that your opponent is as knowledgable as you? Or should we perhaps assume that you have a significant degree of belief in each of these propositions? Or then again, should we assume something altogether different? Moreover, what would be the rationale for making one of these assumptions rather than the others? Why should situations in which you have one of these beliefs rather than another be of special interest? Why are they privileged? Why should the odds that you would set in them be taken as a measure of your degrees of confidence?

There are yet other difficulties. If we say that your confidence in a proposition is to be measured by the odds you would set on it were you in a betting situation of a specified kind K, there are problems with propositions that are concerned with the betting situation itself. In particular, consider the proposition P, that you are now in a betting situation of kind K. Suppose that P is false: you are alone in your office, no one is offering you any bets, and moreover you have no evidence that anyone is doing so. As a result, you have a low degree of confidence in P. But what the above proposal tells us is that your degree of confidence in P is to be measured by the odds you would set on it were you in a situation of kind K. But of course, if you were in a situation of kind K instead of being alone in your office, you might very well post very high odds on the truth of P, since P is the proposition that you are in a situation of kind K. But this in no way shows that you now have a high degree of confidence in P. It only shows that had you been in situation K instead of alone in your office, your degree of belief in P would have been different.[13]

Problems analogous to the above ones will face any other proposed test as well. For example, there is no way to read off precise degrees of belief from your expressed preferences about bets. Consider a test in which you are asked to pick a sum of money such that you would be indifferent between receiving this amount and receiving a ticket that pays you $100 if P is true and $0 if P is false. If you pick, say, $75 as the point of indifference, your strength of belief in P, it might be argued, must be 0.75.[14] The assumption is that your preferences between alternatives reflect your subjective estimated utilities. Thus, if your degree of belief were anything other than 0.75, you would not be indifferent with respect to the two alternatives.[15]

Suppose we ignore any worries about money's not being a suitable unit of value. Even so, the same kind of problems as above arise once again. With most propositions you would feel discomfort at having to state a precise point of indifference. You wouldn't do so willingly. If we force you to do so, then the sums you pick need not reflect your degrees of belief. You simply had to pick some sum.[16] Moreover, whatever sum you choose can be affected by the desirability of P itself, as well as the desirability of the consequences you believe it to have. We might try to handle this problem by imposing yet further conditions, but such conditions cannot themselves make specific presuppositions about what you believe and the degree to which you believe it, since this is what we are trying to measure.[17] Suppose, then, that we ask you to make your choice as if you were indifferent with respect to P and notP considered in themselves and as if you were indifferent as well to whatever you believe their consequences would be. The advantage of this tack is that it does not make specific presuppositions about what you believe. On the other hand, you are now being asked to tell us what sum you *would* pick *were* certain conditions to be met. In effect, we are asking you to make a hypothesis about yourself and your preferences. This is a step yet further away from a natural expression of your preferences, and hence there is even less reason to think that this test invariably provides an accurate measure of your present degrees of belief.

Thus, none of these proposed tests succeed, and no other betting test can succeed either. They cannot succeed even if we grant their theoretical presuppositions. What these tests presuppose is that beliefs and desires are dispositions that combine to produce behavior and that the measure of beliefs and desires is not casual introspection or observation but rather the behavior or the preferences exhibited in these specifically designed tests. The problem is that no piece of betting behavior and no expression of betting preferences is indicative of a specific degree of belief with a specific content. Rather, any number of combinations of degrees of beliefs and desires in any number of propositions might account for the behavior or the preferences, and account for them not just in the sense that they might possibly be the product of any of these combinations. The point here is not one that presupposes some sort of verificationism. The point, rather, is that any number of vastly different combinations will be equally plausible, given the theoretical presuppositions of the tests themselves.

What is true of betting tests is true of behavioral and preferential tests in general. And to make matters worse, it's not just that we cannot go from specific behavior or preferences to specific beliefs and desires. We cannot go in the other direction either. Even if we assume that you have a strong desire for _____ and a strong belief that X will produce _____ , we cannot assume that you prefer X over the other alternatives. Your other beliefs and desires can defeat this belief and desire, so that your strongest disposition may be to do or to prefer something other than X. This is just to say that the worst distorting factors of any proposed behavioral test for beliefs are the presence of phenomena of just the sort that we are trying to measure: other beliefs and desires.

Even if we grant that beliefs and desires are best understood as dispositions that combine to produce behavior, there is a special problem of measurement. The problem is not just the standard one of there possibly being distorting factors. An analogy is not that of measuring the weight of an object by putting it on a scale and then worrying about various factors that might possibly distort the result.[18] A better analogy is that of trying to determine the weights of the various parts of an object when our only tests involve placing the entire object on a scale.

The problem cannot be made to go away by gathering more data. It might seem otherwise. If we found a way for you to express your preferences over a huge range of alternatives, we might seem to be in a better position to assign precise degrees of belief and desire to you. We could proceed in the usual way, assuming that the preferred alternative is always the one with the greater subjective estimated utility, only now we would have many more preferences with which to work. But in fact, gathering more information of the same kind does not help. The problem is still there smirking at us. Different combinations of beliefs and desires will still provide equally plausible interpretations of even these extended preferences.

The extra preferences do make a difference, however. They make the problems of measurement worse, since the more of your preferences we have to work with, the less likely it is that they can be represented as following subjective estimated utilities. For them to be so represented, they must be transitive and trichotomous, and they must also satisfy what Savage calls 'the sure thing principle'.[19] Unfortunately, the empirical evidence indicates that if you have preferences concerning a wide and complex range of alternatives, they are unlikely to satisfy these conditions. Like your subjective perceptions of sweetness for beverages that differ minutely in sugar content, they are unlikely to have the requisite orderliness.[20]

Lack of orderliness isn't at all surprising. It's just what common sense would lead us to suspect. However, it does create a dilemma for anyone who thinks that precise degrees of belief and desire can be teased out from your preferences with the help of the assumption that preference follows subjective estimated utility. On the one hand, the method requires that we have access to a huge number of your preferences; otherwise, we won't have enough data even to begin making fine distinctions with respect to your strengths of belief. On the other hand, if we have access to a huge number of your preferences, they are unlikely to satisfy the ordering conditions that they must satisfy if they are to be represented as following subjective estimated utilities. Moreover, if we fiddle with them to get the required orderliness, or if we ask you to do so, we lose whatever reason we had for thinking that they reflect your current dispositions. It is no longer plausible to think that they can be used to measure your actual degrees of belief.[21]

Of course, we can always fall back on the normative claim. We can insist that if your preferences are to be rational, they must meet these conditions and, thus, they must be representable as following subjective estimated utility. This may be so, but it simply changes the subject. The argument we have been discussing requires assumptions about how we in fact make decisions and what in fact shapes our preferences. The hope was that a requirement of coherence could be made to look more substantial if it could be shown that we typically have precise degrees of belief in a wide variety of propositions, and the further hope was that we could show this by using a theory about our actual preferences—namely, that they follow subjective estimated utility—to generate a plausible and precise measure of our degrees of belief.

The conclusion is inescapable. There are no tests for measuring precise degrees of belief. To be sure, for any proposition P, it will be possible to devise a test that will allow us to extract a number that you can be interpreted as assigning to P. The difficulty is one of finding a rationale for thinking that it is your current degree of belief in P that we are measuring. There isn't a solution to this difficulty.

Might not we nonetheless insist that the problem is merely one of measurement, that you do have precise degrees of belief but that we lack a way of determining what they are? This once again misconstrues the nature of the problem. It's not as if common sense or introspection or something else suggests that you really do have precise degrees of belief but that we run into troubles when we try to determine what they are. The difficulty, rather, is finding any reason whatsoever for thinking that you or anyone else typically do have precise degrees of belief in a wide variety of propositions. Casual introspection and casual observation suggest just the opposite. The strategy was to counter this initial appearance by finding an acceptable test for measuring degrees of belief, but all the proposed tests are inadequate.

In the end we shall just have to admit that you typically do not have precise degrees of confidence.[22] This is especially obvious when you have never explicitly considered the propositions, but it is also obvious for the propositions about which you do have an explicit opinion. Even these opinions are often irremediably vague. You are more confident that your keys are somewhere in your house than in your office, and likewise you are more confident that I will be on time for dinner tonight than that I will remember to bring the book you lent me, but there may be no precise way to rank your degree of belief in either of the first two propositions against your degree of belief in either the third or fourth proposition. Sometimes the most that can be said is that you are highly confident of a proposition's truth, or you are somewhat more confident of its truth than you are of the truth of its negation, or you are roughly as confident of it as its negation.[23]

Probabilists have been increasingly willing to admit that sometimes this is the most that can be said.[23] Consider Bas van Fraassen's views, for example. He concedes that we commonly have only vague degrees of belief, but he nonetheless insists that the probability calculus can be used as a logic of opinion. To illustrate how, van Fraassen introduces the notion of a representor. Your representor is the class of all those probability functions that satisfy your vague degrees of belief. For example, suppose you are more confident that the Yankees will win next year's World Series than you are that the Red Sox will win, and you are more confident of either club's winning than you are of the Cubs' doing so. Only those functions that make the probability of the Yankees' winning greater than that of the Red Sox' winning, and that make the probability of the Red Sox' winning greater than that of the Cubs' winning can satisfy these degrees of belief. The total set of your degrees of belief is rational, then, only if there is some probability function capable of satisfying them all. Of course, if there is one such function, there will be many, but this shows only that there is a variety of ways of making your degrees of belief more precise. On the other hand, if your representor is empty—if no possible assignments of probabilities can satisfy all of your degrees of belief—then there is no way compatible with the probability calculus to make your opinions more precise. On any interpretation, your opinions violate the probability calculus, and thus, says van Fraassen, they are irrational. This is irrationality by way of commission. There is also irrationality by way of omission. If every member of your representor class (that is, if every assignment of probabilities that satisfies your overt judgments) entails that the probability of X is greater than Y but less than Z, then you are committed on pains of irrationality to believing X with greater confidence than Y but with less confidence than Z.[24]

Van Fraassen's kind of view leaves intact the basic idea of probabilism—the idea that it is irrational for your degrees of belief to violate the probability calculus—and it has the advantage of doing so without unrealistic psychological assumptions about the precision of your degrees of belief. The disadvantage of the view is that it leaves untouched the worry with which we began—namely, that no such account is demanding enough. In recognition of this, it is not unusual for probabilists to admit that the avoidance of incoherence is only a necessary condition of rationality. It is not sufficient. There are other requirements as well.[25]

Unfortunately for probabilists, there are even more devastating problems lurking in the other direction. To be sure, coherence isn't nearly sufficient for rationality, but it isn't really necessary either. Thus, the avoidance of incoherence is not only too little to ask for in the name of rationality but also far too much. This is what I will be arguing in the following sections.

4. Inconsistency, Incoherency, and Dutch Books

Why is coherence thought to be a necessary condition of rationality? One answer appeals to the irrationality of making yourself vulnerable to a Dutch book. Suppose that your degree of belief in P is about twice as much as your degree of belief in its negation, and your degree of belief in Q is about the same as its negation. Suppose also that P implies Q . Since a proposition cannot be more probable than a proposition it implies, your degrees of belief violate one of the rules of the probability calculus; they are probabilistically incoherent. If you post odds that reflect these incoherent degrees of belief—for example, if you post 2:1 odds on the truth of P and 1:1 odds on the truth of Q—you will be vulnerable to a Dutch book, which is to say that your opponent can make a series of bets against you such that you will suffer a net loss, no matter how the events you are betting on turn out.[26] For instance, your opponent can bet $1.50 on the truth of Q and $1 on the falsity of P. If Q is true, you will lose $1.50 on Q. You still could win the $1 bet on P, but even if you do, you will suffer a net loss of $.50. On the other hand, if Q is false, you will win $1.50 from your opponent's bet on Q. But since P implies Q , P is false. So, you will lose $2 to your opponent on P. Thus, once again you will suffer a net loss.

This result can be generalized. It can be proved that if your degrees of belief violate the probability calculus and you are willing to post odds that reflect these degrees of belief, then a skillful enough opponent can make a Dutch book against you. From this one might try inferring that it is always irrational to have incoherent degrees of belief, but there is no proof of this.[27] There is no proof even if we assume that it is always irrational for you to make yourself vulnerable to a Dutch book, for even with this assumption, what follows is that it is irrational to accept bets at odds that reflect your degrees of belief when these degrees are incoherent. What degree of confidence it is rational for you to have in a proposition is one matter, what odds if any it is rational for you post on it is another.[28] It does not help to stipulate that the situation is one in which you are forced to bet in accordance with your degrees of belief, for then the conclusion is that it is irrational for you to have incoherent degrees of belief if you find yourself in this kind of forced betting situation. Another argument would be needed to show that this is irrational when you are not being forced.

Besides, any assumption about your being willing or being forced to bet in accordance with your degrees of belief brings in considerations that are irrelevant to your epistemic concerns. It brings in pragmatic considerations.[29] These considerations may give you a reason not to have incoherent degrees of belief, providing that you are willing or forced to bet in accordance with them, but the reasons are not epistemic ones. Rather, they are the kind of reasons that, according to Pascal, everyone has to be a theist.

Still, there may be something here short of a proof. The argument is perhaps best construed as one from analogy. It begins with the assumption that it is irrational for you to allow Dutch books to be made against you. It is next noted that there are important structural similarities between a situation in which you allow book to be made against you and one in which you have incoherent degrees of belief, the hypothesis then being that the features that make the former irrational also make latter irrational.

What are the features? If the odds you post are incoherent and if as a result book is made against you, you will lose money however the events you are betting on turn out. Thus, you can know in advance that your betting goals will be frustrated. But it is irrational to do that which you know cannot possibly be an effective means to your goals. Hence, it is irrational to post incoherent odds. This is an instance of practical irrationality, since the goal you would be frustrating is a practical one. Analogously, it is irrational to have incoherent degrees of belief. As with Dutch books, you can know in advance that if you have incoherent degrees of belief, a goal of yours will be frustrated, only here the goal is an intellectual one and hence the irrationality is epistemic, not practical.

For the moment, set aside the question of what your goal is, and consider instead the related question that arises for the epistemology of belief, assuming for the time being that such an epistemology is not to be abandoned. The question is whether beliefs *simpliciter* must be consistent if they are to be rational. Even if there is no non-question-begging way of proving that it is always irrational to have inconsistent beliefs, we might be able to offer something short of a proof. We might be able to explain or at least illustrate what is wrong with having inconsistent beliefs. Indeed, the explanation might seem to be obvious: if you have inconsistent beliefs, you can know in advance that whatever kind of place the world is, at least some of your beliefs are false. Thus, you can know in advance that one of your intellectual goals will be frustrated—the goal of having accurate beliefs.

What is the analogous goal that incoherence inevitably frustrates? The natural answer is, the goal of having accurate degrees of beliefs. But degrees of belief, unlike beliefs *simpliciter*, are not straightforwardly true or straightforwardly false. So, there is a problem as to what this answer amounts to. But here, F. P. Ramsey hinted at a promising approach: degrees of belief are accurate if they match the objective probabilities.[30] So, the role that truth plays for belief, objective probabilities play for degrees of belief.

To be sure, the approach leaves us with the problem of saying what these objective probabilities are, and there are philosophers who so despair of finding a satisfactory solution to this problem that they have made themselves content with the idea that there are only subjective probabilities. Indeed, much of the classic work on rational degrees of belief is inspired by the prospect of getting along without objective probabilities. Doing so turns out not to be so easy. Our best ways of understanding the world seem to require some notion of objective probability. For example, we need to be able to talk about the probability of a tritium atom's decaying within six months. There is no reason in principle why philosophers who endorse probabilistic coherence as the central normative requirement governing our degrees of belief cannot also endorse this kind of talk of objective probabilities. And an increasing number of philosophers are doing precisely that.[31]

Besides, we are not altogether without ideas about how to understand objective probabilities, and among the most promising are those that allow a subjective contribution to the notion of objective probability. This may sound like an oxymoron, but it's not. Our choices, or our beliefs, or our conventions, may have some role to play in shaping the notion of objective probability without its being the case that the truth of objective probability assertions is ultimately dependent upon these choices, beliefs, or conventions. Once we have made our subjective contribution to these assertions, the matter of their truth is out of our hands.

Thus, for example, van Fraassen suggests that one's degrees of belief are accurate if they conform to the objective probabilities, and for him this is ultimately a matter of their being calibrated with actual frequencies. To take the simplest of cases, if you have degree of confidence 0.6 that it will rain today, you have an accurate degree of confidence just in case it rains on 60 percent of the days that are relevantly similar to today. What makes a day relevantly similar to today? Van Fraassen suggests there is no determinate recipe for the selection of an appropriate reference class. Accordingly, on this question he departs from a standard frequentist program. He insists on allowing an element of subjective choice in the selection of the reference classes that determine the objective probabilties of an event. However, once you have made your choice, it is an objective matter whether or not your degrees of beliefs are calibrated with the actual frequencies. This depends on the world, not on you (except in the special case where you have control over the events in question). In addition, van Fraassen points out that your freedom to choose is not unconstrained. Once you have chosen (at least implicitly) reference classes in arriving at your degrees of confidence for some propositions, your freedom to choose reference classes and to arrive at degrees of belief for other propositions is constrained by the requirement that your judgments not violate the probability calculus.[32]

The approach, no doubt, will have its share of difficulties. Still, the core idea is so simple and appealing that it demands tolerance. The idea is that there are objective probabilities as well as subjective degrees of belief and that one of our intellectual goals is to have our subjective degrees of belief conform to the objective probabilities, however exactly these are to be understood, whether as frequencies or propensities or in some other way. We want in this sense to be calibrated with the objective probabilities. The further suggestion is that this may help explain why it is irrational to have incoherent degrees of belief: if your subjective probabilities are incoherent, you can know that the goal will be frustrated however things turn out. You can know in advance that calibration is impossible.

Thus, at least at first appearance, there seem to be useful analogies among these three proposed requirements of rationality: (1) the requirement that rational bets not be vulnerable to Dutch books, (2) the requirement that rational beliefs not be inconsistent, and (3) the requirement that rational degrees of belief not be incoherent. Indeed, the analogies are close enough that the same general assumption about rationality can apparently be used to explain why each is a requirement of rationality—namely, the assumption that it is irrational for you to do or believe that which you can know in advance cannot possibly be an effective means to your goals.

Nevertheless, the explanation won't do. On the contrary, none of these are strict requirements of rationality. More exactly, they are not strict requirements of egocentric rationality. It is not always and everywhere egocentrically irrational to have inconsistent beliefs, nor is it always and everywhere egocentrically irrational to have incoherent degrees of belief, nor is it always and everywhere egocentrically irrational to make oneself vulnerable to a Dutch book.

None of the conditions are strict requirements of egocentric rationality, if for no other reason than at least some Dutch books, some incoherencies, and some inconsistencies are beyond the cognitive powers of normal humans to discern. Thus, it is not the case that whenever book is made against you, or your beliefs are inconsistent, or your degrees of belief are incoherent, you will be able to know in advance that one of your goals will be frustrated. No matter how careful and thorough you are, some Dutch books and some inconsistencies and some incoherencies may escape you. But the above requirements demand in the name of rationality not just that you try to avoid inconsistency, incoherency, and Dutch books. The idea is not simply that this is a goal that you must strive for. The idea, rather, is that if you are to be egocentrically rational, you must actually succeed. A failure to do so is always and everywhere irrational.

Thus, each of these three conditions in effect presupposes the perspective of a perfect calculator. The condition prohibiting inconsistency presupposes the perspective of a perfect calculator of logical relations, and the other two conditions presuppose the perspective of a perfect calculator of probabilities. Something is rational for you to believe or do only if it is something that a perfect calculator would believe or do in your situation. But a perfect calculator is always able to detect and hence avoid inconsistency. Likewise, a perfect calculator is always able to detect assignments of probabilities that violate the probability calculus and as a result is always able to detect incoherent degrees of beliefs and Dutch books.

Unfortunately, you are not a perfect calculator. Nor can you be. Some logical and probabilistic relations are so complex that you are not capable of understanding them. This is so even if in principle all such relations could be broken down into simpler ones that you can understand. Combinations of these simpler relations can still be so complex as to exceed your capacities. You do well enough in most circumstances, no doubt. Indeed, it may be a condition of your believing something at all that you recognize many of its most obvious implications. Likewise, it may be a condition of your having beliefs at all that there is a limit to your inconsistency and incoherency. You must be an adequate enough calculator. Your status as a believer and agent may depend upon it. On the other hand, it does not depend upon your being a perfect calculator.[33] Indeed, you lack the cognitive powers to be such. Why, then, should we be interested in a theory of rationality that presupposes the perspective of a perfect calculator?

The lack of concern that probabilists have shown for this question might suggest that there is an easy answer to it. And in fact, there does seem to be. The perfect calculator represents an ideal to which you aspire. As such, it can be used to measure your irrationality, and this is so even if it is an ideal you are incapable of satisfying. It is enough that you can do better or worse jobs of approximating it. The more closely you approximate it, the more rational you are.

Compare this with idealizations in science. Scientists theorize about idealized entities in idealized circumstances, ones that model the real phenomena less than perfectly. The gas laws apply first and foremost to perfect gases. The laws of conservation and momentum apply first and foremost to closed and isolated systems. Nonetheless, such laws help explain real phenomena. They do so because the actual phenomena approximate the workings of the idealized model.

Why shouldn't we use analogous idealizations in the theory of rationality? In particular, suppose we take it as a working assumption, a presupposition for our theorizing about rationality, that the best way to measure your rationality is to compare what you do and believe with what an ideally rational being would do or believe in your situation.[33] Doesn't this presupposition solve the difficulty?

It would if it were both relevant and plausible, but it cannot be both. If construed in one way, the presupposition is irrelevant to the question at hand; if construed in another, it is implausible. If by an ideally rational agent we mean someone who is like you but who does and believes only what is rational, then your rationality can indeed be measured by comparing what you do and believe with what this ideally rational agent would do and believe in your situation. However, this makes the above presupposition irrelevant to the question at hand, since such an agent is no more or less capable of determining logical and probabilistic relations than you are. Insofar as the problem is showing that even the incoherencies, inconsistencies, and Dutch books that are beyond your ken can make you irrational, an appeal to what this kind of ideally rational agent would do or believe is useless. Indeed, it is worse than useless, for if there are incoherencies, inconsistencies, and Dutch books that not even this ideally rational agent would avoid, then the same incoherencies, inconsistencies, and Dutch books need not make you irrational either.

On the other hand, the above presupposition is implausible if by an ideally rational agent we mean someone whose cognitive capacities exceed yours. The problem now is that although it may always be rational for such an agent to avoid incoherencies, inconsistencies, and Dutch books, it is no longer clear what this has to do with you. What is the concrete action that it would be rational for Superman to take if he finds himself in the path of a speeding train? Perhaps to stick out his hand, since given his abilities, the act would stop the train. No one will suggest that this is the rational thing for you to do in such a situation. It is no more plausible to suggest that it is always and everywhere egocentrically rational for you to believe only that which a logical Superman would believe in your situation. It is one thing to measure your rationality by comparing what you do and believe with what you or someone with abilities recognizably similar to yours would ideally do and believe. It is quite another to do so by comparing what you do and believe with what some ideally powerful being would do or believe.

Idealizations in epistemology have their limits. The limits are vague, just as they are in science, but if our theory is to be one of human rationality, the limits cannot be allowed to exceed that which is recognizably human. Theories of human rationality must be concerned with human points of view. The relevant point of view might be your point of view idealized. It might be a matter of what you would do or think were you to be ideally reflective and ideally careful. However, it cannot be a matter of what someone with ideal cognitive powers would do or think in your situation. The rough rule is that we are to limit ourselves to idealizations of the conditions under which you, as a normal human being, employ your various cognitive abilities and skills. Thus, we can legitimately idealize away various distorting conditions, ones that interfere with the operation of these abilities and skills, and similarly we can idealize away constraints on the time you have available to employ these abilities and skills. We can imagine, for example, that you have only one end—say, to discover the truth about a proposition P—and that all your time can be devoted to using your abilities and skills in pursuit of this end. But we are to avoid idealizations of the abilities and skills themselves. Ideal-observer theories are no more plausible in epistemology than they are in ethics.[34]

The temptation to deem ideal-observer theories plausible can be discouraged by remembering that not every intellectual ideal is an ideal of rationality. It may be ideal to believe with full confidence all and only the propositions that are true, but no one thinks that the distance that you depart from this ideal is in general a measure of your irrationality.[35] Or alternatively, it may be ideal to have degrees of belief that are perfectly calibrated with objective probabilities, but again no one should think that the distance you depart from this ideal is in general a measure of your irrationality. Being ideally rational is not the same thing as being ideally accurate. Indeed, any notion of rationality is in part a notion of understandable mistakes. The fact that you have made a mistake of belief indicates that your belief system is less than ideally accurate, but it need not indicate that it is less than ideally rational.

This raises a more radical suspicion about consistency, coherency and the avoidance of Dutch books. The suspicion is that not only are they not prerequisites of egocentric rationality, they are not prerequisites of human rationality in any other interesting sense either. Any theory that incorporates these as utterly strict conditions of rationality would be presupposing the perspective of someone who is logically perfect but empirically imperfect. In effect, such theories ask us to imagine what someone with perfect logical knowledge but limited empirical knowledge would do or believe in your situation. Since such a being would recognize and avoid inconsistency, incoherency, and Dutch books, it is supposed to be irrational in the designated sense for your beliefs to be inconsistent, your degrees of belief to be incoherent, and your bets to be vulnerable to Dutch books. On the other hand, since such a being need not be able to recognize all beliefs that are only contingently false, or all degrees of belief that are only contingently inaccurate, or all bets that are only contingently losing bets, it is not always irrational for you to have such beliefs or make such bets.

The question is why the perspective of beings with a combination of logical savvy and empirical ignorance should be of particular interest to us in our evaluations of one another's beliefs? Any epistemology presupposing such a perspective asks us to think about questions of rational belief in a peculiar way. It asks us to use the extent to which you depart from logical omniscience as a measure of your irrationality but not to use the extent to which you depart from empirical omniscience as a comparable measure. But if a logically omniscient perspective, one in which we make no mistakes in calculating logical implications and probabilities, is an ideal perspective, one to which we aspire and one that we can do a better or worse job of approximating, so too is an empirically omniscient perspective. If this were a reason to regard all departures from logical omniscience as departures from ideal rationality, it would be an equally good reason to regard all departures from empirical omniscience as departures from ideal rationality. But of course, no one wants to assert this.

Why, then, are many epistemologists inclined to regard all departures from logical omniscience as departures from some kind of ideal rationality? I have two conjectures, neither flattering. The first is that it is largely a matter of theoretical convenience. Epistemologists want rational belief-systems to have a characteristic structure. Logic and probability theory conveniently provide epistemologists with such a structure. So, they are seduced into thinking that mistakes in calculating logical implications and probabilities are always symptomatic of irrationality and other mistakes are not, despite the fact that there is no obvious rationale for such an asymmetry and despite the fact that it forces us to conclude, for example, that Frege's beliefs about how to axiomatize set theory, as expressed in *The Basic Laws of Arithmetic*, were irrational, since they turned out to be inconsistent.[36]

The second conjecture is that the temptation arises out of a view of human reason that has largely been discarded but whose influence nonetheless lingers. According to this view, reason is conceived as a special faculty that is tacked onto our other cognitive faculties and whose operations are sharply distinct from them. The other faculties—those associated with perceiving, remembering, introspecting, and imagining, for example—are arational. They simply provide raw data for reason. Reason's job is to work with these data. It is to perform calculations upon them, correcting inconsistencies as well as drawing out implications.[37] Without this special faculty of reason, we would be arational. With it, we are capable of both rationality and irrationality. When reason performs its calculations well, we are rational. Otherwise we aren't.[38]

Radical empiricist positions—phenomenalism, for example—constitute the purest expressions of such views. Our various senses provide reason with arational data—sense data—and then reason performs its complicated computations on it. Of course, not many philosophers are prepared to defend phenomenalism anymore,[39] and likewise not many would be prepared to defend the view of rationality it presupposes. A more plausible view, we think, is that our cognitive faculties are reason-saturated. Judgment and hence reason pervade everything: perceiving, remembering, introspecting, and so on. Correspondingly, sheer calculation is a relatively minor part of our rationality.

Still, the outlines of the older picture can be discerned in views that make consistency and coherency strict requirements of rationality. Beliefs have merely replaced sense data as the input. Perception, memory, introspection, imagination, and the like are belief-producing mechanisms. They produce a huge range of beliefs, from the relatively simple perceptual to the more complex theoretical ones. However, reason's function is essentially the same. It is to take the data that are given to it from other sources and perform calculations upon them, checking them for inconsistency, incoherency, and the like. If the checks are not done accurately, if some inconsistencies and incoherencies remain, we are to that extent irrational. Thus, mistakes of logic and the like are invariably symptomatic of irrationality and other kinds of mistakes are not. The former are symptomatic of irrationality because they are due to less than perfect workings of the special faculty of reason, and our other mistakes are due to the less than perfect workings of essentially arational processes such as perceiving, introspecting, remembering, imagining, and so on.

In any event, the important point for purposes here is not so much whether these conjectures are correct or not. Rather, it is the more modest point that avoiding inconsistency, incoherency, and Dutch books is not a strict condition of egocentric rationality. Otherwise, every logical mistake and every mistake in calculating probabilities that manifests itself in your beliefs would be irrational; you would never make such mistakes insofar as you are rational.[40] This would be so even if from your point of view there would seem to be overwhelming evidence in favor of the mistaken conclusion. But then, even if we grant that which is doubtful—namely, that there is some interesting sense in which all such mistakes are irrational—the sense cannot be one of egocentric rationality. By definition what is egocentrically rational for you is a matter of your own perspective. It is a matter of what is within your ken. To be egocentrically rational is essentially a matter of being invulnerable to self-criticism. But not all logical and probabilistic relations are within your ken, and hence not all logical and probabilistic mistakes need make you vulnerable to self-criticism. Some are too complicated for you. Perhaps any logical relation can in principle be broken down into a series of simpler relations, each of which taken individually you could grasp. Still, the thing in its entirety may be beyond you.

5. Being Knowingly Inconsistent

Neither coherency nor consistency nor the avoidance of Dutch books is a strict prerequisite of egocentric rationality. Still, on the assumption that one of your goals is to have an accurate belief system and another is to win your bets, it might be irrational to violate any of these conditions knowingly. After all, were you to do so, you would be knowingly frustrating one of your goals.

Philosophers have shown little interest in this as a fallback position,[41] perhaps because it leaves us within the circle of epistemic terms from which we are trying to escape. We will now need to say what it is to be knowingly incoherent or knowingly inconsistent. In addition, the position threatens the simplicity of our epistemological models. We can no longer read off strict conditions of rationality from the rules of logic and probability.

Despite these drawbacks, a position of this sort does have an initial appeal. Think of Dutch books, for example. Granted, you might unknowingly post incoherent odds. This is understandable, given your limited abilities. But isn't it always irrational to post such odds if you recognize they will allow your opponent to make book against you and if in addition you value money (or whatever else that is at risk from the bet)? And by analogy, isn't it also always irrational for you knowingly to have inconsistent beliefs or incoherent degrees of belief?

Later I will argue that the answer to even the first of the questions is no.[42] For the moment, assume that it is always irrational for you knowingly to allow someone to make book against you. Nevertheless, this doesn't commit us to answering yes to the second question. On the contrary, the analogy between having a book made against you on the one hand, and having inconsistent beliefs and incoherent degrees of beliefs on the other, is weak. The distinguishing feature of the first is that no matter how the events you are betting on turn out, you will suffer a net loss. The distinguishing feature of the other two is that no matter how the world turns out, you will do less well than what is ideal. If your beliefs are mutually inconsistent, then not all of them can be true; and if your degrees of belief are incoherent, not all of them can be calibrated with the objective probabilities. Hence, if you know that your beliefs are inconsistent or that your degrees of belief are incoherent, you know that they are less than ideally accurate. But to say that an option is sure to be less than ideal is not yet to say that it is sure to be irrational. In fact, it often isn't. Moreover, there are betting situations that provide clear illustrations of this. These kinds of betting situations are more directly relevant to cases of inconsistent beliefs and incoherent degrees of belief than situations in which you are vulnerable to a Dutch book. So, if we are going to rely on betting analogies to draw lessons about rational belief, one of the lessons will be that it can be rational for you to choose options that you know are less than ideal.

I have in mind betting situations in which you agree to a series of bets despite the fact that you are guaranteed to lose at least one of them. Nonetheless, it can be rational for you to agree to the series. Indeed, the series may even be optimal for you. It can be optimal even if it is not ideal. The ideal would be to win each and every bet, but your situation may be such that the necessarily flawed strategy is preferable to any that keeps open the possibility of an ideal outcome.

Imagine that you are given the opportunity to play the following game. There are ten cups on a table, numbered 1–10, and you know that nine of the ten cups each cover a pea. You are asked to predict of each cup whether or not it covers a pea. For each correct answer you receive $1 and for each incorrect answer you pay $1.

What is the best strategy for you in the game? Bet 'pea' on each cup. The payoff from this strategy will be $8, with your winning nine of the bets and losing one. What are your alternatives? One alternative is to guess which cup doesn't have a pea under it and to bet 'nonpea' on it. By doing so, you keep open the possibility of an ideal result, one in which you win every bet, but your estimated payoff is only $6.40.[43] Another alternative is to bet 'pea' on nine of the cups while refusing to bet on some arbitrary cup. This strategy precludes the possibility of an ideal outcome, since you do not even try to win every bet. However, it does leave open the possibility of a flawless outcome, one in which you win each of your bets. Nevertheless, the estimated payoff of $7.20 is still below that of betting 'pea' on each cup.[44] Finally, if you were to refuse all the bets, the payoff would be $0.

The lesson is that it can be rational for you to prefer a strategy that you know precludes an ideal outcome over one that does not. This is as true of doxastic strategies as it is of betting strategies. What is wrong with consistency requirements on belief and coherency requirements on degrees of belief is that they fail to recognize the lesson.

Consider inconsistency first, leaving incoherency until the next section. The issue is whether with respect to the synchronic goal of having accurate and comprehensive beliefs, it can be egocentrically rational for you knowingly to have inconsistent beliefs. The issue is not what you can responsibly believe, given constraints on your time and given your other goals.[45] If it were, it would be easy to defend a tolerant attitude toward inconsistency. Putting up with a minor inconsistency will sometimes be preferable to going to the trouble of correcting it. The matter may not be important enough to warrant your giving it a second thought. Even so, this is irrelevant to the challenge at hand, which is to defend the idea that sometimes it is rational even in a purely epistemic sense for you to tolerate inconsistency. This is rational, in other words, even if your only concern is the accuracy and comprehensiveness of your beliefs. Of course, you know that inconsistent beliefs cannot possibly be ideal. You know that at least one is false. Nevertheless, this doesn't rule out the possibility of their being rational. There are situations in which it is egocentrically rational for you to have beliefs that you know are neither ideal nor even flawless.[46]

This is the real lesson of the lottery and the preface. It can be rational to believe that the lottery is fair and that as such exactly one ticket will win and also rational to believe of each and every ticket that it will not win. After all, if the lottery is large, the evidence that you have in favor of the proposition that ticket #1 will not win is extremely strong, as strong as you have for almost any empirical proposition whatsoever. But of course, you have equally strong evidence for the proposition that ticket #2 will not win, the proposition that ticket #3 will not win, and so on.

Similarly, it can be rational for you to believe each and every proposition that you defend in your book even though it is also rational for you to declare in the preface that at least one of these propositions is false. Once again, you might have enormously strong evidence for each of the propositions in the body of the book, and yet given their huge number, you might also have enormously strong evidence for the proposition that at least one of them is false.

Situations of this sort are not even uncommon. Most of us have very strong but not altogether certain evidence for a huge variety of propositions, evidence that makes these propositions rational for us. And yet we also have strong evidence for our fallibility about such matters, evidence that can make it rational for us to believe of a set of such propositions that at least one is false. If it were always and everywhere irrational to be knowingly inconsistent, this would be impossible. It would be impossible for us knowingly and rationally to have these kinds of fallibilist beliefs. But it isn't impossible, and any theory that implies otherwise should be rejected for this reason.[47]

Part of the reluctance of philosophers to admit that it is sometimes rational to be knowingly inconsistent stems from a fear that if mutually inconsistent propositions can be rational, then so too can explicitly contradictory ones. In the lottery, for example, the fear is that we will be forced to say that it is rational for you to believe the proposition that some ticket will win as well as the proposition that it's not the case that some ticket will win. These fears would be justified if it were rational for you to believe the conjunction of each and every proposition that is rational for you, but precisely what the lottery, the preface, and other such cases illustrate is that this need not be so. In the lottery, you have enormously strong evidence for the proposition that some ticket will win as well as for the proposition that ticket #1 will not win, the proposition that ticket #2 will not win, and so on. The conjunction of these propositions is that (ticket #1 will not win & ticket #2 will not win . . . & ticket #n will not win), which is logically equivalent to the proposition that it's not the case that some ticket will win. However, you do not have strong evidence for this conjunction. On the contrary, you have strong evidence for its denial. Similarly for the preface case. You have strong evidence for each of the assertions you make in your book. Nevertheless, you do not have strong evidence for their conjunction. Indeed, you have strong evidence for its denial.[48]

Contrast this treatment of lottery and preface cases with the treatment described earlier.[49] There the suggestion was that these cases show the inadequacy of the Lockean thesis and thus by extension show that the epistemology of belief ought to be abandoned in favor of an epistemology of degrees of belief. The argument was based on the assumption that any adequate theory of rational belief must contain a conjunction rule—that is to say, it must make rational belief closed under conjunction. The preface and the lottery were then used to show that any such theory of rational belief faces absurd consequences, from which it was inferred that we ought to abandon the theory of rational belief.

My strategy is to stand this argument on its head. I begin by presuming that the project of formulating an epistemology of belief, at least on the face of it, is a legitimate project. The second premise is the same as above: any theory of rational belief must either reject the conjunction rule or face absurd consequences. I conclude that we ought to reject the conjunction rule, which in any event is not a plausible rule. After all, a conjunction can be no more probable than its individual conjuncts, and often it will be considerably less probable.

Why, then, has it so often been unquestioningly presumed that an adequate theory of rational belief must contain a conjunction rule? Part of the explanation may be that knowledge is commonly thought to be closed under conjunction, and knowledge is also commonly thought to be roughly a matter of having a rational true belief. However, considerations of this sort are irrelevant when questions of egocentric rationality are at issue. They are irrelevant because a belief can be both true and egocentrically rational and yet still not be a particularly good candidate for knowledge.[50]

But it isn't simply a failure to distinguish rational belief from knowledge that accounts for the hold of this idea. There are also more serious worries at work here, ones that go to the heart of how we think and argue. If we are not required on pains of irrationality to believe the conjunction of propositions that we rationally believe, we might seem to lose some of our most powerful argumentative and deliberative tools. Indeed, it might even seem as if deductive reasoning entirely loses its force, since without a conjunction rule, we can believe each of the premises of an argument whose deductive validity we acknowledge and yet deny that this commits us to believing its conclusion.[51]

Anyone who rejects a conjunction rule for rational belief must find a plausible way of dealing with this worry. A good way of beginning is to admit that some sort of conjunction rule is essential for deductive reasoning. This much is undeniable. What can be denied, however, is that the relevant conjunction rule is one for beliefs. A conjunction rule does govern many belief-like attitudes. For example, it governs presuming, positing, assuming, supposing, and hypothesizing. Each of these attitudes is a form of commitment that, unlike belief, is context-relative. You don't believe a proposition relative to certain purposes but not believe it relative to others. You either believe it or you don't. But presuming, positing, and assuming are not like this. Having such attitudes toward a proposition is a matter of your being prepared to regard the proposition as true for a certain range of purposes or in a certain range of situations. Moreover, relative to these purposes or situations, the attitudes are conjunctive. If for the purposes of a discussion you assume (suppose, posit, and so on) P and if for that same discussion you also assume (suppose, posit, and so on) Q, then you are committed within that context to their conjunction, and you are committed as well to anything their conjunction implies.

Purely deductive reasoning is typically carried on in terms of such attitudes rather than beliefs. Suppose, for example, that you deduce R from P and Q. If you don't believe either P or Q, the reasoning process cannot be characterized as one that directly involves beliefs. It is not a matter, for example, of your moving from your beliefs in P and Q to a belief in R. The attitudes involved are weaker than beliefs. For purposes of your deliberations, you have assumed or posited P and you have done the same for Q.

Suppose, on the other hand, that you do believe both P and Q. This doesn't alter the nature of the deductive reasoning, and one sign of this is that the deduction has no determinant consequences for what you believe. In deducing R from P and Q, you can just as well abandon P or abandon Q (or both) as believe R. The deductive reasoning considered in itself is neutral among these alternatives. Thus once again, it cannot be construed as a matter of moving from belief to belief. You may be engaging in the reasoning in order to test your beliefs P and Q, but the reasoning itself must be regarded as involving attitudes that are distinct from belief. For the purposes of the test, you hypothetically suspend belief in P and Q and adopt an attitude toward each that is weaker than belief. You assume or posit both P and Q and from these assumptions deduce R. You are then in a position to deliberate about whether to abandon P or Q (or both) or to believe R. The latter kind of deliberation does directly concern your beliefs, but on the other hand it is not deductive reasoning.[52]

But even if this is admitted—that is, even if it is admitted that deductive reasoning must be regarded as involving attitudes distinct from belief—it doesn't end the worries. After all, without a conjunctive rule governing beliefs, wouldn't we lose the regulative role that considerations of consistency play in our deliberations about what to believe? Suppose, for example, that someone constructs a *reductio* argument out of a number of propositions that you believe. If rational belief need not be conjunctive and if as a result you can knowingly but rationally have inconsistent beliefs, it seems as if you could acknowledge the validity of this *reductio* without its having any effect whatsoever on your beliefs.

The way to deal with this worry is to be clear about the nature of *reductios*. *Reductios* prove that the conjunction of their premises cannot possibly be true. They prove inconsistency. However, they need not show which of the presupposed premises is false. They only sometimes do this and then only in a derivative way by proving that the conjunction is false. If all of the premises but one are uncontroversial for you, with the remaining one posited for the purpose of the *reductio*, then a valid *reductio*, in proving the conjunction to be false, gives you a decisive reason to reject this premise. More generally, in proving that the conjunction is false, *reductios* provide a potentially powerful argument against any given premise of the argument, but the strength of this argument is a matter of how closely the truth of this premise is tied to the truth of the conjunction.

Suppose, for example, that the premises are so theoretically intertwined with one another that they tend to stand or fall together. An argument against the truth of their conjunction will then constitute a strong argument against each premise as well. Alternatively, the truth of a premise might be tied to the truth of the conjunction not so much because it is theoretically interdependent with the other premises but rather because the other premises are so strong in comparison with it and so few in number. The weaker the premise and the fewer the number of other premises, the stronger is the argument against that premise. So, if one premise is distinctly weak while the others are strong and if there is a relatively small number of premises, a *reductio* will provide a devastating argument against this weakest premise.

On the other hand, there are examples of *reductios* whose premises are not like this. Their premises aren't so theoretically intimate that they tend to stand or fall together. Moreover, even the weakest premise is relatively strong and the number of premises is large. But if so, the strength of the argument against even this weakest premise may be only negligible. This is the reverse of the idea, common enough in contemporary epistemology, that although consistency among a very small or theoretically untight set of propositions doesn't have much positive epistemic significance, consistency among a very large and theoretically tight set does.[53] My assertion is that although inconsistency among a very large and untight set of propositions need not have much negative epistemic significance, inconsistency among a very small or very tight set does. The latter precludes each member of the set's being rational for you to believe, but the former need not.

This is not to say that the discovery of inconsistency among a very large and untight set of propositions is irrelevant epistemically. It isn't. Inconsistency is always an indication of inaccuracy, and because of this, it always will be a relevant consideration insofar as your aims are epistemic. It must always be taken into account. But as I will later argue, there are ways of doing so short of an absolute prohibition on knowingly believing inconsistent propositions. In particular, the prohibition may be one not so much of belief as evidence. Even if you are sometimes permitted to believe such propositions, you might not be permitted to base further inquiry on them. The idea, in other words, is that something can be rational for you to believe without its being the case that you can unrestrictedly use it as evidence to argue for or against other propositions.[54]

So, a convincing *reductio* does show that it is irrational for you to believe the conjunction of its premises, and it puts you on alert about each of the individual premises as well. This, in turn, may result in restrictions on how these propositions can be used as evidence. Even so, the case against the individual premises need not be so great as to make it irrational for you to believe them. The lottery, the preface, and the more general case of a fallibilist belief about your other beliefs provide particularly clear examples of this. In each of these cases, it is possible to construct a *reductio* entirely out of propositions that you believe, but a huge number of propositions are needed for these *reductios*. So, despite the fact that a *reductio* can be constructed out of them, the propositions aren't serious competitors of one another. Nor are they so deeply intertwined with one another theoretically that they tend to stand or fall together.

Such cases are by no means rare, but they aren't the rule either. The discovery of inconsistency typically does make for effective *reductios, reductios* that constitute powerful arguments against one or more members of the inconsistent set of propositions, and when they do, it is irrational to believe the propositions.

But it is precisely the rejection of the conjunction rule that allows us to say when *reductios* can be so used and when they cannot.

Of course, rejecting the conjunction rule does preclude one use of *reductios*. It precludes their being used to prove that knowingly believing inconsistent propositions is always and everywhere irrational. But this is hardly a criticism, since precisely the issue in question is whether this is always and everywhere irrational. I say that it is not; that the lottery, the preface, and the case of a fallibilist belief about one's other beliefs plainly illustrate this; and that attempts to deny the obvious in these cases are based in part upon a failure to distinguish various senses of rational belief, in part upon a failure to distinguish evidence from rational belief, and in part upon the unfounded worry that if inconsistencies are allowed anywhere they will have to be allowed everywhere.[55]

Besides, what are the alternatives to rejecting the conjunction rule? They are to give up on the epistemology of belief altogether or find some other way of dealing with the preface and the lottery within the confines of a theory of rational belief that retains the conjunction rule. But on this point, the critics of theories of rational belief are right: if we retain the conjunction rule, there is no natural way to do justice to the controlling intuitions of both the lottery and the preface.

The controlling intuition in the lottery is that it can be rational for you to believe that the lottery is fair and that as such exactly one ticket will win—ticket #1 will win or #2 will win . . . or ticket #n will win. But then we are forced to conclude that it cannot be rational for you to believe of any given ticket that it will lose, for if this were rational, it would be rational to believe of each ticket that it will lose, since by hypothesis your evidential position with respect to each is the same. But if it were rational for you to believe of each ticket that it will lose, then given the conjunction rule, it would also be rational for you to believe that (#1 will not win & #2 will not win . . . & #n will not win). This proposition is logically equivalent to the proposition that it's not the case (#1 will win or #2 will win . . . or #n will win). If you realize this, then it would be rational for you to believe the latter proposition as well, in which case it would be rational for you to believe explicitly contradictory propositions. But we have assumed that this is impossible: explicitly contradictory propositions cannot be simultaneously rational for you. And so, we are forced to conclude that it cannot be rational for you to believe of any given ticket that it will not win.

Unfortunately, if we were to reason in a parallel way about the preface, we would find ourselves denying the controlling intuition about it—namely, that it is rational for you to believe the individual propositions that constitute the body of your book. On the other hand, if we grant that each of the propositions can be rational for you, we are forced to conclude that it is also rational for you to believe the conjunction of the propositions despite the fact that the conjunction is highly unlikely to be true.

To be sure, there are important differences between the lottery and the preface. It's just that the differences are not ones of rationality. One difference is that while you can know many of the propositions that make up the body of your book, you do not know of any given ticket in the lottery that it will lose. However, this difference is to be explained not by citing the conditions of egocentrically rational belief but rather the conditions of knowledge. The precise form of the explanation will depend on one's account of knowledge. For example, according to one kind of account, to know a proposition P you must have evidence for it that does not support a relevant proposition that is false.[56] For our purposes here, we need not be overly concerned with what makes a proposition relevant to P. Simply assume that however the notion is explicated, the propositions that ticket #1 in the lottery will lose, that ticket #2 will lose, that ticket #3 will lose, and so on are relevant to one another. But one of these propositions, you know not which, is false. Moreover, it is the same evidence that supports each. So, your evidence for any one of these propositions, say the proposition that ticket #23 will lose, is evidence that supports a relevant false proposition. Thus, given the above requirement for knowledge, you cannot know this proposition.

By contrast, the evidence that you have for each of the individual propositions in your book need not be like this. You have different evidence for the different propositions. Thus, even if one is false, the various kinds of evidence you have for the others do not necessarily support the false proposition. And so, nothing in the above requirement implies that you cannot know these other propositions.

But all this is irrelevant to the main point at hand, which is not one of knowledge but rather one of rational belief. In particular, the point is that there is a straightforward way of dealing with the lottery and the preface without repudiating the epistemology of belief. It is to reject the assumption that rational belief is closed under conjunction. This allows us to stipulate a threshold for belief, if only a vague one, without paradox.

Still, it is worth asking why we nonetheless shouldn't abandon the epistemology of belief for an epistemology of degrees of belief? Doing so makes it easy to deal with the lottery and the preface. We simply say that it is rational for you to have a high degree of confidence in each of the particular assertions in those cases and a low degree of confidence in their conjunction, and we leave the matter at that, refusing even to entertain the question of what it is rational for you to believe *simpliciter*. Moreover, abandoning the theory of rational belief would seem to have the advantage of simplifying our theorizing, especially if we assume that the doxastic inputs for rational decision making must be degrees of belief rather than beliefs *simpliciter*. This suggests that we cannot do without a theory of rational degrees of belief but that we might be able to do without a theory of rational belief. But then, why have two theories when one will do just as well? The answer is that one won't do just as well. There are deep reasons for wanting an epistemology of beliefs, reasons that epistemologies of degrees of belief by their very nature cannot possibly accommodate.

Consider again the betting situation in which you know that nine of the ten cups on the table cover a pea, and you are offered the opportunity to bet 'pea' or 'not-pea' on any combination of the ten cups, with a $1 payoff for each correct guess and a $1 loss for each incorrect guess. In such a situation, a decision to bet 'pea' on each of the ten cups can be rational, even though you realize that this series of bets precludes an ideal outcome. But notice, the number of options available to you in this case is sharply limited. You must either bet 'yes' or 'no' to there being a pea under a cup, accepting without alteration the stipulated payoffs for successful and unsuccessful bets, or you must refuse to make any bet at these payoffs. Of course, we can imagine situations in which you have a greater range of betting options with respect to the cups. We can imagine, for example, that you yourself get to determine the payoff scheme for the bets and your opponent then gets to choose the side of the bets. You are able to post whatever you take to be fair odds. In this kind of betting situation you are not limited to three betting options. Your options are more fine-grained. According-ly, you have a greater range of betting strategies from which to choose.

The theory of rational belief is concerned with doxastic situations that resemble the more restricted of the above betting situations. The three betting options—betting 'pea' at odds X, betting 'not-pea' at these odds, and refusing to bet at these odds—correspond to the three doxastic options with which the theory of rational belief is concerned: believing, disbelieving, and withholding. To be sure, not every betting situation is one in which our options are limited to just three. So too, there is nothing in principle that limits our doxastic options to just three. We can and do have various degrees of confidence in propositions, and we can and do ask whether or not our degrees of confidence are appropriate. Even so, in our deliberations we often to want to limit our doxastic options to just three, and likewise in gleaning information from others we often want to limit them to just three. We often find it useful or even necessary to do so. We exert pressure upon others and upon ourselves to take intellectual stands.

In reading a manuscript of this sort, for example, you expect me to say what I think is true and what I think is false about the issues at hand. You expect me not to qualify my every assertion. You do not want me to indicate as accurately as I can my degree of confidence in each assertion that I defend. You want my views to be more economically delivered than this. And so it is with a host of other informative, argumentative, and decision-making activities.

In decision making, for instance, we need the general parameters of at least some decisions to be set out without qualification. We first identify what we believe to be the acts, states, and outcomes that are appropriate for specifying the problem. It is only after we make this specification that there is a decision upon which to deliberate. It is only then that our more fine-grained doxastic attitudes—in particular, our degrees of confidence that various acts will generate various outcomes—come into play.[57]

Similarly, in expository books and articles, in department reports, in financial statements, in documentaries, and in most other material that is designed to transfer information, we want, all else being equal, a black-and-white picture.[58] We want a definite yes or no on the statements in question while at the same time recognizing that this is not always feasible. Often the information available is not sufficiently strong one way or the other to allow the author to take a definite stand on all of the issues, in which case we tolerate a straddling of the fence.

Even so, the overall pattern is clear. If all of the information provided to us by others were finely qualified with respect to the provider's degree of confidence in it, we would soon be overwhelmed. It is no different with our private deliberations. We don't have finely qualified degrees of confidence in a wide variety of propositions, but even if we did, we would soon find ourselves overwhelmed if we tried to deliberate about complicated issues on the basis of them.[59] We would need to force ourselves to take definite stands in order to to make our deliberations about these issues manageable.

Of course, we don't always need to take definite stands. Sometimes we want probabilities, and we force ourselves or others to provide them. But even here it needs to be emphasized that we arrive at the probabilities only against a backdrop of black-and-white assumptions—that is, a backdrop of belief. I calculate what to bet before I draw my final card, and I note to myself that the probability of the drawn card's being a heart, given the cards in my hand and the exposed cards of my opponents, is 0.25. Or I note that the probability of the die coming up six is 0.16667, or that the probability of an American male's dying of a heart attack prior to age forty is 0.05. The assignment of each of these probabilities depends on antecedent black-and-white beliefs. I believe that the deck of cards is a standard deck, that the die isn't weighted, and that the statistics on heart attacks were reliably gathered. Probabilists might argue that these background beliefs are so close to certain that we ignore their probabilities. But this is just the point. There are so many potentially distorting factors that we need to ignore most of them. We couldn't possibly keep track of all of them, much less have them explicitly enter into our deliberations. Therefore, we ignore them. We ignore them despite the fact that we recognize that there is some probability of their obtaining. We are content with our black-and-white beliefs about these matters.

On the one hand, then, even our probabilistic reasonings require a background of belief. And on the other hand, we try to minimize the need for such probabilistic reasonings. To the extent possible, we try to avoid probabilistic qualifications, both in our own case and in the case of others. Indeed, a penchant for making such qualifications is often regarded as a character flaw. It is a mark of an overly cautious and perhaps even slippery personality. We do not want to get our information from the overly opinionated but neither do we want to get it from the overly diffident. We commonly need others to provide us with a sharply differentiated picture of the situation as they see it.[60]

In effect, we expect others, whether they be scientists, teachers, butchers, journalists, plumbers, or simply our friends, to act as jurors for us, delivering their black-and-white judgments about the facts as best they can. Indeed, legal judgments provide a good paradigm for this kind of judgment. In the American legal system, juries have three options in criminal proceedings. Each particular juror has only two options—to vote 'innocent' or to vote 'guilty'—but collectively they have three. If each individual juror votes 'innocent' the jury reaches a collective verdict of innocence and thereby acquits the defendant; if each votes 'guilty' the jury reaches a collective verdict of guilt and thereby convicts the defendant; otherwise the result is a hung jury, in which neither innocence nor guilt is declared.[61]

No room is left for judgments of degree here. Juries are not allowed to qualify their judgments. They cannot choose among 'almost certainly guilty' as opposed to 'highly likely to be guilty' as opposed to 'more likely than not to be guilty'. *A fortiori* they are not given the option of delivering numerically precise judgments. They cannot, for example, judge that it is likely to degree 0.89 that the defendant is guilty. There is nothing in principle that precludes a legal system from allowing such fine judgments and then adjusting the punishment to reflect the degree of belief that the jury has in the defendant's guilt. But of course, there is no legal system of this sort and for good reasons. Any such system would be horribly unwieldly. Besides, it would invite injustice, since it would increase the percentage of innocent people who are punished.

Taking stands is an inescapable part of our intellectual lives, and the epistemology of belief is the study of such stands. Your options are restricted to just three: to say yes to a proposition, to say no to it, or to remain neutral on it. The project is then to describe what is the best, or at least a satisfactory, combination of yes, no, and neutral elements for you—not for all time but for now.

Admittedly, sometimes it may be odd for you to report your opinion within the belief/disbelief/withhold judgment trichotomy. Doing so might even be misleading. This is especially likely to be so with respect to games of chances and other situations in which it is natural for you to work with precise probabilities. In lottery cases, for example, you will be reluctant to say without qualification that you believe, say, that ticket #23 will not win. You will be especially reluctant to say this if #23 is your ticket. To do so would be to underdescribe your opinion, and as a result it might encourage misunderstanding ("Well, if you believe it will lose, why are you buying it?"). Thus, it will be natural for you to resist reporting such opinions in a black-and-white way. Even so, we can still ask, if you had to give a black-and-white picture, what picture should it be? Could it be rational for you to say yes to the propositions that ticket #1 will not win, that #2 not win, and so on, even though you realize one of the tickets will win?

I have been arguing that this can be rational for you. A combination of yes, no, and neutral elements that you know to be somewhat flawed can nonetheless be a satisfactory one for you, given your situation and given the alternatives. The lottery, the preface, and the more general case of having fallibilistic beliefs about your other beliefs all illustrate this. To be sure, in each of these cases you realize that alternatives keep open the possibility of a flawless outcome, but only a misplaced fastidiousness would insist that it is condition of egocentric rationality that you always and everywhere do so.

6. *Being Knowingly Incoherent*

Sometimes the best strategy is one you know to be flawed. This is so for beliefs as well as actions, and it is so for degrees of beliefs as well as beliefs. It can be rational for you to have degrees of belief that you know to be incoherent.

Consider the discovery of a logical paradox. Suppose there is a set of propositions, numbered from #1 to #10, each of which you realize is either necessarily true or necessarily false. After having considered them, you think that each is necessarily true. Indeed, each strikes you as being self-evident. Accordingly, you believe each with maximal confidence. But then you discover the paradox. You come to see that the denial of any of these propositions can be deduced in a surprising way from the others. Thus, you realize that at least one is false. For simplicity, assume you also know that at most one is false. You commit yourself to finding a solution, but for the moment you cannot see which one is the culprit. Each is equally plausible, seemingly equally undeniable. What should your attitudes be in the interim, given that your goal is to have accurate and comprehensive degrees of belief?

A natural suggestion is to believe each with great but no longer maximal confidence. In particular, if you are capable of such precision, a natural suggestion is to believe each with precisely 0.9 degree of confidence, since the number of such propositions is ten and all but one is true. However, these degrees of belief are incoherent. Suppose you realize this. You realize that what is necessarily true has a probability of 1 and what is necessarily false has a probability of 0. You are aware, then, that these degrees of belief cannot possibly conform to the objective probabilities. Even so, need it be irrational for you to have 0.9 degree of confidence in each? First appearances would suggest not. But if not, you can knowingly but rationally have incoherent degrees of belief.

Unproved mathematical theorems provide other examples. The theorems are necessarily true or necessarily false, and so have a probability of either 1 or 0. However, you cannot prove which. But of course, even if you lack a proof of the truth (or falsity) of a proposed theorem, you might have good reasons to be confident of its truth (or its falsity). No one has proved Goldbach's conjecture, but since no one has ever succeeded in finding an even number greater than two that is not the sum of two primes, there are reasons to have confidence, albeit not full confidence, in its truth. There are reasons, in other words, to have a degree of belief in it that you know cannot possibly be accurate.[62]

It is the same even with truth-functional tautologies. Not every tautology is one that you will recognize to be such. Some are too complex. Suppose then that you are confronted with a complex statement and are told that either it or its negation is a tautology. You try to come up with a proof of one or the other but you fail to do so. However, a friend then tells you that she has succeeded in proving its truth, but at the same time she warns you that her proof is so complicated that she herself has some doubts about its validity. Her testimony does not make it reasonable for you to have full confidence in the proposition's truth, but it may very well make it reasonable for you to have more confidence in its truth than its falsity, although once again you know that this degree of belief cannot possibly be accurate. You know that the objective probability is either 1 or 0.[63]

Is there any way of explaining away the force of these kinds of examples? No plausible way. For instance, one way of trying to deal with them is to search for some contingent proposition to serve as a surrogate for the necessary propositions. Distinguish the above propositions #1–#10 from the following proposition: that a proposition chosen at random from this set of ten propositions is true. This proposition is contingently true if true at all. It is contingent, since the randomly chosen proposition might be the one false proposition in the set. So, the suggestion might be that it is the failure to distinguish propositions #1–#10 from this contingent proposition that creates the appearance that it might be rational to have 0.9 degree of confidence in the former propositions. Each of the former is either necessarily true or necessarily false. Thus, none of them can have an objective probability of 0.9, but this contingent proposition might.

This simply changes the subject, however. We divert attention from propositions #1–#10 and toward some other proposition, despite the fact that our puzzlement is about what degrees of confidence you should have in #1–#10. You know that one of the propositions is false and the remaining nine are true, and yet if coherence is a prerequisite of rationality, it cannot be rational for you to have 0.9 degree of confidence in each. In an attempt to explain away the counterintuitiveness of this result, the present suggestion is that we cast about for some other proposition that you could legitimately believe with 0.9 confidence. However, the only motive for looking for another such proposition is that you know that none of the propositions #1–#10 can possibly have an objective probability of 0.9. But precisely the question at issue is whether this in itself is sufficient to make a 0.9 degree of confidence in them irrational.

A related tack is to insist that it is not possible for you genuinely to understand a necessarily true proposition and yet not realize it is true. Correspondingly, it is not possible for you to understand a necessarily false proposition and yet not realize it is false. If we assume this is so and assume also that you understand each of the propositions #1–#10, then contrary to the above hypothesis, you must know which one is false. On the other hand, if we grant that you do not know which one is false, you must not understand them all. But if you do not understand a proposition, you cannot have any degree of belief in it whatsoever.

This is contrary to appearances, of course. It certainly looks as if you might have degrees of belief in each of the propositions #1–#10. But it might be argued that what you really are believing are some closely related propositions. Suppose that sentence 1* in the present context expresses proposition #1, sentence 2* expresses proposition #2, and so on. Then it is possible for you to believe with 0.9 confidence the proposition that sentence 1* is true. You can do so because this proposition is either contingently true or contingently false. It is not a necessary truth that sentence 1* expresses proposition #1. Similarly, it is possible for you to believe with 0.9 degree of confidence the proposition that sentence 2* is true, and so on for propositions corresponding to each of the other sentences. If you have these degrees of belief, you must be ignorant of some crucial information, but your ignorance need not be the sort that results in a violation of probability calculus. It is semantic ignorance.

The most obvious difficulty with the foregoing tack is that it presupposes an implausibly strong theory of understanding. The assertion is that you don't *really* understand a necessarily true proposition unless you see that it is true. This may have some plausibility for very simple necessary truths, but as a general assertion, it has all the appearances of an overly convenient stipulation, although its stipulative character is partially disguised by the word 'really'. Think of the skeptic who asserts that you cannot *really* know that you are now seated at your desk. The insertion of 'really' has the effect of raising the standards of knowledge beyond the normal ones.[64] The skeptic first points out that you are not ideally situated to determine the truth of this proposition. It is at least conceivable that you are being deceived. It is then asserted that this is enough to show that you cannot *really* know that you are at your desk. Knowledge has come to involve absolute and utter certainty.

Only an analogous shift in standards can make the above thesis concerning understanding look respectable. The presupposition is that if you ideally understood a proposition that is necessarily true, you would see that it is true. Thus, if you don't see this, you must not *really* understand it. Genuine understanding of a proposition thus comes to involve something like a complete and perfect grasp of its implications, or at the very least a grasp of something sufficient to identify its truth value. But of course, this is beyond what we normally expect. What, then, is the difference? It is hard to resist the thought that the difference is mere convenience. The higher standards help rule out embarrassing cases of incoherence.

Nor is this kind of strategy made any more plausible by embedding it within a broader theory of beliefs and propositions—for example, one according to which you cannot help but believe everything implied by a proposition you believe.[65] This has the effect of making it impossible for ignorance of necessary truths to produce probabilistic incoherence, since there is no ignorance of necessary truths. You believe with full confidence everything implied by that which you fully believe, and accordingly if you fully believe anything at all, you fully believe all necessary truths. And so, you cannot help but believe with full confidence nine of the above ten propositions—namely, the nine that are necessarily true—and likewise you cannot help but believe with full confidence the negation of the tenth.[66] Moreover, appearances to the contrary are once again to be explained away linguistically. What appears to be logical ignorance is really semantic ignorance.

There is a sense of magic to this solution. We theorize logical ignorance out of existence, replacing it with semantic ignorance, despite the fact that antecedently it would have seemed implausible to assert that we cannot help but believe all the implications of what we believe. This seems especially implausible in light of the fact that we sometimes believe the negations of propositions that are implied in complex ways by other propositions we believe. One might try responding that this illustrates only that we believe explicitly contradictory propositions far more often than would seem to be the case at first glance. We believe a proposition P and a proposition not-Q, but since P implies Q we *must* also believe it, even if for all appearances we are not aware of the connection between P and Q and even if we would sincerely assert that Q is false.[67] However, this only reinforces the feeling that extreme consequences are being embraced for reasons of theoretical convenience. We rule out logical ignorance. We decree that when it comes to questions of logic, there are no mistakes of omission, but we do so only by making the most blatant kind of logical mistake of commission a common occurrence: beliefs in explicitly contradictory propositions.

In any event, whatever there is to be said for the theory of propositional belief at work in these suggestions, the strategy of turning logical ignorance into semantic ignorance does not affect the most basic epistemological issue that is at stake here: the issue of whether it is always irrational for you to have degrees of belief that you know in advance to be flawed. I assert that this is not always irrational and that there are various cases that plainly illustrate this, including cases involving the discovery of logical paradox and cases involving unproven mathematical theorems. Moreover, this is so even if your ignorance in these cases is best construed as semantic ignorance. The same problems still arise, although in a somewhat different form.

To see how the same problems arise, suppose we adopt the above theory of belief. Then you cannot believe the above propositions #1–#10 with 0.9 degree of confidence. However, you can believe the sentences 1*–10* with 0.9 degree of confidence, where 'believing sentence 1* with 0.9 degree of confidence' is shorthand here for 'believing with 0.9 degree of confidence the proposition that sentence 1* is true'. The degrees of belief need not be incoherent. Your semantic ignorance shields you from incoherence.

On the other hand, your avoidance of incoherence is now less interesting, and it is less interesting precisely because logical ignorance has been turned into semantic ignorance. The result is that semantic ignorance begins to function epistemically in much the same way that logical ignorance had been thought to function. It puts you into similar sorts of binds. If you believe sentences 1*–10* with 0.9 degree of confidence but do not know what proposition each expresses, then you can avoid incoherence. Nevertheless, you still do know that there is a sense in which these degrees of beliefs cannot possibly be accurate. You know that this is so relative to the correct semantics for these sentences. You don't know what the correct semantics is, but by hypothesis you do know that given it, the objective probability of all but one of the sentences is 1.0 and the objective probability of the remaining one is 0. Moreover, this has familiar consequences. If you believe each of these sentences with 0.9 degree of confidence and if you are willing or are forced to post odds corresponding to your degrees of belief in the truth of these sentences, an appropriately skilled opponent—namely, one who knows the correct semantics—will be able to make bets against you that you cannot help but lose.[68]

So, with respect to epistemic concerns, there is little to choose between your incoherently believing each of the propositions #1–#10 with 0.9 degree of confidence and your coherently believing each of the sentences 1*–10* with 0.9 degrees of confidence. In either case you know in advance that you cannot help but be guilty of a certain kind of inaccuracy, and in either case you know that posting odds in accordance with your degrees of beliefs will make you vulnerable to bets that you cannot help but lose. In the first case your opponents need only the appropriate logical knowledge (or more generally, the appropriate knowledge of necessary truths) to be able to make such bets against you, and in the second case they need only the appropriate semantic knowledge. However, on the theory of propositional belief in question, this is really no difference whatsoever, since what we had previously regarded as logical knowledge is really semantic knowledge.[69] The perfect logician is really just the perfect semanticist.

Thus, the most basic epistemological issue here is unaffected by such theories of belief. For this issue it doesn't really matter whether one adopts such a theory or a more traditional theory, one that allows for logical ignorance. If there were good reasons, given a traditional theory, for insisting that it cannot be rational to have 0.9 degree of confidence in propositions #1–#10, then there would be equally good reasons, given a theory that turns logical ignorance into semantic ignorance, for insisting that it cannot be rational to have 0.9 degree of confidence in sentences 1*–10*. If, for example, the reasons require you to avoid degrees of belief that you know in advance to be mistaken, they cut the same way in both cases. Similarly, if the reasons require you to avoid degrees of belief that could be exploited in a betting situation, they once again cut the same way in both cases.

Accordingly, if someone wishes to introduce a theory of propositional belief that attempts to explain away what is commonly taken to be ignorance of necessary truths as semantic ignorance, then so be it. Such theories may be metaphysically interesting, but they will have little relevance for epistemology. Like other basic epistemological problems, the problem here cannot be solved by metaphysics, in this case a metaphysics of beliefs and propositions. It merely reappears in somewhat altered form.

For simplicity's sake, then, I will set aside theories of propositional belief that preclude ignorance of necessary truths. I will be assuming, for example, that it is possible for you to believe the proposition that $21 \times 30 = 630$ without believing the proposition that if something is red all over, it's not blue all over, and that in turn it is possible for you to believe either of these without believing that every even number greater than 2 is the sum of two primes (even assuming that this is necessarily true).[70] The most basic issues that are at stake are not affected by this assumption.

One of the unaffected issues is familiar: the extent to which it is appropriate to idealize in doing epistemology. The above example and others like it raise the question of idealization in its most pressing form. The nature of these cases is such that you realize your capacity to distinguish necessarily true from necessarily false propositions is limited. Moreover, you realize this not just in a general way, not just as a pious recognition of your fallibilism. Rather, you are aware of it concretely. You realize that the ten propositions, each of which you previously took to be self-evident, collectively lead to paradox. They cannot possibly all be true. The question that is commonly idealized away now becomes unavoidable. What is the rational reaction to this situation? Since logically equivalent propositions must have the same probability, probabilists commonly presuppose that an ideally rational being is always able to identify logically equivalent propositions. A being with this ability also has the ability to distinguish necessarily true from necessarily false propositions. But then, propositions #1–#10 cannot possibly present a serious problem. It is rational for such a being to believe all but one of the ten with full confidence and to believe the negation of the remaining proposition with full confidence.

The problem is that this is not a plausible strategy for you. Indeed, it seems inapplicable to you, since by hypothesis there is nothing within your current perspective to indicate which of the ten propositions is false. On the other hand, if someone were to insist that this is the rational strategy for you, then the suggestion would be strongly counterintuitive. It would be arbitrary for you to believe nine of the propositions with full confidence and the negation of the remaining one with full confidence. After all, you have no idea how to pick out the one that is necessarily false.

There is no way to glide over the problem of idealization in this kind of case. It is of no help to say: "Of course we are not ideal cognizers, and there is no way that we can be. Nonetheless, we ought to strive for perfection. No doubt there are many situations in which we unknowingly have incoherent degrees of belief. This is perfectly understandable. What cannot be excused is knowingly having incoherent degrees of belief." This is of no help in the case here because you know that your degrees of belief are incoherent and you know how to avoid being knowingly incoherent. If you believe with full confidence nine of the ten propositions as well as the negation of the tenth, you will not know that your degrees of belief are incoherent. Thus, you can avoid being knowingly incoherent. It's just that it is not rational for you to do so.

This is not to say that the discovery of incoherence is epistemically irrelevant. It obviously isn't. Like inconsistency, incoherency is a sign of inaccuracy. As such, it must always be taken into account insofar as your aims are epistemic. But there are ways of doing so short of an absolute prohibition on having degrees of belief that you know to be incoherent. For example, there can be restrictions on how you use incoherent degrees of belief in further inquiry. To use them in an unrestricted way risks spreading the inaccuracy. So, the avoidance of incoherence may be a requirement for those propositions that you use as evidence.[71] Moreover, it will ordinarily be rational for you to avoid incoherence among your other degrees of belief as well. The point here is simply that there are some exceptions. It is not always and everywhere irrational to be knowingly incoherent. This is not an epistemic categorical imperative, and we should not allow considerations of theoretical convenience to convince us otherwise.

Nor should we allow analogies with betting situations to convince us otherwise. Any such analogies will encounter all of the familiar complications—for example, what if you are not willing to post odds, or if we suppose you are forced to do so, what do the odds that it is rational for you to post indicate about the degrees of belief that it is rational for you to have when you are not being so forced? But for purposes here, I will ignore these problems. I grant that betting analogies can be useful in thinking about questions of rational degrees of belief. Even so, the real force of these analogies is in the opposite direction. They help reinforce the idea that it can sometimes be rational for you to have incoherent degrees of belief.

This idea is apt to seem surprising, given Dutch book theorems, but it begins to look less surprising when two points are made. First, it is not always irrational to accept bets that you know will result in a net loss. Whether it is irrational depends on what the alternatives are. Second, what odds it is rational for you to post vary with the nature of the betting situation. Thus, insofar as the odds it is rational for you to post are supposed to be indicative of the degrees of belief it is rational for you to have, everything will depend upon the rationale for using one kind of betting situation rather than another as providing the proper analogy.

Begin with the former point. When might it be rational for you to make a bet that you are sure to lose? A situation in which you have no alternative but to do so is one such case. Suppose that you are forced to choose between two betting options, each of which cannot help but lead to losses but one of which is nonetheless superior to the other. "Yes," you may say, "but as long as I have other options, ones that don't guarantee a loss, it is irrational for me to make bets that I'm sure to lose." This isn't so either. Keeping open the possibility that you won't lose sometimes involves unacceptably high risks. But if so, it may be preferable to accept bets that guarantee modest losses.

Here is an example. When I was an undergraduate, my friends and I sometimes played a seven-card poker game with several special rules. One was that a player could not fold on the first round of betting. Three of the seven cards were dealt face up. The player to the right of the dealer began the betting. All the other players, including the dealer, were compelled to match the opening bet, which in effect was a variable ante (although there was an upper limit on its size). On the first round the dealer was the only one with the option of raising the initial bet. If the dealer refused to raise, the other players were called, in which case the best of the dealt hands won. On the other hand, if the dealer raised, this gave all of the players the option of discarding one of their unexposed cards and drawing another. This was followed by a second round of betting in which each player had the usual poker options: to fold, match, or raise.

The game's rules sometimes presented me as dealer with a situation in which

I knew, given the distribution of the exposed cards, that at least one of the other players had a better hand than I. Hence, I knew that if I called, I was guaranteed to lose an amount equal to the opening bet. On the other hand, if I raised, there was a chance that I would win. The raise gave me an opportunity to improve my hand in the draw, and if the raise was aggressive enough it might even bluff some of the other players into folding during the second round. But of course, while opening up the possibility of a win, this strategy also opened up the possibility of even greater losses. In such situations, I sometimes opted to call, forgoing the possibility of a win and guaranteeing modest losses. Was I being irrational? Not always. Sometimes it is rational to accept losses with the idea of limiting them.

Keeping this in mind, suppose we grant that the odds it is rational for you to post on the truth of various propositions is indicative of the degrees of confidence it is rational for you to have in the propositions, and suppose we then show that the posting of a certain combination of odds is certain to lead to losses. In itself this is not enough to show that posting these odds is irrational, and hence not enough to show that it is irrational to have degrees of belief corresponding to these odds. What has to be shown is that posting such odds would have unacceptable consequences in comparison with the alternatives. This is where the second of the above points becomes relevant. What consequences you can expect from the posting of a set of odds depends upon the nature of the betting situation.

Suppose that you are forced to assign probabilities to propositions #1–#10, the ten propositions that have generated paradox, and that you are then forced to accept bets on the truth of these propositions. The betting is carried on by selling and buying $1 tickets, with the cost of the tickets determined by your assignment of probabilities. If you assign 0.9 to a proposition, say to proposition #3, you are setting 9:1 odds, and thus your opponent can buy from you a ticket on #3 for $.90, hoping to secure the $1 payoff if #3 is true. Alternatively, your opponent can sell you such a ticket for $.90, hoping to avoid a $1 payoff to you. On the other hand, if you assign a probability of 0 to #3, you must be willing to give away for free (or as close to free as you please) a ticket that would entitle your opponent to collect $1 from you if #3 is true. If you assign a probability of 1, you must be willing to buy for $1 (or as close to $1 as you please) a ticket that will pay you $1 if #3 is true.

You know that nine of the ten propositions are necessarily true, with the tenth being necessarily false, but you do not know which is the false one. What assignment of probabilities would be best for you? It depends. It depends against whom you are betting and the nature of the betting situation.

Assume that the betting situation is such that after you determine the odds for each of the ten propositions, your opponent determines not only which side of the bets she will take but also the number of such bets made. On these matters she has complete discretion. Suppose also that your opponent is logically omniscient and you realize this. In particular, you realize that whenever a proposition is necessarily true, she knows that this is so. Then you should try to avoid betting altogether, since your opponent has a tremendous advantage. But if you must bet, you have no choice but to opt for a probability of 1 for nine of the ten propositions and a probability of 0 on the remaining proposition. Of course, you do not know which proposition is necessarily false, and hence you do not know which proposition should be assigned 0. Still, you must guess, even though from your point of view—that is, relative to your background information—you have only a 10 percent chance of guessing correctly. You must guess because any other strategy guarantees that your opponent can win as much as she pleases from you. This is the only strategy that has any chance at all of making your probability assignments coherent, and hence it is the only strategy that has any chance at all of limiting your losses against a logically omniscient opponent who can choose the side and the number of bets.

However, suppose we limit the number of $1 tickets that your opponent is allowed to buy or sell. She is limited to a single ticket on each of the ten propositions. What odds is it best for you post in this kind of betting situation? Suppose you assign 0.9 to each of the propositions. Nine of the propositions, you know, have an objective probability of 1. Your opponent, being logically omniscient, knows which propositions these are. So, she will bet on their truth, paying $.90 for a ticket and collecting $1, for a profit of $.10 on each. The remaining proposition has a probability of 0. So, your opponent will bet against it, selling you a $.90 ticket. Her total gain and your total loss are each $1.80. You can know in advance that this is exactly what you will lose. Still, the fact that you are sure to incur this loss does not in itself show that such a strategy is unacceptable. That can be determined only by a comparison with your other options.

One of the other options is to assign a probability of 1 to nine of the ten propositions and a probability of 0 to the tenth. If you guess correctly, there will be a $0 payoff, but you realize that you have only a 10 percent chance of your getting every assignment correct. If you do not guess correctly, there is one proposition to which you assign 1 whose real probability is 0 and one proposition to which you assign 0 whose real probability is 1. You are committed to buying for $1 a ticket on the latter; you lose $1. Moreover, you are committed to giving away a ticket on the former that has a payoff of $1; you again lose $1. There are then two possibilities: from your point of view there is 90 percent chance of a $2 loss and a 10 percent chance of a $0 loss. Your total estimated loss is $1.80.

So, from your point of view, there is little to choose between the two strategies. The assignment that you know to be incoherent (the one that involves assigning 0.9 to each proposition) will result in a loss of $1.80. This is exactly equal to the estimated loss you will incur from the the assignment that, relative to what you know, keeps open the possibility of coherence (the one that involves assigning 1 to all of the propositions but one and assigning 0 to that one).

There are still other options, however, one of which is to assign 1 to each of the ten propositions. This too is an assignment that you know to be incoherent, and moreover at first glance it would seem to be a strange one, since it ignores the fact that you have discovered a paradox among the ten propositions. Despite this, you continue to assign a maximum probability to each. On the other hand, you know that nine of these assignments are correct. Hence, you are guaranteed to lose only $1, as opposed to the $1.80 you are guaranteed to lose if you assign 0.9 to each and as opposed to the $1.80 you are estimated to lose if you assign 1 to nine of them and 0 to the tenth.

Thus, assigning 1 to all of the propositions is your best option in this kind of betting situation. Why is this so? Why does it fare so well, despite the fact that initially it seems counterintuitive? Because it is the assignment of probabilities that allows your opponent the least flexibility to take advantage of her superior knowledge. It allows her the least room for maneuvering, the fewest opportunities to exploit you.

The two kinds of betting situations—the one in which your logically superior opponent has discretion with respect to the side and number of bets and the other situation in which the number of bets is limited—illustrate that insofar as the odds that it is rational for you to post on the truth of propositions #1–#10 are supposed to indicate by way of analogy the degrees of confidence it is rational for you to have in these propositions, everything will depend upon the nature of the betting situation that is chosen for the analogy. Different betting strategies are best, depending on the situation. Of course, the two kinds of situation also illustrate that if you are forced to bet against an ideal opponent, you are going to have problems no matter what.

Suppose we drop the assumption that you are betting against a superior opponent. Then matters change once again. In particular, suppose you are betting against a peer, someone who is no more knowledgeable than you. She too knows that nine of the ten propositions are necessarily true and one is necessarily false, but she does not know which. Both you and she are forced to bet on each of the ten propositions, with you determining the odds and she then being allowed to pick the side. What is your best strategy in this kind of betting situation?

If you assign 0.9 to each proposition and your opponent decides to buy tickets from you, betting on the truth of each of the propositions, she will win nine of the bets (at a $.10 profit on each) and lose one (at a loss of $.90). Your payoff is $0. You can know this in advance. If she sells tickets to you, she will win one (at a profit of $.90) and lose nine (at a loss of $.10 on each). Once again your payoff is $0. If she mixes her bets, buying tickets from you on some of the propositions and selling tickets to you on others, then regardless of the mix, your total estimated payoff is $0.

Suppose you assign a probability of 1 to nine of the propositions and a probability of 0 to the tenth, and suppose also that you guess correctly about which one is necessarily false. Your opponent can sell you $1 tickets on the nine propositions to which you assign 1 and can take your free ticket on the remaining proposition. Since you have guessed correctly, you will win back $1 on each of the nine tickets that you have bought and you won't have to pay on the ticket that you have given away. So, there will be a $0 payoff. But from your point of view, there is only a 10 percent chance of your guessing correctly. There is a 90 percent chance of your assigning 1 to a proposition that has a probability of 0 and assigning 0 to a proposition that has a probability of 1. Thus, there is a 90 percent chance of your losing $2. So, your total estimated loss is $1.80. Suppose, on the other hand, that you assign 1 to all of the propositions. Then your opponent can accept all of your free tickets and she will win $1 from you. Thus, in this kind of betting situation, it is best for you to assign 0.9 to each of the propositions #1–#10. Indeed, it alone among your options is neither guaranteed nor estimated to lead to a loss.

We now have three kinds of betting situations in which you are forced to post odds on propositions #1–#10, and it is best for you to post different odds in each of the three situations. Where does this leaves us? It leaves us yet again with the lesson that if betting situations are to help us think about what degrees of belief it is rational for you to have—the assumption being that the odds it is rational for you to post indicate by way of analogy the degrees of belief it is rational for you to have—everything will depend upon the nature of the betting situations that it is appropriate to use.

There are two ways of reacting to this lesson. One is to give up entirely on the idea that betting situations can be of much help in thinking about rational degrees of belief. The other is to meet the challenge by arguing that some betting situations are more appropriate than others for thinking about questions of rational belief. This is what I will be arguing. Specifically, I will be arguing that betting situations in which we conceive our opponent to be logically omniscient are the betting equivalents of evil demon and brain-in-the-vat hypotheses, and that as such they do not provide an appropriate test of the rationality of our opinions.

7. Pessimistic Scenarios

Skeptical conjectures sometimes provoke epistemologists into endorsing antecedently implausible metaphysical positions, but they can also bludgeon them into a defensive posture from which it can seem that consistency and coherency are the least that rationality requires of us. The connection is this: if we grant there is no way of marshaling our resources that will provide us with non-question-begging assurances that skeptical hypotheses are false, it can seem as if we are condemned to proceed defensively. There is no intellectual strategy that can assure us of success, but there are strategies that we know will result in error. It thus becomes tempting to think that rationality minimally requires that we avoid these strategies. It requires that we avoid certain error.

This is Cartesianism stood on its head. The certainty of success eludes us. However we marshal our cognitive resources, there are no guarantees of truth or even likely truth. Nevertheless, we can at least protect ourselves against the certainty of failure. If our concern is with the epistemology of belief, this translates into a requirement that we not have beliefs that we recognize to be inconsistent. Otherwise, we would be knowingly forgoing the opportunity of having only true beliefs. On the other hand, if our concern is with the epistemology of degrees of belief, it translates into a requirement that we not have degrees of belief that we recognize to be in violation of the probability calculus. Otherwise, we would be knowingly forgoing the opportunity of having degrees of beliefs that conform to the objective probabilities. In either case, the spirit of the recommendation is the same. If we are consistent and coherent, we keep open the possibility of a flawless belief system. We avoid certain error.

The implicit message of such epistemologies is a defensive one. Whatever positive things there are for us to do intellectually must be secondary to our defensive strategy. We must first put up our barricades with the idea of staving off certain intellectual defeat. It is only within the confines of this defensive posture that we are to wield whatever offensive intellectual strategies we might have at our disposal.

What is the certain defeat that we stave off by being consistent and coherent? Only this: that of having something less than an altogether flawless belief system. Is this really such a crushing defeat? It is hard to think so, especially since it is unlikely that our belief systems will be flawless in any event. After all, we are not logically and probabilistically omniscient. So, even if we were never knowingly incoherent, we are likely to be incoherent nonetheless. And of course, there is always contingent error.

Suppose, on the other hand, that we refuse to conceive of intellectual success in absolute terms. Grant instead that something less than perfection is required for success. This makes room for intellectual strategies that deliberately court error. It can be rational for us knowingly to allow ourselves to be in error if there are benefits to be won by doing so. And often enough there are benefits to be won. We want our beliefs to be both comprehensive and accurate, and only persons who are obsessed with avoiding error will not be prepared to allow some trade-offs between the two. The rest of us will sometimes be willing to put up with opinions that we know to be less than perfectly accurate in order to have some opinion about the matters in question.

Strategies in which we deliberately court a less than ideal outcome are often rational in nonintellectual contexts. Indeed, this is understating the case. They are often indispensable. Our choice is often between such a strategy and one that holds out the hope of a flawless outcome only because it is either far too cautious or far too daring.

Recall the betting situation in which nine of the ten cups on the table have peas under them and you are asked to predict of each cup whether or not it covers a pea. For each correct answer you receive $1 and for each incorrect answer you pay $1. The best strategy is to bet 'pea' on each of the ten cups, but this will not result in a flawless outcome. You are sure to lose one of your bets. Nevertheless, all of the options that keep open the possibility of a flawless outcome are overly daring or overly cautious. If you bet 'not-pea' on one of the cups, the chances are good that you will lose two bets instead of just one, and if you refuse to bet on one of the cups, the chances are good that you will still lose one bet and in addition you have passed by a bet that you were likely to win. Either way your estimated payoff is lower. Your choice is between a strategy that is sure to be somewhat flawed and one that might possibly turn out to be flawless but whose estimated return is inferior.

The example is not an isolated one. Our lives are filled with such situations. As a result, our strategies of finance and politics and even love are commonly ones in which we deliberately forgo the opportunity of securing a flawless outcome because we recognize that any strategy that holds out the hope of such an outcome is either unduly cautious or unduly risky. Thus, we balance our investments. Some of them hold out prospects of high returns but with a correspondingly high risk. Others are secure but have only modest returns. Some will do well in times of high inflation, others in times of low inflation. The package as a whole protects us against what we take to be unacceptable risks, but the cost of such protection is that we forgo a chance of having all of our investments do well. Similarly, we often opt for moderate political reforms, reforms that we recognize will work to the disadvantage of some. We do so despite there being radical proposals that have at least some small chance of working to everyone's benefit. Still, we prefer the moderate course, since we judge the risks of the more radical reforms to be unacceptably high. Likewise, we live with our imperfect relationships, patching them up as best we can as we go along rather than force the kind of confrontation that might possibly remove the misunderstandings. We do so because we realize that such a confrontation might also altogether end the relationship.

It is not always rational to prefer the moderate but necessarily flawed strategy over the possibly flawless one, but it is not always irrational either. This is a modest enough point, but it sometimes is a difficult one for us to keep in mind. There is even experimental evidence of our difficulty. Julian Feldman describes experiments in which subjects are presented with a random series of X's and O's, 70 percent of which are X's. Subjects are then asked to make predictions about the next string of symbols and are rewarded for making correct ones. The best strategy is always to predict X's, but subjects rarely do this. They usually try to anticipate when an O will come up.[72]

This same tendency shows up in our theories of rationality, especially our theories of rational belief. We insist upon consistency and coherence because we are reluctant to be content with an outcome that we know in advance will involve us in error. This is so even if all of the other options would force us to be unduly cautious or unduly daring. Thus, if the avoidance of recognizable inconsistency were an absolute prerequisite of rational belief, we could not rationally believe each member of a set of propositions and also rationally believe of this set that at least one of its members is false. But this in turn pressures us to be unduly cautious. It pressures us to believe only those propositions that are certain or at least close to certain for us, since otherwise we are likely to have reasons to believe that at least one of these propositions is false. At first glance, the requirement that we avoid recognizable inconsistency seems little enough to ask in the name of rationality. It asks only that we avoid certain error. It turns out, however, that this is far too much to ask.

The recommendation that we always avoid incoherence encounters similar difficulties. They merely manifest themselves in different examples. Recall the set of ten propositions, each of which, you know, is necessarily true or necessarily false, and one of which, you also know, is false, only you don't know which. If rationality required you to avoid certain error, then you must not be knowingly incoherent. However, the only way to do this is for you to believe nine of the ten propositions with maximum confidence and the tenth with minimum confidence. But this forces you to be unduly daring.

Nor can such consequences be made to look more palatable by analogies with betting situations. Even if it is granted that our degrees of belief cannot be rational unless posting odds in accordance with them would be rational, nothing immediately follows about the irrationality of our knowingly having incoherent degrees of belief. This follows only if we make pessimistic assumptions about the nature of the betting situation. If we assume we are in a hostile betting situation, one in which we face logically superior opponents who are able to exploit their superior knowledge without limit, then it will be irrational to be knowingly incoherent. But this is merely the pragmatic counterpart of skeptical hypotheses. Evil demons have been replaced by superior betting opponents who can bet as much as they please against us, but the effect is precisely the same. It is to induce an overly defensive attitude in us, one that encourages us to design our epistemologies with the worst possible case in mind. For Descartes, the result was a search for certainty, a search for propositions of whose truth he could be assured in even the most hostile environment. For today's probabilists, the result is a search for degrees of belief that we could use even in a hostile betting environment.

The danger of such scenarios is the danger of all overly pessimistic assessments. They either intimidate us into being unduly cautious or they lure us into taking desperate risks. Of course, sometimes we have no alternative. Think of the maximin principle of decision making. There are conceivable situations in which the kind of conservatism that this principle calls for is appropriate. Suppose you are aware that when you make your decision, your enemy will have immediate access to it and will be able instantaneously to arrange the world so as to ensure that the decision will have its worst possible outcome. You would then have good reasons to be defensive. It would be rational for you to adopt a barricades mentality.

Analogously, in a desperate enough situation it may be rational for you to take risks that in other situations would be reckless. Suppose all of your options are bad. Each is such that it will almost surely result in an unacceptable outcome. However, one option holds out a significant but low probability of a satisfactory outcome, but it does so at the likelihood of even greater losses than the other options. Still, the kind of daring that a maximax principle of decision making calls for might be appropriate in such a situation. It might be rational for you to pick the option whose best possible outcome is at least as good as the best possible outcome of any other option.

No one suggests that in general it is rational to act in accordance with a maximin principle or a maximax principle. There is no reason to suppose that in general your enemy will have control over the states of the world that will determine the outcome of your decisions, and there is no reason to suppose that in general your situation is so desperate as to make it reasonable for you to go for broke.

Analogously, there may be some intellectual situations in which extreme caution or extreme daring are appropriate, but in general our intellectual situations are not of this sort. It is necessary to keep this in mind when using betting situations as epistemological models—models that are to help us think about what degrees of belief it is rational for us to have. To be sure, if we know that a betting situation is stacked against us, this will affect the odds that it is rational for us to post. We will need to find a way to protect ourselves as best we can. Exactly how to do so will depend upon the way in which the situation is stacked against us. If our betting opponent is logically omniscient but empirically ignorant, it will not be so important to avoid contingent error in the odds we post, but it will be rational for us to go to great lengths to avoid logical error. By contrast, if our opponent is superior to us with respect to identifying contingent truths, it can be rational for us to go to what would otherwise be extreme lengths to avoid contingent error.[73]

But insofar as we are interested in questions of egocentrically rational degrees of belief, all these pessimistic scenarios are beside the point. In thinking about the confidence it is egocentrically rational for us to have in various propositions, it may occur to us that the world is somehow conspiring against us, but this should not be our working assumption. The relevant question is not what degrees of belief we should have, given that nature behaves as if it were a malevolent demon. If this were our assumption, there might be a point to the idea that the degrees of confidence it is rational for us to have in propositions correspond to the odds that it would be rational for us to post on them were we betting against a vastly superior opponent. But this is not our assumption, and because it is not, the whole idea is misconceived. When questions of egocentric rationality are at stake, our degrees of confidence are more naturally construed as bets that we make against ourselves rather than bets against a vastly superior opponent. To assume otherwise is to construe our intellectual projects in an overly defensive manner, encouraging the equivalent of a siege mentality for our intellectual life. In the name of rationality it would require that we be obsessively concerned with the kind of mistakes that would allow a superior opponent to take advantage of us.

The most pernicious influence of skeptical hypotheses and other pessimistic scenarios, such as those commonly imagined in Dutch book arguments, is that they tempt us to do epistemology as if it were a matter of plotting strategies against a far superior opponent. What I have been advocating, in contrast, is a nondefensive epistemology, one that refuses to be either submissive or dismissive in the face of skeptical or other pessimistic hypotheses. It recognizes that circumstances can conspire against us but insists that the proper attitude toward this possibility is one of insolence. A nondefensive epistemology refuses to be apologetic for the lack of positive guarantees. It is not a prerequisite of your being rational that you avoid radical error, and it is not even a prerequisite that you succeed in making this objectively unlikely. Similarly, a nondefensive epistemology refuses to be apologetic for the lack of negative guarantees. It is not a prerequisite of your being rational that you opt for strategies that avoid certain error. A necessarily flawed strategy is sometimes preferable to strategies that are possibly flawless. Egocentric rationality requires no guarantees whatsoever, positive or negative.

8. Evidence

If coherence is neither necessary nor sufficient for rational degrees of belief, what is it that makes your degrees of belief rational or irrational? I will sketch the outlines of an answer to this question, and it is an answer that depends on there being a distinction between your evidence and what your evidence makes rational for you.

To the uninitiated it seems obvious that there is a such a distinction, but during the last half of this century an increasing number of epistemologists and philosophers of science have despaired of finding an acceptable way to make the distinction, and hence have felt forced to deny the obvious. They have been driven to holistic epistemologies, which make every rational belief, or every degree of belief, part of your evidence. Everything is always in principle available as a test for everything else.

A holism of such a sort encourages the idea that consistency and coherency are strict requirements of rationality, and this in turn produces spectacularly implausible results. In the theory of rational belief, we are forced to say that it can never be rational for you to believe of the other propositions that are rational for you that even one is false. Similarly, it cannot be rational for you to believe of a given ticket in a lottery that it will lose, and this is so no matter how large the lottery and hence no matter how small the chance of error. In the theory of rational degrees of belief, there are equally implausible results. If you discover paradox among a set of ten propositions each of which is necessarily true or necessarily false but you cannot yet see which one is false, it cannot be rational for you in the interim to believe these propositions with great but no longer maximum confidence.

Results such as these are avoidable if we give up the idea that consistency and coherency are strict requirements of rationality. And one way of discouraging this idea is to distinguish your evidence from that which your evidence makes rational. We can then grant that it might be rational for you to believe of the other propositions that are rational for you that at least one is false. We can grant this because not all of these propositions need be part of your evidence. All are adequately supported by your evidence. That's why they are all rational. But not everything you rationally believe is available for you to use in evaluating the truth of other propositions.

Similarly, we can grant that in the case where you have discovered paradox in the set of ten propositions but you do not yet know which one is false, it can be rational for you to believe each of the ten with great but not maximum confidence. It's just that these propositions can no longer be part of your evidence. They are no longer available for use in proving or disproving other propositions.

The distinction between evidence and that which evidence makes rational is thus a welcome one. Still, we need a plausible way to make it, and the record of such attempts is not encouraging. It is easy enough to provide an abstract schema for evidence: one proposition A is evidence of another proposition B's truth for you if you stand in the appropriate relation to A and if in addition from some appropriate perspective A seems to be mark of B's truth.[74] The trick is to fill in this schema. It is to say what the appropriate relation is and what the appropriate perspective is.

Infallibility, incorrigibility, direct accessibility, self-presentingness, and observability have all been suggested as the appropriate relation, and have all been found wanting. At best only a very few beliefs, or at least only a very few contingent beliefs, are infallible. So, if your evidence were restricted to that which you infallibly believe, you wouldn't have adequate evidence for much of anything. The same is true of incorrigibility. Very few of your beliefs are incorrigible either. Appealing to direct accessibility or self-presentingness only makes matters worse, since these notions are little more than metaphors that derive whatever plausibility they have from the fact that we sometimes know what we are thinking and feeling without observing our behavior. To be sure, there are those who have tried to make these notions precise,[75] but given all of the usual explications there are only a precious few propositions whose truth is either directly accessible or self-presenting. So, once again your body of evidence will be excessively narrow.

One way to correct the narrowness problem is to conceive your evidence, or at least your empirical evidence, as what you believe as the result of observation. Unfortunately, this creates other problems. Much of what you observationally believe is a function of what else you believe, including what you believe about matters that are not observational. You believe that you see the meter ticking or the rabbit fleeing only against a backdrop of general beliefs about the world and its makeup. Thus, at best there is a difference only of degree between those beliefs that are observational and those that are not. Besides, even if there is a rough-and-ready distinction between the two, there is no rationale for thinking that a belief is epistemically privileged merely because it is observational. After all, not everything you observationally believe is the result of a clear perception. Often enough, it is an unclear perception that causes your beliefs. You believe you see something moving in the fog, for example.

Why not say, then, that your empirical evidence consists of your observational knowledge rather than your observational beliefs. Or why not even say more generally that your evidence consists of whatever you know. This was Locke's view, but it was also part of his view that we know only that which is certain for us and there are internal marks of certainty and hence of evidence. None of this will do for us. It would not do even if we were to agree that knowledge has to be utterly certain. Knowledge does not come with its own internal mark. Nor does observational knowledge. You can fail to know or observe something even though there is nothing in your perspective that provides you with any indication of this. So, evidence cannot be equated with what we know or what we know through observation. Or at least this is so if the notion of evidence is to be at all relevant to questions of egocentric rationality.[76]

All of the above proposals assume that evidence is of necessity pinned to reality, either a subjective reality presented to you in introspection or an objective one presented to you in perception and the like. Either way evidence is extradoxastic. It is not a matter internal to your beliefs. We are asked to look beyond the circle of your beliefs in determining whether or not a proposition is part of your evidence. We need to determine whether your belief in the proposition is infallible or incorrigible, or we need to determine whether its truth is directly accessible to you or self-presenting for you or observed by you or known by you.

Insofar as our interest is egocentric rationality, this cannot be the right approach. Egocentric rationality is a matter of how things would look from your own perspective were you to be sufficiently reflective, but there is nothing in your perspective that guarantees an escape from the circle of your beliefs. Thus, if your evidence is to be distinguished from what your evidence makes egocentrically rational for you, the criteria for doing so cannot be extradoxastic. The criteria must instead be internal to your own perspective. They must be reflected in your own deepest epistemic standards.[77]

There can be no absolute assurances that your standards will allow such a distinction. Being egocentrically rational is essentially a matter of believing what your deepest epistemic standards permit you to believe, and your standards might be such that they never permit inconsistent beliefs or incoherent degrees of belief. If so, there will be no room for a significant distinction between your evidence and what your evidence makes rational for you. If a proposition is rational for you, it is also part of your evidence. Your deepest epistemic standards are holistic. Everything that it is rational for you to believe is available for you to use in arguing for or against anything else.

On the other hand, your deepest epistemic standards need not be like this. Indeed, I have suggested they are probably not like this. Most of us would be prepared to admit that sometimes our best option is one that is sure to be somewhat flawed. This is as true of our beliefs as it is of our actions. As a result, our deepest epistemic standards don't imply that inconsistency and incoherency are always be avoided. On the contrary, sometimes they can be avoided only by strategies that we are apt to regard as spectacularly implausible.

Suppose, then, that your deepest epistemic standards are such that they sometimes permit you to have beliefs that you know to be inconsistent and degrees of belief that you know to be incoherent. It wouldn't be surprising if these same standards imposed restrictions upon how you can use such beliefs or degrees of belief in arguing for or against other claims. But this is just to say that such standards permit a distinction between your evidence and what that evidence makes rational for you.

So, taking seriously the idea that there is no guaranteed escape from the circle of beliefs does not make holism inevitable. It does not preclude an ordering of your belief system, one that distinguishes your evidence from that which your evidence makes rational. It's just that the ordering must be internally motivated.

Let me illustrate one way in which an internally motivated ordering might arise. Think of your evidence as the propositions that are uncontroversial for you to use in arguing for or against other propositions. They are uncontroversial given your own perspective—that is, given your own epistemic standards and what you believe. They need not be uncontroversial come what may. They are only provisionally uncontroversial. Something might alter this. Something might give you an internal motivation to reconsider them, to be suspicious of using them in your evaluations of other propositions. However, for the time being you have no such motivation. They are temporarily settled, or at least this is so from a purely epistemic point of view. There may be a reason for further inquiry if something else of value is at stake. Prudence might then demand it. But insofar as your concern is to have accurate and comprehensive beliefs, there is no such motivation. From the epistemic point of view, then, the plausibility of these propositions is not in question. Quite the opposite. They are the tools for you to use in evaluating other propositions and hypotheses. They are the bases of argument and inquiry, not the object of them.

This is uncomfortably vague, but it is also suggestive. It suggests why it is unlikely to be the case that recognizably inconsistent propositions are part of your evidence. They are unlikely to be so even if you believe each of the propositions with great confidence. After all, inconsistency is a sign of inaccuracy. It is a sign that at least one of the propositions you believe must be false. Inconsistency thus puts you on guard, and in doing so it may indicate to you, at least on reflection, that your views about these propositions are not settled to the point where you can safely base inquiry into other matters upon them. Or more exactly, this is so once again from an epistemic point of view. You may have other pressing needs, needs that make it unwise for you to spend time inquiring further into the truth of these matters. If so, it might be reasonable, all things considered, for you to go ahead and base inquiry on these propositions, especially if the inquiry concerns relatively trivial issues. This might be reasonable, given all of your ends and given that there are constraints on your time. Nevertheless, the essential point here remains: recognizable inconsistency among a set of propositions that you believe is an indication to you that something is wrong. Thus, to use these propositions in evaluating the truth of other propositions would be to risk spreading the error. And hence, your deepest epistemic standards are likely to prohibit or at least restrict your using them in this way.

A similar restriction applies to propositions that are jointly improbable. If you recognize that a set of propositions is such that the negation of any proposition in the set is highly probable, given that the rest are true, then once again you are put on guard. Your own perspective indicates that in all probability at least some of these propositions are false, and hence from your own perspective you have a reason to be cautious about basing further inquiry upon them.

A somewhat more precise way of making these points is to say that a proposition P is unlikely to be part of your evidence unless it is argument-proof for you. It must be the case that nothing you believe with comparable confidence can be used to argue against P in a way that conforms to your epistemic standards, unless the force of this argument is defeated by something else within your doxastic system. Suppose, for example, there are other propositions that you believe with as much confidence as you believe the premises of the argument against P, and moreover these propositions defeat the force of that argument. If so, P can still be an evidential proposition for you. On the other hand, if there are no such defeating propositions, then there are reasons, given your own perspective—that is, given your other beliefs and your own epistemic standards—to be wary of using P to evaluate the truth of other propositions.[78]

Suppose, then, that all this is so. Suppose, in other words, that for a proposition to be part of your evidence, it must be argument-proof relative to what else you believe. Much of the bite of this requirement derives from the fact that it is relatively easy for propositions that you believe to be recognizably inconsistent or recognizably improbable with respect to one another. But if propositions are recognizably inconsistent or improbable with respect to one another, not all of them will be argument-proof. Take any set of propositions you believe. If you believe even tacitly of this set that at least one member is likely to be false, the resulting beliefs are jointly improbable. If in addition you believe this at least as confidently as you believe some of the propositions in the original set, then at least some of these latter propositions—namely, the least confidently believed ones—will not be part of your evidence.[79]

On the other hand, if you are very confident of a proposition's truth and if in addition you don't think that the proposition is strongly competitive with other propositions about whose truth you are comparably confident, it is a good candidate for evidence. Among the very best candidates, for example, are simple propositions about your own current psychological states, simple propositions about what you observe or remember, certain fundamental propositions that most of us take for granted, and simple necessary truths. Not all propositions of these sorts need be part of your evidence. You can have substantial doubts about, say, whether you are perceiving or remembering something correctly, and if so, these propositions need not be part of your evidence. Nevertheless, there typically will be a large number of such propositions about which you don't have substantial doubts. You believe that you have a headache, that you see a cat on the mat, that you remember being at the zoo last Saturday, that there are material objects, that the world has had a significant past, that $2 + 3 = 5$, and so on. You may acknowledge that these beliefs are not utterly certain. There is, you admit, some chance that at least one is false, and this in turn creates a measure of competition among them. Still, you need not regard them as being strongly competitive with one another, especially if they otherwise hang together well. For then, even if their number is great, you are unlikely to believe with great confidence that even one is false. And in any event, you are enormously confident of such propositions. So, even if you do believe with some significant degree of confidence that at least one is false, you are unlikely to believe this with the degree of confidence that you believe them. But then, each might be argument-proof for you. Hence, each might be part of your evidence.

There may be additional constraints that have to be met in order for a proposition to be part of your evidence, but for purposes here it is more important to be clear about the general conception than its details.[80] This conception allows us to separate out some of what you believe as having a privileged position of evidence, but it does so in a frankly belief-laden way. Your evidence consists of the propositions that are uncontroversial for you to use in arguing for or against other propositions, and this in turn is a function of your degrees of belief and your epistemic standards.

Your evidence so conceived can then be used to determine the confidence with which it is egocentrically rational for you to believe other propositions, and it can do so in accordance with the Lockean thesis. For one proposition to be evidence of the truth of another, the first must seem, from an appropriate perspective, to be a mark of the second's truth. The greater the apparent reliability of the mark, the more strongly the evidence supports this proposition, and hence the greater should be your confidence in it. Since the kind of rationality that is at issue here is egocentric rationality, the appropriate perspective is your own deeply reflective one. Thus, the support relation, like the notion of evidence itself, is to be understood in terms of your own deep epistemic standards. It is egocentrically rational for you to believe a proposition with the degree of confidence that these standards warrant, given the degrees of belief you have in your evidential propositions. More precisely, this is so subject to the restriction that these latter degrees of belief are not recognizably incoherent, for if they are incoherent, basing inquiry on them would risk contaminating the rest of your belief system with their inaccuracy.

Consider a simple example. You might have a greater degree of belief in one evidential proposition than a second, despite the fact that on reflection you would see that the first implies the second. If so, these degrees of belief cannot possibly be accurate, and moreover you yourself would see this were you to be reflective. Thus, your own perspective gives you a reason not to use these degrees of belief in determining what degrees of belief to have in other propositions. Instead, you have a reason to correct the inaccuracies before proceeding. How to do so is up to you. The degrees of belief that it is egocentrically rational for you to have in these propositions is determined by what you yourself on reflection would take to be the best way of correcting them. There is no algorithm for making the corrections. You might think it best to lower your confidence in the first, or you might think it best to raise your confidence in the second or perhaps to adjust both. Similarly with other such incoherencies among your evidential propositions. We can imagine your tinkering in a way that removes them as well. You make these adjustments in the manner that seems best to you, given that your goal is to have accurate and comprehensive degrees of belief.

None of this need be or even can be very precise, since your degrees of belief in evidential propositions will typically not be precise. Notice, moreover, that the more vague these degrees of belief are, the less opportunity there is for incoherence in the first place. So, there may be little if any adjusting to be done, in which case the degrees of confidence that you actually have in these propositions are the ones it is rational for you to have. On the other hand, if adjustments are necessary, they will be all the easier to make, given that your degrees of belief are vague. Whatever degrees of belief you would have after such adjustments are the degrees of belief it is rational for you to have in these evidential propositions. They, in turn, help determine what degrees of belief it is rational for you to have in other propositions.

In particular, it is egocentrically rational for you to believe a proposition with the degree of confidence that your epistemic standards warrant, given the degrees of beliefs that it is rational for you have in your evidential propositions. Suppose it is rational for you to have degree of confidence x in an evidential proposition E. The propositional counterpart of this degree of belief is the proposition that E is likely to degree x. To determine the degree of confidence it is rational for you to have in a nonevidential proposition P, take the propositional counterparts of all those evidential propositions that your epistemic standards imply are relevant to P. Make these the premises of an argument that has P as its conclusion. The degree of belief that it is rational for you to have in P is a matter of what your deepest epistemic standards imply about the likely truth preservingness of this argument. It is a matter of what you would think on deep reflection about the strength of this argument.

Once again, vagueness will be the rule. Your epistemic standards need not imply anything precise about how likely a proposition is, given your evidence for it. They might do so if the issue at hand concerns a game of chance or a matter involving statistical frequencies, but it will be far more common for you to have a only a vague view about these matters. Your reflective view might be that given the evidence, it is much more likely that your misplaced key is in your office than in your car and that it is about as likely to be in your car as in your briefcase. This vagueness is in turn transported onto the degrees of belief that it is rational for you to have. It is rational for you to have much more confidence that your key is in your office than in your car and about as much confidence that it is in your car as in your briefcase.

This, then, is one way in which a rational belief system might come to have a hierarchical structure. I am not suggesting that it is the only way. I don't even suggest that a rational belief system must of necessity have some kind of hierarchical structure. My most basic assertion about egocentric rationality remains the same: egocentric rationality is essentially a matter of having beliefs (or degrees of belief) that you could produce no stable criticism of were you to be reflective; it is a matter of what your deepest epistemic standards permit. This general conception is compatible with holism. Your epistemic standards might categorically disallow inconsistency and incoherency, and in so doing might place all rational beliefs (or degrees of belief) at the same level. Every rational belief or degree of belief can be used as evidence. It is freely available for you to use in arguing for or against anything else. But the general conception is also compatible with a rational belief system's having a hierarchical structure. It can be the case—indeed, I have suggested that it is likely to be the case—that your epistemic standards create an ordering among your rational beliefs. If so, some of the propositions that you believe constitute your evidence, and your degrees of belief in these propositions in conjunction with your epistemic standards determine the degrees of beliefs it is rational for you to have in other propositions.

But notice, even if your epistemic standards do create this kind of hierarchical structure, there will still be an important kernel of truth in holism. In particular, which propositions are part of your evidence is a global matter. It is a matter of your doxastic system in its entirety. A proposition is part of your evidence, on this view, only if it is argument-proof, given what else you believe and given your epistemic standards. So, holistic considerations are relevant for determining what your evidence is, but they are not always directly relevant for determining what beliefs are rational for you. Not everything it is rational for you to believe need be available as a test for everything else. It is your evidential propositions that determine what else it is rational for you to believe. As a result, even recognizably inconsistent propositions can sometimes be rational for you.

This is one of the differences between your evidence and what your evidence makes rational for you. If you recognize that a set of propositions is inconsistent, then it's unlikely to be the case that all of these propositions are part of your evidence. Your own perspective indicates that your views about them contain at least some inaccuracies. In so doing, it also gives you a reason not to base further inquiry on them, since to do so would be to risk infecting the rest of your belief system with their inaccuracies. Nevertheless, it might be rational for you to believe all of these propositions. That is, it might be rational for you to include them in your best black-and-white picture of the world, despite the fact that you know in advance that this picture is sure to be flawed. It is not always rational to keep open the possibility of flawless outcomes. Sometimes it is rational to involve yourself in error knowingly. The distinction between evidence and what evidence makes rational allows for this. Knowingly involving yourself in error is sometimes to be tolerated, but on the other hand you also have reasons to contain the error. You have reasons not to use that which you know to be flawed as evidence.[81]

Philosophers who want to make the avoidance of detectable inconsistency into a strict prerequisite of rational belief for you thus make the mistake of trying to extend what can be plausibly regarded as a characteristic of evidence to your doxastic system generally. It is plausible to think that your evidence cannot be recognizably inconsistent. Your own epistemic standards are likely to prohibit this. It is also plausible to think that a proposition doesn't become part of your evidence just by virtue of your rationally believing it with a sufficiently great degree of confidence. This is one of the lessons of the lottery. But it is a mistake to try to extend this lesson to the broader class of propositions that are rational for you to believe. This is a mistake, in turn, that is the result of another: the mistake of assuming that only that which can be used as evidence can be rationally believed.

Philosophers who want to make coherence into a strict prerequisite of rational degrees of belief make the same mistake. They too try to make what is plausibly regarded as a characteristic of evidence into a general characteristic of rationality. It is plausible to think that the degrees of belief you use to determine what degrees of belief to have in other propositions should not be detectably incoherent. Your epistemic standards are likely to demand that you not base inquiry on degrees of belief you know to be inaccurate. To do so would be to risk spreading the error. On the other hand, there are situations in which it seems appropriate for you to have recognizably incoherent degrees of belief—for example, situations involving the discovery of paradox. Only a view that distinguishes evidence from what evidence makes rational allows us to say the intuitively correct thing about such situations. We can say that it might be rational for you to believe each of these propositions with a high degree of confidence, but on the other hand these propositions are no longer argument-proof for you. On the contrary, they can be used to argue against one another. So, they don't have the status of evidence for you. This is the price of paradox.

This view restricts the requirements of consistency and coherency, but it does not junk them. It is natural to make the avoidance of recognizable inconsistency and incoherency a requirement governing evidence. Moreover, inconsistency and incoherency is typically to be avoided even among nonevidential propositions. However, there are important exceptions, ones that defeat the hope that logic and probability theory can be harnessed in a mechanical way to give us conditions of rational belief.

9. Belief as Epistemic Commitment

Locke had the structure of egocentric rationality essentially right but the spirit wrong. By contrast, probabilists and like-minded theorists have the structure wrong but the spirit essentially right. They are right and Locke wrong about there being no guaranteed exit from the circle of beliefs, but Locke is right and they are wrong about the need to allow an ordering of claims into those that are evidential and those that are rational but not evidential.

What emerges is a hybrid view. The view follows Locke in allowing us to make a distinction between your evidence and what your evidence makes rational. It likewise follows Locke in allowing us to say that the degree of confidence it is rational for you to have in a proposition is proportionate to the strength of your evidence for it. On the other hand, there is no presumption that your evidence must be restricted to that which you know with certainty. Nor is there a presumption that there is always some precise degree of confidence it is rational for you to have in a proposition. Both your degrees of belief and your epistemic standards are commonly vague, and this vagueness is reflected in the confidence it is rational for you to have in various propositions.

This hybrid view allows us to think about the relationship between theories of rational beliefs and theories of rational degrees of belief in a natural way. We are not forced to choose between them. Rather, we can say that what seemed right from the start really is right. Namely, questions about the rationality of beliefs are not fundamentally different from questions about the rationality of degrees of belief. The latter simply uses more fine-grained categories than the former. Indeed, there is a systematic relationship between the two, expressed by the Lockean thesis: it is egocentrically rational for you to believe a proposition just in case it is egocentrically rational for you to have a sufficiently great degree of confidence in it, sufficiently great to make your attitude toward it one of belief.

What is a sufficiently great degree of confidence? It doesn't matter much insofar as the concern is to avoid the threat of paradox. That threat was based on the assumption that it is always rational for you to believe the conjunction of any two propositions you rationally believe. Once this assumption is rejected as implausible, we can stipulate pretty much any degree we like as the threshold for belief, making the needed allowances for the vagueness of our degrees of belief.

Still, within the wider context of our epistemology, the threshold will make a difference. If it is low enough, there will be much that we rationally believe; if it is high enough, there will be relatively little. The difficulty is that wherever we choose to place the threshold, our choice is apt to look arbitrary. What we would like is some principled way to pick out the threshold.

Our everyday ascriptions of belief don't help much in this regard. They don't tell us how to pick out the threshold. A good place to begin looking is within the conception of egocentrically rational belief itself. The conception presupposes that you have a purely epistemic goal: the goal of having accurate and comprehensive beliefs. In effect, we suppose that your task is to say yes, say no, or remain neutral on every proposition you understand. It is egocentrically rational for you to believe a proposition, then, just in case it seems appropriate, given your perspective, to say yes to it.

But what would make it appropriate for you to say yes to it?

Assume that your evidence supports the proposition to degree x. Now imagine yourself reflecting on the question of whether a likelihood of degree x would be sufficiently great to make saying yes to this proposition a part of the best combination of yes, no, and neutral elements that you can put together. Suppose you would think that x is sufficiently great, and suppose further that you have a degree of confidence in this proposition that is equal to or greater than x. Then at least for the purposes of epistemology, where our concern is with what it is rational for you to believe insofar as your goal is to have accurate and comprehensive beliefs, we can say that you believe this proposition and that it is rational for you to do so. It doesn't matter if your degree of confidence in it is somewhat less or more than the degree of confidence that it is rational for you to have in it. It still can be the case that you rationally believe the proposition. You believe it because the degree of confidence you have in it corresponds to a likelihood that you yourself would think warrants saying yes to it, and it is rational for you to believe it because it is rational for you to have at least this degree of confidence in it.

Call this 'the epistemic sense' of belief. Whether or not you believe something in this sense depends upon your degree of confidence x in it, but it also depends on whether you would commit yourself to saying yes to it were you forced to take a stand on it and were you to think that it is likely to this degree x, where x can be and usually is vague. We suppose that you have only three options: to believe, disbelieve, and withhold judgment. Your project is to choose one of these three options for each proposition that you understand. It is to construct the best black-and-white picture of the world that you can at the moment. If on reflection you would think that a likelihood x of this proposition's being true would make it worth the risk—that is, make it worth including in this picture—then the corresponding degree of belief is sufficient for belief. Otherwise not.[82]

Belief thus involves an element of commitment, and commitments are context relative. You might be willing to commit yourself to the truth of a proposition in one context but not in another. If you are a scientist, for example, you might be willing to commit yourself to the truth of a hypothesis in designing your experiments but not be willing to do so when deliberating about political issues to which the hypothesis is relevant. But at least for the purposes of epistemology, we want a notion of belief that is not like this. Assuming, postulating, supposing, hypothesizing, and other kinds of intellectual commitment are relative to a purpose. Thus, they can be fragmented, but we want a notion of belief that cannot be fragmented in this way. We want a notion such that either you believe a proposition or you don't. We want to avoid a notion that has you believing it relative to one purpose and yet at the same time not believing it relative to some other purpose.

Nevertheless, the context independence of belief is compatible with the view that belief involves an element of commitment and hence an element of will. The element of commitment enters only to establish the threshold of belief. What is to count as a degree of confidence sufficient for belief is a matter of the will, but your degree of confidence in a proposition ordinarily is not. So, belief is still rigid. It is not relativized to a context. You either believe the proposition with the requisite degree of confidence or you do not.

The threshold of belief is determined by how on reflection you would resolve a hypothetical decision problem. The problem is framed in terms of a purely intellectual aim, that of providing an accurate and comprehensive black-and-white picture of the world. There are various strategies you might adopt with respect to this aim. If you are daring, you will say yes to everything that you think is more likely to be true than not, and no to everything that is less likely to be true than not. You will rarely remain neutral. You thereby increase the sharpness of your image, but you also increase the risk of inaccuracies. If you are conservative, you will say yes only to that which is nearly certain to be true and no only to that which is nearly certain to be false. Thus, you will often be neutral. You thereby reduce the risk of inaccuracies, but you also reduce the sharpness of your overall image of the world. These are the extreme alternatives. The two risks also can be balanced in a variety of more moderate ways, but there is no one correct answer about how to do this balancing. The relevant balancing for you is one that conforms to your own deep standards, one that further reflection would not prompt you to retract. This is ultimately a matter of your intellectual character. Or perhaps more accurately, it is a matter of the kind of intellectual being that on reflection you would want yourself to be.

It is as if you are taking a true-false test in which there is a special cost to error. So, you are given the additional option of not answering as many questions as you like. Suppose, for example, there are one hundred questions. You get one point for each correct answer, no points for not answering a question, and minus two points for each incorrect answer. Thus, you can score anywhere from $+100$ to -200. Since there is a special cost to error, you need to be relatively sure of the claims you mark 'true' and those you mark 'false'. Here the cutoff point is 0.667. It is best to be at least this sure of a claim's truth before answering 'true', and correspondingly it is best to be at least this sure of a claim's falsehood before answering 'false'. Now add this wrinkle. You yourself determine the special cost of error. If your distaste of error is great, the scoring range of the test is enlarged on the negative side and the corresponding cutoff points for 'true' and 'false' answers go to the extremes. If the distaste is great enough, it may be unwise for you to answer any of the questions. You will then find yourself in a skeptical position, but it is your own attitude, your own horror of error, that has put you in this position. Thus, the solution to this kind of skepticism must also be one of attitude. The trick is not to find a better argument but rather a better attitude.

Indeed, the reaction to this kind of skepticism must be doubly a matter of will and attitude. I have already argued that for the epistemologist *qua* epistemologist, the proper attitude toward skepticism is one of disdain. Disdain not because skeptical worries are incoherent—they are not—and not because they are refutable—again they are not. There are no non-question begging-guarantees of truth or reliability. Regardless of how we marshal our cognitive resources, there are no guarantees that we will not be seriously misled. We are working without nets. We have no assurances that radical error will not be our reward for honest intellectual effort. Still, in fashioning our theories of rational belief we can refuse to be intimidated by the lack of guarantees. We can opt for nondefensive epistemologies.

And now, with this epistemic notion of belief in hand, it can be seen that a complete response to the skeptic depends not just upon the attitudes of the epistemologist but also upon those of the believer, for ultimately it is for each of us to determine how much subjective risk we are willing to put up with in making an intellectual stand. We determine how likely a proposition must be if it is to be included in our best black-and-white picture of the world. In so doing, we ourselves, not the epistemologist, determine the degree of confidence we must have in a proposition for our attitude to be one of belief in the epistemic sense.

Skeptics try to work their wills on us *qua* epistemologists by emphasizing the ineliminability of objective risk, but they also try to work their wills on us *qua* believers. They do so by trying to coax us into raising our standards. We are asked not to commit ourselves to hypotheses with any significant level of subjective risk. But in fact, we are by nature inveterate believers. Most of us prefer being the kind of intellectual being who takes stands rather than the kind who sits idly by on the sidelines. We prefer intellectual engagement, not because we are capable of proving that this will have happy results but rather because we prefer an intellectual life of risk to one of sterile subjective certainty.

Notes

1. More precisely, assume that this is so unless your having this degree of confidence in the proposition would itself alter your evidence. See sec. 1.5.

2. Locke, *An Essay Concerning Human Understanding*, especially Book IV, chaps. 15 and 16.

3. Ibid., chap. 15, 5.

4. According to Locke, we do not believe what we know. Belief is a matter of opinion, whereas knowledge goes beyond mere opinion. It is a matter of directly perceiving agreement or disagreement among our ideas. Questions of rationality, then, arise only with respect to those propositions that we do not know.

5. See sec. 4.8.

6. There are those who argue that despite initial appearances, we have numerically precise degrees of confidence in a wide variety of propositions and, moreover, that there are tests that can be used to reveal these precise degrees of confidence. None of these tests are uncontroversial, however, and none are simple. See sec. 4.3. So, even if these tests are in principle defensible, the vagueness of belief-talk may be just what is needed for everyday purposes.

7. This forces us to bracket for the moment the conclusion of the lottery argument.

8. "Once a subjective or epistemic probability value is assigned to a proposition, there is nothing more to be said about its epistemic status." Robert Stalnaker, *Inquiry* (Cambridge: MIT Press, 1987), 91.

9. Most probabilists require not just finite additivity but also countable additivity. However, there are those (e.g., de Finetti) who resist this on the grounds that it might be rational to believe that the tickets in a denumerably infinite lottery are equally likely to win. For a defense of the stronger and mathematically more convenient form of additivity, see Brian Skyrms, *Pragmatics and Empiricism* (New Haven: Yale University Press, 1984), 21–23.

10. See F. P. Ramsey, "Truth and Probability," in Ramsey, *Philosophical Papers*, ed. H. Mellor (London: Routledge and Kegan Paul, 1978).

11. "One plausible measure of a man's partial belief is thus the odds he will determine to bet where his greedy but otherwise mysterious opponent subsequently decides both the stake size and the direction of the bet. From this situation the irrelevant effects are absent of a man's other beliefs, of his itch or distaste for gambling, or his preference for high or

for low stakes, of his desires that some things should be true and others not and of the variable utility of money. The claim is that the only remaining factor disposing a man to settle on some odds in preference to others just is the strength of his partial belief, of which the odds are therefore a fair measure." D.H. Mellor, *The Matter of Chance* (Cambridge: Cambridge University Press, 1970), 37. See also F. Jackson and R. Pargetter, "A Modified Dutch Book Argument," *Philosophical Studies* 29 (1976), 403–7.

12. See secs. 4.5 and 4.6.

13. Another complication is the phenomenon of anchoring. The odds you would post on a series of propositions can be affected by the order in which you consider them. See Jon Elster, *Ulysses and the Sirens* (Cambridge: Cambridge University Press, 1984), 128–33.

14. See, e.g., with H. Raiffa, *Decision Analysis* (Reading: Addison-Wesley, 1968).

15. The assumption is not that you consciously make calculations of estimated utility but only that you rank your preferences just "as though" you did. See Richard Jeffrey, "Ethics and the Logic of Decision," *Journal of Philosophy* 62 (1965), 528–39; and Ellery Eells, *Rational Decision and Causality* (Cambridge: Cambridge University Press, 1982), 33–34.

16. Compare with Mark Kaplan, "Bayesianism without the Black Box," *Philosophy of Science*, 6 (1989), 49–69.

17. Ramsey's method suffers from such problems. The first and most basic step in his method is to determine your degree of belief in an "ethically neutral" proposition. A proposition P is ethically neutral for you if two possible worlds differing only in regard to the truth of P are always of equal value for you. Suppose P is such a proposition, and suppose in addition that you are not indifferent between outcome A and outcome B but that you are indifferent between the gambles (A if P, B if ¬P) and (A if ¬P, B if P). Then, says Ramsey, your degree of belief in P must be 0.50. But why? The definition of ethical neutrality guarantees that you don't intrinsically value P, but in certain situations you might nonetheless value it for the consequences you think it would produce. Ramsey attempts to rule this out by stipulating that A and B are as specific as it is possible for them to be, subject to the constraint that each is compatible with either the truth or falsity of P; they are thus close to being alternative possible worlds. This stipulation is so strong that the test is no longer a feasible one, but it is not a theoretically sound one either, since what is relevant here is what you *believe* about A, B, and P. Suppose you believe with some degree of confidence that, say, ¬P in conjunction with whatever is the less desirable of the two outcomes, A or B, would produce something else of value. Then even on the assumption that your preferences follow subjective estimated utility, you can be indifferent between the above two gambles even if your degree of belief in P $\neq$ 0.50. Ramsey needs to rule out such possibilities, but he cannot do so simply by stipulating, e.g., that you believe with full confidence that A and B are as specific as it is possible for them to be, since the point of his procedure is to determine your degrees of belief by your preferences. See Ramsey, "Truth and Probability."

18. See Eells, *Rational Decision and Causality*, 43.

19. See L.J. Savage, *The Foundations of Statistics*, 2d ed. (New York: Dover, 1972). Transitivity requires you to prefer A to C if you prefer A to B and B to C. Trichotomy requires that for any two outcomes A and B in the domain in question, either you prefer A to B or you prefer B to A or you are indifferent between them. The surething principle requires that if acts A and B would have the same outcome, given a possible state of

nature, then which act you prefer is independent of that outcome; your preference of one over the other is instead wholly a matter of those states of nature in which the two acts would have different outcomes.

20. See, e.g., K. R. MacCrimmon, "Descriptive and Normative Implications of the Decision-Theory Postulates," in K. Borch and J. Mossin, (eds.) *Risk and Uncertainty* (New York: St. Martin's Press, 1968), 3–23; P. Slovic and A. Tversky, "Who Accepts Savage's Axiom?" *Behavioral Science* 19 (1974), 368–73; A. Tversky, "Intransitivity of Preferences," *Psychological Review* 76 (1971), 105–10; D. Kaheman, P. Slovic, and A. Tversky (eds.), *Judgement under Uncertainty: Heuristics and Biases* (Cambridge: Cambridge University Press, 1982); D. Kahneman and A. Tversky, "Prospect Theory: An Analysis of Decision under Risk," *Econometrica* 47 (1979), 263–91.

21. There are various ways of trying to explain away the empirical evidence that indicates our preferences don't always follow subjective estimated utility. We might try doing so in terms of a special aversion to risk or a second-order uncertainty about first-order desires and beliefs. These maneuvers might have some plausibility if we could presume that you typically have precise degrees of belief and desire, for then the problem would merely be one of reconciling this presupposition with the recalcitrant empirical data. But in fact, this is not our situation. What we are looking for and what we need is some argument for thinking that you really do have precise degrees of beliefs. But insofar as this is what we are looking for, all of these maneuvers are *ad hoc*. Indeed, they all make the overall problem of measurement even more complex. They thus make it more difficult to argue, as opposed to assume, that we typically have precise degrees of belief in a wide variety of propositions. Contrast with Eells, *Rational Decision and Causality*, especially 33–41.

22. Suppose it is instead claimed that you have precise confidence-intervals for almost every proposition that you can understand, the idea being that although you may be of many minds about a proposition, there is nonetheless a unique upper bound to your confidence in a proposition as well as a unique lower bound. Your overall attitude toward the proposition is defined by these upper and lower bounds. Proposals of this sort have been forwarded by Henry Kyburg, *Probability and the Logic of Rational Belief* (Middletown, Conn.: Wesleyan University Press, 1961), and I. J. Good, *The Estimation of Probabilities* (Cambridge: MIT Press, 1965). For a related view, see Levi, *The Enterprise of Knowledge*. However, none of these proposals avoid the basic difficulty here either. Casual introspection and observation do not reveal that our confidence in various propositions typically have precise upper and lower bounds, and no behavioral test can plausibly be construed as revealing such bounds. We always can imagine a series of tests that would elicit precise bounds from an individual, but then the question is why this series of tests rather than a somewhat different one should be taken as a correct measure of actual individual's confidence intervals.

23. Might it be a condition of rationality that you strive to make your degrees of belief as fine as possible? Even if it were, we would be still left with the question of what degrees of belief are rational for you in the interim. But in fact, it isn't always rational to try to make your degrees of belief more precise. For starters, there may not be much that you can do to make them more precise, but in addition, it would not always be rational for you to do so even if you could. You have better things to do. Doing so would sometimes even be positively harmful. The finer your degrees of belief, the more complicated your deliberations and inquiries become, and this in turn may increase the likelihood of your

making mistakes, Indeed, having extremely fine degrees of belief might make deliberation on all but the simplest matters next to impossible. See Harman, *Change in View*, especially chap. 3.

24. Bas van Fraassen, "Empiricism in the Philosophy of Science," in P. Churchland and C. Hooker (eds.), *Images of Science* (Chicago: University of Chicago Press, 1985), 245–308.

25. "Indeed, the Bayesian framework is too roomy in that it permits belief functions that would be entertained only by a fool, and value assignments that would be entertained only by a monster. But I take it that the formulation and critique of particular probability and value assignments must be largely conducted in situ, with the aid of facts about the agent, his language, his community, and his special situation; and that although such activity should use the Bayesian framework, it belongs to other disciplines—say, to inductive logic, and to ethics." R. Jeffrey, *The Logic of Decision*, 211. See also van Fraassen, "Empiricism in the Philosophy of Science," and Skyrms, *Pragmatics and Empiricism*.

26. See, e.g., B. DeFinetti, "Foresight: Its Logical Laws, Its Subjective Sources," trans. H Kyburg; reprinted in H. Kyburg and H. Smokler (eds.), *Studies in Subjective Probability* (New York: Wiley, 1964). Also see Ramsey, "Truth and Probability."

27. "The cunning bettor is simply a dramatic device—the Dutch book a striking corollary—to emphasize the underlying issue of coherence." Skyrms, *Pragmatics and Empiricism*, 22.

28. Compare with Henry Kyburg, who argues: "No rational person, whatever his degrees of belief, would accept a sequence of bets under which he was bound to lose no matter what happened. No rational person will in fact have a book made against him." From this Kyburg concludes: "The Dutch Book argument gives excellent reasons for adopting a table of odds or publishing a list of preferences which conform . . . to the probability calculus, but it does so at the cost of severing the . . . connection between odds and degrees of belief." It severs this connection, according to Kyburg, because "however irrational and strange my degreee of beliefs, I will, under compulsion, post odds that are coherent." Kyburg, "Subjective Probability: Criticisms, Reflections, and Problems," in Kyburg, *Epistemology and Inference* (Minneapolis: University of Minnesota Press, 1985), 79–98.

29. See Ralph Kennedy and Charles Chihara, "The Dutch Book Argument: Its Logical Flaws, Its Subjective Sources," *Philosophical Studies* 36 (1979), 19–33. See also Pollock, *Contemporary Theories of Knowledge*.

30. See Ramsey, "Truth and Probability," especially sec. 4.

31. " We subjectivists conceive probability as the measure of reasonable partial belief. But we need not make war against other conceptions of probability, declaring that where subjective credence leaves off, there nonsense begins. Along with subjective credence we should believe also in objective chance. The practice and analysis of science require both concepts. Neither can replace the other." David Lewis, "A Subjectivist's Guide to Objective Chance," in Lewis, *Philosophical Papers*, vol 2 (New York: Oxford University Press, 1983). See also Mellor, *The Matter of Chance*.

32. "Suppose that you choose reference classes for *rain all day* and *dry all day* and announce your personal probabilities as .2 for today's having the first attribute and .3 for its having the second. Now I ask you about its having the attribute *rain all day or dry all day*. Why should you stop to consult a recipe for choosing a reference class? You know now that whatever one you choose, you will be irrational unless you come up with the

answer .5." Bas van Fraassen, "Calibration: A Frequency Justification for Personal Proba-bility," in R. S. Cohen and L. Laudan (eds.), *Physics, Philosophy, and Psychoanalysis* (Dordrecht: Reidel, 1983), p. 311.

33. Compare with Ellis, *Rational Belief Systems*. See also Stalnaker, *Inquiry*, espe-cially 84.

34. Contrast with Roderick Firth, who in an uncharacteristically infelicitous phrase makes reference to an omniscient, omnipercipient, disinterested, dispassionate but "in other respects normal" observer. This cannot be read as anything other than an unintended joke. See Firth, "Ethical Absolutism and the Ideal Observer," in W. Sellars and J. Hospers (eds.), *Readings in Ethical Theory* (New York: Appleton-Century-Crofts, 1970), 200—221.

35. "In this ultimate meaning it seems to me that we can identify reasonable opinion with the opinion of an ideal person in similar circumstances. What, however, would this ideal person's opinion be? As has previously been remarked, the highest ideal would be always to have a true opinion and be certain of it; but this ideal is more suited to God than to man." Ramsey, "Truth and Probability."

36. Compare with Ramsey, who distinguished formal logic from human logic. The latter, according to Ramsey, tells us how to think. Ramsey went on to complain that "nearly all philosophical thought about human logic and especially about induction has tried to reduce it in some way to formal logic." Ramsey, "Truth and Probability."

37. Some would add that it is also reason's job to provide some sort of certification of the accuracy of these data. As Thomas Reid understood, this is a view that encourages skepticism: "The sceptic asks me, Why do you believe the existence of the external object which you perceive? This belief, sir, is none of my manufacture; it came from the mint of Nature; it bears her image and superscription; and, if it is not right, the fault is not mine; I ever took it upon trust, and without suspicion. Reason, says the sceptic, is the only judge of truth, and you ought to throw off every opinion and every belief that is not grounded on reason. Why, sir, should I believe the faculty of reason more than that of perception? They both came out of the same shop, and were made by the same artist, and if he puts one piece of false ware into my hands, what should hinder him from putting another." Reid, "An Inquiry into the Human Mind," in *Thomas Reid's Inquiries and Essays*, ed. R. Beanblossom and K. Lehrer (Indianapolis: Hackett 1983), 84–85. For a contemporary version of the kind of view that Reid is attacking, see Bonjour, *The Structure of Empirical Knowledge*. Bonjour insists that empirical reasons for belief need an *a priori* meta-justification, a justification that shows that the thing cited as a reason really is a mark of truth. On the other hand, he requires no such metajustification for *a priori* reasons for belief. So, reason is given the job of certifying our other faculties but it itself needs no independent certification.

38. Theological concerns can also be seen at work here. We have higher and lower faculties, the lower ones (e.g., perception) we share with the animals and the higher one (reason) we share with God. This encourages the view of reason as an altogether discrete faculty, one whose operations are fundamentally different from those of other cognitive faculties. Compare with Edward Craig, *The Mind of God and the Works of Man* (New York: Oxford University Press).

39. There are exceptions. For the most subtle defense of phenomenalism in the litera-ture, see Fumerton's *Metaphysical and Epistemological Problems of Perception*.

40. Compare with *The Republic*, Book I, where Socrates gets Thrasymachus to admit that the mathematician *qua* mathematician never makes mistakes. Such mistakes are the

product of biases and the like, which to the extent they are operative imply that the individual is not really doing mathematics.

41. One of the exceptions is Ian Hacking. See his "Slightly More Realistic Personal Probabilities," *Philosophy of Science* 34 (1967), 311–25.

42. See sec. 4.6.

43. Your estimated payoff on each of the nine 'pea' bets = .9($1) + .1(−$1) = $.80, and your estimated payoff on the 'nonpea' bet = .1($1) + .9(−$1) = − $.80.

44. Your estimated payoff on each bet = .9($1) + .1(−$1) = $.80, and you make nine such bets.

45. See sec. 3.2.

46. Contrast with Jordan Howard Sobel: "A person has a stake in intellectual perfection, a deeply personal stake, and compromises made here are always degrading in a sense . . . " Sobel, "Self-Doubts and Dutch Strategies," *Australasian Journal of Philosophy* (1987), 75.

47. There are many such theories. A sampling: Keith Lehrer, *Knowledge* (New York: Oxford University Press, 1974); Bonjour, *The Structure of Empirical Knowledge*; Harman, *Thought*; Marshall Swain, *Reasons and Knowledge* (Ithaca: Cornell University Press, 1981).

48. Compare with Henry Kyburg, "Conjunctivitis," in M. Swain (ed.), *Induction, Acceptance, and Rational Belief* (Dordrecht: Reidel, 1970), 55–82.

49. See sec. 4.2.

50. See sec. 2.6.

51. Both Robert Stalnaker and Mark Kaplan have expressed worries of this sort. See Stalnaker, *Inquiry*, especially 92; and Mark Kaplan, "A Bayesian Theory of Rational Acceptance," *Journal of Philosophy,* 78 (1981), 305–30.

52. Points of this sort have been especially emphasized by Gilbert Harman. However, he regards reasoning as essentially a matter of moving from one belief state to another. As a result, he concludes that there is no such thing as deductive reasoning, only deductive argument. This is a needlessly controversial conclusion. If we distinguish believing from assuming and the like, we can admit what in any event seems obvious—viz., that there is such a thing as deductive reasoning—while retaining what is really essential in Harman's position, viz., that there is no simple way to get principles of rational belief revision from the principles of deductive argument. See Harman, *Change in View*.

53. And so, in constructing theories, including philosophical theories, a high premium is placed on consistency. The mistake is trying to turn this into an altogether general requirement on rational belief.

54. See sec. 4.8. Contrast with Harman, who says: "Belief in or full acceptance of P involves . . . [allowing] oneself to use P as part of one's starting point in further theoretical and practical thinking." *Change in View*, 47.

55. For some other defenses of the idea that one can knowingly and rationally have inconsistent beliefs, see Richard Foley, "Justified Inconsistent Beliefs," *American Philosophical Quarterly* 16 (1979), 247–58; Peter Klein, "The Virtue of Inconsistency," *Monist*, 68 (1985), 105–35; and Paul Moser, *Empirical Justification* (Dordrecht: Reidel, 1985).

56. This is essentially Chisholm's view; see *Theory of Knowledge*, 98.

57. ". . . *whenever we apply decision theory we must make some choices*: At the very least, we must pick the acts, states, and outcomes to be used in our problem specification. But if we use decision theory to make these choices, we must make yet another set of

choices." Michael Resnik, *Choices* (Minneapolis: University of Minnesota Press, 1987), 11.

58. Compare with Kaplan, "A Bayesian Theory of Rational Acceptance."

59. Compare with Harman, *Change in View*, especially chap. 3.

60. Recent work in cognitive science reinforces this picture by suggesting that the human cognitive system displays a propensity toward full acceptance. See J. A. Feldman and D. H. Ballard, "Connectionist Models and Their Properties," *Cognitive Science* 6 (1982), 205–54. For a brief description of Feldman and Ballard's work, see Alvin Goldman, "The Cognitive and Social Sides of Epistemology," *Proceedings of the Philosophy of Science Association* 2 (1986).

61. Unlike the jury that acquits, a hung jury typically allows the prosecutor the prerogative of retrying the case; it is not a declaration of innocence.

62. ". . . there are mathematical propositions whose truth or falsity cannot as yet be decided. Yet it may humanly speaking be right to entertain a certain degree of belief in them on inductive or other grounds: a logic which proposes to justify such a degree of belief must be prepared actually to go against formal logic; for to a formal truth a formal logic can only assign a belief of degree 1 . . . This point seems to me to show particularly clearly that human logic or the logic of truth, which tells men how they should think, is not merely independent of but sometimes actually incompatible with formal logic." Ramsey, "Truth and Probability."

63. So, the problem here cannot be avoided by offering a more relaxed interpretation of what coherence demands—e.g., one that does not require us on pains of irrationality to believe all necessary truths with degree of confidence of 1.0 but rather only those necessary truths that are truth functional tautologies. Brian Skryms has suggested in passing a position of this sort in *Pragmatics and Empiricism*.

64. Compare with David Lewis's discussion of Peter Unger's theory of knowledge in "Scorekeeping in a Language Game," in his *Philosophical Papers*, vol. 1 (New York: Oxford University Press, 1983).

65. For the most well worked out theory of this sort, see Stalnaker, *Inquiry*.

66. On Stalnaker's possible-worlds semantics, there is only one necessarily true proposition, although there are many different sentences that express it. So, Stalnaker would insist that of the ten sentences in the above case, nine express the same proposition, the one that is necessarily true.

67. Again see Stalnaker, *Inquiry* especially chap. 5. His basic idea is that particular beliefs belong to more general belief-states, and that it is possible to be in more than one belief-state at a time. The beliefs within any given belief-state are governed by a conjunctive rule. Thus, if you believe P and believe Q and both of these beliefs are part of the same belief-state, then you believe (P & Q) and anything that it implies. On the other hand, beliefs that belong to different belief-states are not conjunctive, and thus you can have explicitly contradictory beliefs without believing everything whatsoever.

68. Is this a counterexample to the so-called converse Dutch book theorem, which states that if your betting quotients don't violate the probability calculus, no Dutch book can be made against you? No; genuine Dutch bookies do not require any special empirical knowledge, but your opponents here do need special empirical knowledge in order to exploit your odds. On the other hand, the special empirical knowledge that they need is only semantical knowledge. If they know what propositions the sentences 1*–10* express, they will be able to place bets against you that you cannot help but lose. They will be able to do so despite the fact that your degrees of belief are coherent.

69. Stalnaker, *Inquiry*, again chap. 5.

70. I am thus assuming that propositions need to be more finely individuated than, say, Stalnaker's theory allows.

71. I discuss this issue in sec. 4.8.

72. Julian Feldman, "Simulation of Behavior in Binary Choice Experiments," in E. Feigenbaum and J. Feldman (eds.), *Computers and Thought* (New York: McGraw-Hill, 1963), 329–46.

73. Suppose that a ball has been drawn from a basket containing 100 red balls and 100 green balls and that you are forced to assign a probability to the proposition that the ball is red. The probability you assign will be used to post odds and you will be forced to accept a bet on the proposition at the corresponding odds, with your opponent being free to choose both the side and the size of the bet. There is a hitch, however: your opponent has seen the color of the ball, whereas you have not. Moreover, you know this. Then of course, you should try to avoid assigning any probability at all to the proposition, but if you must, what should it be? Not 0.5. The posted odds would then be 1:1, and your opponent, with her superior knowledge, will win whatever she declares to be the size of the bet. If she declares the bet to be $1,000, that's what she will win. If she declares it to be $1,000,000, she will win $1,000,000. Your only choice is to be daring. You must assign either a probability of 1 or a probability of 0 to the proposition, despite the fact that you would be merely guessing. If you assign 1 to the proposition and the ball turns out to be red, you will win nothing; if it is green, you will lose a sum equal to the size of the bet. If you assign 0 and the ball is green, you will win nothing, but if it is red, you will again lose a sum equal to the size of the bet. Even so, this is your best option, since it is the only one that gives you any hope of preventing your opponent from winning as much as she pleases from you.

74. See sec. 1.3.

75. See, e.g. Chisholm, *The Theory of Knowledge*; Fumerton, *Metaphysical and Epistemological Problems of Perception*; and William Alston, "Varieties of Privileged Access," in Alston, *Epistemic Justification* (Ithaca: Cornell University Press, 1989), 249–85.

76. Compare with Mark Kaplan, "It's Not What You Know That Counts," *Journal of Philosophy* (1985), 350–63.

77. In itself even infallibility is irrelevant insofar as the issue is egocentric rationality. After all, your beliefs in some propositions may be infallible unbeknownst to you. From your perspective there might even be indications that these propositions are false. The most obvious examples are necessarily true propositions that you have reasons to regard as false, but there may be examples involving contingent propositions as well. Suppose that unbeknownst to you the nature of belief is such that it is impossible to believe something without being in state x. Suppose also that you happen to believe that you are in state x. Then your belief is infallible; it is impossible for you to believe this and for it to be false. Still, this tells us nothing about the egocentric rationality of your belief.

78. The argument against P does have to be a relevant one, however. It's not enough for its premises simply to imply notP. After all, jointly inconsistent propositions will trivially imply any proposition whatsoever. For example, even if you were to believe jointly inconsistent propositions with great confidence (as you might in lottery cases), you need not think that these propositions give you a reason to be on guard about P, since you need not think that they are relevant to P. You need not think they are relevant even if you realize that they imply notP (as well as P).

79. Suppose you believe each of the propositions in the set (P1, P2, . . . Pn) and you also believe of this set, with as much confidence as you believe some of these propositions, that at least one of its members is likely to be false. Does this mean that none of the propositions in the set are part of your evidence? No; it only means that some are not. Suppose P1 is the least confidently believed member of the set. Then P1 is not part of your evidence, since there are propositions you believe as confidently as it that can be used to argue against it. So, delete it from the set. Now ask of the reduced set (P2, P3, . . . Pn) whether you believe with as much confidence as you believe some of these propositions that at least one of its members is false. If you do, then not all of the members of this set are part of your evidence. Suppose P2 is the least confidently believed of these propositions. Then it is not part of your evidence. Delete it from the set and then ask the same question of the smaller set (P3, P4, . . . Pn). As this process continues and the sets gets smaller and smaller, two things will ordinarily happen: (1) the least confidently believed proposition in the revised set will be believed with more confidence than the least confidently believed proposition in the preceding sets, and (2) your confidence that at least one member of the set is likely to be false will decrease. So eventually, the result will be a set of propositions that are not recognizably improbable with respect to one another. If there is nothing else wrong with these propositions, they all can be part of your evidence.

80. For some of these details, see Foley, *The Theory of Epistemic Rationality*, especially secs. 1.5–1.7.

81. The problem is not merely that anything whatsoever is implied by inconsistent propositions. If this were the only problem, we might be able to deal with it by insisting that classical logic is to be replaced with a relevance logic or by insisting upon a strategy of fragmentation, as David Lewis has suggested. Either strategy would prevent us from deducing just anything from inconsistent propositions. On the other hand, neither addresses the more basic problem, which is that basing inquiry on propositions that you recognize to be inconsistent risks contaminating the rest of your belief system with the error that you know to be contained somewhere among these propositions. This problem remains even if you restrict yourself to the relevant implications of these propositions and even if you fragment them in the way that Lewis suggests. Contrast with Lewis, "Logic for Equivocators," *Nous* 16 (1982), 431–41. See also S. Shapiro and J. Martins, "A Model for Belief Revision," *Artificial Intelligence* 35 (1988), 25–79

82. Compare with Kaplan, "A Bayesian Theory of Rational Acceptance". Also Bas van Fraassen, "Belief and the Will," *Journal of Philosophy*, 81 (1984), 235–56; and R. B. DeSousa, "How to Give a Piece of Your Mind: Or, the Logic of Belief and Assent," *Review of Metaphysics* 25 (1971), 52–79.

Index